collaborators

SBTD

UK DESIGN FOR PERFORMANCE

2003 • 2007

This catalogue of Design for Performance accompanies the Collaborators exhibition. It is a celebration of the richness and diversity of work made between 2003 - 2007 by designers born or based in the UK. Opera, dance, drama, performance/installations and the design of theatre space are included here and accompanied by five essays written by, or from interviews with, notable British designers in which they reflect on their own collaborative process.

Compiled by Kate Burnett

Published in Great Britain
by The Society of British
Theatre Designers
4th Floor, 55 Farringdon Rd,
London EC1M 3JB

Registered Charity No.
800638

Text copyright © 2007

ISBN
978 - 0 - 9529309 - 4 - 5

British Library Cataloguing in
Publication Data:
a catalogue record of this
book is available from the
British Library

Design and typography
Simon Head

Compiled by Kate Burnett

Edited by Keith Allen

Printed by
Tadberry Evedale Ltd

Photographs and illustrations
are by the contributing
designers unless otherwise
stated.

Information in this catalogue
has been provided by
contributing designers and
is published in good faith.

The Society of British Theatre
Designers is deeply grateful
to all the sponsors, from
private individuals to large
organisations who have
made this exhibition, its
catalogue and programme of
educational events possible.

Funded by The National
Lottery through Arts Council
England.

LOTTERY FUNDED

British Council.

Sincere thanks are due to:
Nottingham Trent University
The Really Useful Group
The Mackintosh Foundation
British Equity
Association of Lighting
Designers
Association of British
Theatre Technicians
Ambassador Theatre Group
AC Lighting Limited
Bentley Chemicals
Bower Wood Production
Services
Delstar Engineering Ltd
DHL Express
Gerriets of Great Britiain Ltd
Richard Hudson
JD McDougall Ltd
Nixon Knowles - Timber
Merchants
Northern Light
Opera North
Royal Opera House, Covent
Garden
Royal Shakespeare Company
Set One (Derby)
Souvenir Scenic Studios Ltd
Stage One
Stage Technologies Ltd
CH Stead and Son
Talbot Designs Ltd
Vienna Volksoper

Collaborators draws on the
resources and membership of
the following organisations
which include theatre
designers, technicians,
architects and academics:

The Society of British
Theatre Designers
The Association of British
Theatre Technicians
The Association of Courses
in Theatre Design
Equity Register of Designers
Society of Theatre
Consultants

Thanks are also due to the
following for their inspiration,
commitment and practical
help:

Susan Ansell - film maker,
Digital Profiles
Jamie Booker - exhibition
construction
Steven Brown - Sound
Designers Collective
Gareth Chell - technical
assistance
Aby Cohen
Ken Coker - ALD Collective
Lee Dawkins
Mike Elliott exhibition design
and management
Ada Gadomski - exhibition
and SBTD organisation
David Hoskins - Digial Profiles
Katie Jones - Vectorworks
drawings
Roma Patel
Lili Rogué exhibition and
catalogue coordinator
Peter Ruthven Hall - financial
management
Simon Thomas Colquhoun -
lighting
Sophie Tyrrel - education
programme coordinator
Katherine Warman -
education officer (tour)
Louise Weibull - design
coordination assistance

Simon Banham
Paul Brown
Julian Brown
David Cockayne
Greer Crawley
Richard Downing
Johan Engels
Sophie Jump
Ralph Koltai
Fred Meller
Dody Nash
Penny Saunders
Colin Winslow

Mark White, chairman, ABTT
Jenny Straker, ABTT
Francesca Greatorex, ABTT
Helena Easton, ABTT
John Taylor, d&b audiotechnik
Wimbledon School of Art
(ACTD installation)
LIPA (ACTD installation at PQ
and V&A)
Liam Doona
Simon Fitch
Mark Hollander
Gary Kahn
Ian Saunders
Carolyn Downing
(Sound Designers' Collective)

At Nottingham Trent University
16/1/2007 – 4/2/2007:

Professor Simon Lewis
Ann Priest
Professor Terry Shave
Matthew Hawthorn
Maggie Burnett
Roma Patel
Shane Guy
Chris Green
Simon Perkins
Staff, technicians, students
and administrators in Theatre
Design and Mulitmedia
departments and in Waverley
for their generosity in
accommodating the
Collaborators national
exhibition

Also to the following
individuals and their staff at:

The Prague Quadrennial
14 – 24/6/2007;
Milada Novakova
Daniela Parizkova

Northern Stage, Newcastle-
upon-Tyne
30/8/2007 – 22/9/2007;
Neil Murray
Erica Whyman

Inverness Museum and Art
Gallery
6/10/2007 – 3/11/2007;
Muriel McLeod, Highlands &
Islands Theatre Network
Catherine Niven, IMAG

The Victoria & Albert Museum
21/11/2007 – 16/11/2008;
Geoffrey Marsh
Victoria Broackes
Kate Bailey
Helen Crawford
Stewart Airde
Adrian Deakes
Samantha Lane
Alex Bratt

The Collaborators national
exhibition is dedicated to the
memory of Maria Bjornson,
who sadly died in December
2002 shortly after selecting
the award winning UK
exhibition for the Prague
Quadrennial 2003.

The Society of British Theatre Designers

The Society of British Theatre Designers was founded in 1975 by John Bury, with Ralph Koltai, Nicholas Georgiadis and Timothy O'Brien. It started life with the object of deciding on the most appropriate union to negotiate for designers. Since then it has developed and diversified and now has a wide membership.
It aims to enhance the standing of British theatre design at home and abroad in many different ways.
One of these is to organise, every four years, an exhibition of theatre design, which, in part, represents Britain at the international Quadrennial in Prague.
It also arranges seminars and forums for discussion and development of professional practice. Designers are easily isolated by their work. Their Society puts them in touch with one another and with those working in theatre in other countries.
The SBTD and ABTT together form the UK Centre of OISTAT (International Organisation of Scenographers, Theatre Architects and Technicians). SBTD members represent UK Theatre Design practitioners and educators on OISTAT Commissions including Scenography, Education and History & Theory, organising and participating in international meetings and events such as, Scenofest, the Prague Quadrennial and World Stage Design.

4th Floor
55 Farringdon Road
London EC1M 3JB
Tel: +44(0)20 7242 9200
Fax: +44(0)20 7242 9303
Email: sbtd@ntu.ac.uk
www.theatredesign.org.uk
www.oistat.org

The Association of British Theatre Technicians

The Association of British Theatre Technicians was formed in 1961 by leading exponents of the technical side of theatre. The vision was to have a network of technicians who could exchange information, advise each other of safe codes of conduct, good working practice and trade information on new technology. It was also formed to review new theatre buildings and equipment. Forty years on, the need for the Association is as great as ever. EEC directives from Brussels and the Health and Safety Executive, and the growth of increasingly sophisticated equipment have meant that the beleaguered technician needs as much good advice as he or she can get.
The ABTT publishes codes of practice for the theatre industry, influences draft standards and regulations and offers assistance and advice to those involved in planning new or refurbishing old theatres.
ABTT organises an annual Trade Show in London, in addition to the occasional conference; members' meetings and seminars. Members of the ABTT include Flymen, Architects, Consultants, Stage Managers, Lighting Designers, Equipment Suppliers, Teachers, Students, Scenographers and Production Managers. In other words anyone, professional or amateur, in work or training that has any interest in the technical aspects of theatre.

4th Floor
55 Farringdon Road
London EC1M 3JB
Tel: +44(0)20 7242 9200
Fax: +44(0)20 7242 9303
Email: office@abtt.org.uk
www.abtt.org.uk

The Association of Lighting Designers

The Association of Lighting Designers (ALD) is the professional body representing lighting designers in all fields within the United Kingdom and abroad. A voluntarily run association, it exists to provide a resource and forum for the discussion and development of artistic and creative aims amongst lighting designers from the fields of live performance, television, architecture, education, industrial and corporate presentations and manufacturing.
The membership includes leading lighting designers from Britain and many other parts of the world. The ALD holds regular meetings including show briefings, product demonstrations, master classes and discussion groups. The ALD publishes a bi-monthly magazine called *Focus* giving details of meetings, associated events and lighting news.
The Professional Members' Directory is distributed bi-annually to producers and other potential employers to promote professional members of the Association. Corporate members enjoy access to an accurately targeted database of lighting professionals. For details of how to join and the membership categories available, visit the ALD website or contact the office.

P.O.Box 680
Oxford OX1 9DG
Tel: +44(0)7817 060189
Email: office@ald.org.uk
www.ald.org.uk

BritishEquity

Equity is delighted to be associated with the Collaborators exhibition. It welcomes the opportunities afforded by this showcase of members' talent and creativity and applauds the continuing high levels of professionalism shown by designers even in the current, often difficult, financial climate. Equity currently has over 300 designers on its designers' register. It has negotiated agreements with all the major employers' groups: the Theatrical Management Association, the Society of London Theatre and the Independent Theatre Council. These agreements cover everything from billing to model expenses, from copyright to minimum fees. There is a full-time organiser available to help with queries, grievences or disputes arising from any contract of employment. The organiser will also represent designer members in the event of contractual disputes with managers. In addition, all the normal services available to members can be used by designers. Of these, the advice on tax and DSS claims provided by the Welfare Benefits Officer is particularly useful. There is also a legal service provided to members who have legal problems connected with their work. This is much used by members, especially those with personal injury problems. Equity welcomes and encourages the involvement of its designer members, and will continue to strive to maintain and improve its service to them.

Guild House
Upper St. Martin's Lane
London WC2H 9EG
Tel: +44(0)20 7379 6000
Fax: +44(0)20 7379 7001
Email: info@equity.org.uk
www.equity.org.uk

ESSAYS

SIMON BANHAM
7.30 for 8.00
Cooking with my daughters   8

FRED MELLER
Have we started yet?   14

DODY NASH
Futurespace   20

PENNY SAUNDERS
A landscape of possibilities   26

PAUL BROWN
Craft With A Bit Of A Gob On   32

CATALOGUE

INTRODUCTION 6

A RESPONSE TO... 39

DIRECTOR · DESIGNER 69

ART · CRAFT · DESIGN 93

OTHER ART FORMS 123

TEAMWORK 141

RESPONSE TO SPACE+PLACE 171

BIOGRAPHIES 208

INDEXES
  Designers/Collaborators 225
  Productions 226
  Companies 227
  Venues 228

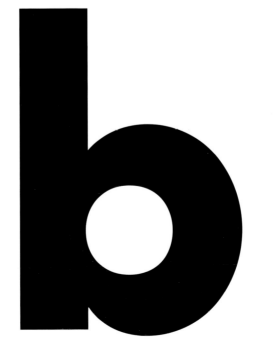

The Collaborators project is, in a sense, a leap into the dark - again, a new team, new venues, new partnerships - and in particular, a relationship that has re-awakened, that of the profession with the training courses. This is exemplified by Nottingham Trent University who have generously hosted and sponsored the national exhibition and are currently home to the Society of British Theatre Designers projects base.

...LET'S DO THE SHOW RIGHT HERE!

As with previous exhibitions, the intention of the theme is firstly, to create a journey through a wide range of work, with headings and questions that stimulate a dialogue with the work on display. Secondly, the theme aims to provide 'handles' with which designers can reflect upon and present key aspects of their work. Almost all of the work presented here could usefully be considered under each of the section headings.

In previous exhibitions we have taken SPACE as our theme, along with its partner TIME, followed by PROCESS in 2D|3D. Now we turn our attention to those we make performance with and for – our COLLABORATORS.

'Collaborators' is preferred to 'collaboration', as it focuses on the people and their / our activity. With this theme we aim to consider shared purpose, shared discovery and our delight in the 'labour' of making (for) performance, which typically involves collaboration with variously skilled artists, technicians and performers.

Exhibiting designers and artists working in performance have been invited to write a brief commentary to accompany their work. Involving key collaborators in their presentations has been welcomed and they are also included in the index, as are the photographers who have allowed us to reproduce their images in the catalogue and exhibition.

Acknowledging the continuing fascination with environment, we feature 'space and place' as both collaborative partners and as sites of collaboration. This includes the design and specification of spaces by theatre architects and consultants. Also exhibiting for the first time are sound designers, significant and inspirational collaborators, who are considering ways in which their work can be presented, outside the production context.

My grateful thanks and admiration go to the designers and their editors, who have written the following five essays, for opening up their thoughts and reflections on the diverse projects they have been engaged in. All have been involved in 'mainstream' performance companies and theatres, as well as collaborations that reach out to the perceived edges of the theatre designers' remit. They have been invited to write, or to be interviewed about their work, considering the detail of particular projects that have been key to their process and that perhaps push the edges mentioned above.

These national exhibitions in the UK are, themselves, major collaborations in both conception and organisation. They provide rare opportunities to reflect - to each other as well as to the wider community – the ideas, issues and forms with which we are engaged. Collaborators has also aimed to create an opportunity, in organising, designing and writing for this catalogue and exhibition, for younger designers to get involved with and take forward the SBTD and its ongoing programme of work - a celebration of art, craft and design for performance.

Kate Burnett

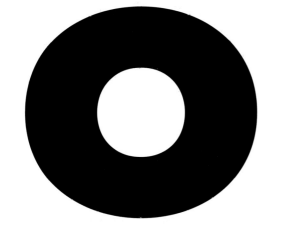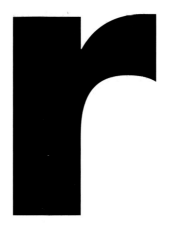

7:30 for 8:00
Cooking with my daughters

The Menu

See Saw
Two slices of seating banks separated by a red silk curtain flowing down the centre.

Something a taxi driver in Liverpool said
A small fragrant room of flowered wallpaper and upholstery served with tea as a preparation for a liquorice black journey of smells and sounds from the edges of your memory.

Frank
A collection of old memories and new experiences housed in private spaces wrapped in a communal corridor with soup at its heart.

Eat Eat
Two slabs of concrete perched on steel legs sandwiching a path of under-lit rice, prepared in the timber-framed Tudor Hall in Leicester.

Rantsoen
Discovered in a crumbled garage in Ghent, and served on a warm red tray, containing a circular table of cherry wood and rice.

Geneva
750 light bulbs on a bed of black cables with a dress of faded flowers

White Trash
A single green pool table on a surface of scuffed vinyl tiles sprinkled with tab ends.

Butterfly
A parquet dance floor spread with white balloons and edged with buffet tables under a glaze of 150 mirror balls, with a side dish of freshly prepared sandwiches and crisps.

Grace
In a mould of shuttering ply under a sagging star cloth nestles an awkward litter of plastic chairs, a pink wall, Lidl bags, a water cooler, a broken neon sign all garnished with a fake palm tree.

Susan and Darren
A squash of spectators at the breakfast bar, layered with the flicker of television screens, the slow pulse of cheap disco light and a sliver of polished dance pole to secure the whole.

Eat Eat

Geneva

Susan and Darren

The Invitation
"What are you making?"

When my daughters ask me about my shows, I can answer very simply or at great length. They are inevitably keener to show their friends the remnants of old models that pile up on the attic shelves: rowing boats beached on scaffolding stages, stained glass windows wedged between Ferris wheels and spiral staircases, the leftover medieval feast shoved into the back of a Fiat 500 and a collection of period figures quizzing the Snow Queen as to the origin of her saucepan hat. Leaving aside their fascination with the miniature, it may seem that the world of make-believe, the sense of illusion that so draws them is less apparent in my work for Quarantine…but is it? I still thrive on spectacle, I still enjoy making something beautiful, I still have to remind myself to stop. Many of the same questions and processes pertain; they are just calibrated differently in Quarantine's work.

Susan and Darren: *Sitting drinking tea in the front room, Sue leaning in the kitchen doorway always on hand to prepare food whilst Darren talks, stretches and watches television, the door to the house left open for the inevitable visitors: this task is a theatrical envisioning of Susan and Darren's living room. Everything present but extended for presentation, on its best behaviour, perhaps a little over-dressed, a space that encompasses both the public and the private – a show that must include a dance class and some sandwich making – one party's ending the next (with our help) in preparation, as they share their 90-minute biography of lost loves, precious childhood memories, violent deaths, living room carpets, rape, cooking, friends and endless fatalism.*

The Guests
"Can we come? What happens?"

We hope to be taken by surprise by our audiences. We want to give them the opportunity to reshape the event by their presence and actions. This is one of the key aims of our work, and for me the hardest to achieve successfully: the integration of the spectators into the space and activity of the performance, not only a physical engagement but also an invitation to act, to partake, be an active presence, and actively contribute to a confusion and fusion between performers and audience. We have often used shared rituals, usually meals or parties, to breach the divide between the audience and performer (*Eat Eat, Rantsoen, Butterfly* and *Susan and Darren*). These familiar social gatherings have their own codes of behaviour that allow and encourage an interaction that may range from the intimate to the public and as such can be exploited within the peculiarities of the theatrical context to extend the experience beyond the moment.

Frank: *On the edge of the stage, sandwiched between fly ropes and prompt corner, you sit awaiting your turn. In front of you the backs of flats and beyond these a variety of half-remembered sounds, underscored by the repeated playing of Frank Sinatra. After a period of waiting, listening and observing from the wings, you enter a perimeter corridor, dimly lit and smelling of boiled cabbage, where some doors are locked (the interiors only accessible through the spy hole) whilst others give access to a variety of rooms and installations, through which you can wander at leisure. There is no limit to how long you spend in the installation and no knowing if the people you encounter are performers or other audience members.*
The process of the individual journey through rooms enables a 'remembering' of self, whether this is by tapping into an old memory triggered by a smell or moments of self-reflection in a mirror, or simply the heightened perceptions enabled by alone-ness (maybe in the cupboard full of old toys and fur coats). Until the penultimate room, a soup kitchen. This, by chance, proves to be a strong focal and gathering point, an accidental success, the threads of which can be traced in our subsequent work. Here complete strangers will settle and talk, creating a strong sense of community, in fact a new community that begins within but develops a life of its own beyond the performance. You reach the soup kitchen with a renewed, heightened, or 'opened' sense of self and this promulgates the extraordinarily intimate communality of the penultimate room. A situation where you can reveal as much or as little as you wish, where you can be as honest or as imaginative as you choose. The making of that choice is interesting and it is both heartening and intriguing that 'in the company of strangers' we choose to reveal rather than disguise.

See-Saw: *Before you arrive at the theatre: a man at the train station with a bunch of flowers waiting for - whom? ; teenagers on opposite sides of the street, swapping chips and flirtatious insults; milk spilt outside the theatre doorway. The very ordinary, un-noticeableness of these actions, by these 'performers', who you will meet later in the theatre, becomes utterly different when you place them under the lights, in a theatre…*
At the theatre: each seating bank (separated by a concealing curtain) is seasoned with audience and 'performers', an unknowing and unknown mixture. The entrance to the performance is through a darkened, gauze maze originating in Door A or Door B (whose traces remain in the Tramway today, used still to divide and allocate tickets printed with the ghost of a previous production) and finally placing you in 'your' auditorium. After suitable anticipation the curtain falls and for a moment you're facing a giant mirror, until the reflection doesn't repeat your wave, until the twins in the front rows

scratch different ears, then surprise turns to laughter, turns to embarrassment, and back to laughter; who is supposed to perform? Then the stories begin, people from Glasgow sharing their memories, their lives, with their neighbours; who is performing?

In the Kitchen
"Do you make the shows on your own?"

Since 1998 Quarantine has made ten pieces of theatre. Initially there were three core members, directors Richard Gregory and Renny O'Shea and myself (the designer). There are many people we have since worked with repeatedly, who have contributed significantly to the shape of the work, in particular the lighting designer Mike Brookes and more recently our administrative producer, Verity Leigh.

It is not possible to disentangle my contribution from that of my collaborators, as the scenography and performance elements are developed interdependently from the first concept, which is almost always presented as a visual idea. This then has to be translated into space, and it is in this transition that it finds a new dimension, as when Mount Everest becomes a field of light bulbs (*Geneva*).

Quarantine is more like a rubber jelly mould that can stretch to fit whatever contents are poured into it. The initial idea may be to make a rabbit, but if it turns out to be an elephant, nobody is too surprised.

Director's note: *I like to picture us arriving at our collaborations hatless - only polite when one's sitting down to eat. Each of us – designer, director, lighting designer, choreographer, writer, producer, whoever is involved at the beginning – start from the same place, interrogating our subject freely, forgetting that we'll have a particular role. At some point, sooner or later, each of us will need to put on the hat labelled 'designer' or 'director' (whatever we happen to have some degree of expertise in) but, at the start, we're just offering the ingredients that our own particular human experience suggest. But of course we need to start with something - a little 'amuse gueule' to get our juices flowing. Any of us might bring this. Most often mine happen to be visual - a formal construct (two seating banks for 'See-Saw'; a pool table for 'White Trash') that might evolve into a trope where our explorations can be sited. Simon takes these and shakes them up and distils them until only the essence remains - sometimes unrecognisable as stemming from the miniature crumb I offered. The visual, spatial, aesthetic choices that Quarantine make are an exact corollary with the way in which we develop live performance material. These elements are inseparable and inextricable -*

White Trash

Grace

the one the function of the other. In rehearsal, I try to develop material with performers that is, at the same time, a genuine reflection of their lived experience and somehow a heightened, theatrical comment upon it - through textual framing and juxtapositions, the choice of performance languages, a host of strategies... Simon's work - those mirror balls floating above the familiar party setting for 'Butterfly', the polished pole linking earth to heaven in 'Susan and Darren' - does something very similar: offering images which are at one and the same moment familiar, mundane even - perhaps 'real' - yet somehow suggesting something beyond the everyday.

Simon's scenography for Quarantine is most definitely and defiantly not simply the table our work is served upon. He chops, stirs, spices and salts like the rest of us. Our collective aim is to try to make something tasty enough to share...
(Richard Gregory - Artistic Director)

The Ingredients
"What's in them?"

We might start with one question and 20 people, perhaps 100 questions and two people, the outcome always confounds expectations and assumptions.

1. What have you forgotten?
2. Name something that you believe in...
3. What was the date of the last time you cried?
4. What stops you?
5...6...7...

Quarantine make theatre with, and arising from, the histories of the people we work with: a Glaswegian family; seven young white men from Manchester; a dancer and his mother who cleans; refugees in Leicester, immigrants in Ghent; a group of performers from various cities, yourselves... Quarantine are not a reality theatre company, we are not the stage version of *Big Brother*, but we do often choose to work with people who are not trained actors, people who are not trained to tell other people's stories and who could not tell stories unless they were true (or their own lies). And we ask these people to share their stories and experiences, to show but never to pretend. We use theatre and its means to develop a context for people to make discoveries for (and about) themselves and we create situations, circumstances and environments that encourage interactions between people, which can be intimate and invisible, public and celebratory. We try to make work where these moments can emerge unforeseen and unscripted, and continue beyond the frame of our work. We want to remove ourselves from the centre, to make space for others (paying guest or paid participant) to meet and determine if there is to be any further outcome; what might exist beyond the moment of connection. The work is a reflection of what we see in front of us, what we think is intriguing or confusing about the world that surrounds us now.

White Trash: *'a dirty ballet' of young, white, working-class men who tell us of their ambitions, their fears, how to survive growing up in Manchester, when they laugh, when they cry - provoking questions about what is 'real' and what is 'true'. A performance that takes place on and around a pool table (in a pub?), in a theatre surrounded by friends for the night, balancing sympathy with respect, eyes opened wide.*
When you book a ticket you are given the choice of sitting within the performance space or standing outside the space - on chairs on the stage surface within low boundary walls or standing outside the walls looking in - but it becomes clear that when the audience enter the space they adjust their preferences according to their immediate reaction upon viewing the options, the choice effectively between being onstage or offstage, participant or observer, active or passive.
"The seven are finding themselves as they perform, because their performance is their triumph, their nightly act of self-definition. In short, you're not told what happened; you're there as it happens."
(Peter Preston)

Grace: *A collection of people who are accustomed to performing are asked to present themselves, to be the person they are, perhaps to tell us things they should only tell their friends, to bring their cultural and social individualities together to squeeze a city into a theatre and see what happens next; tiny moments with huge consequences, can we recognise them? Can we change them? The set is slightly too big for the stage: it contains an arbitrary assemblage of glimpses from a city life, a collection of objects that, like the people that inhabit the city, have to find some way of functioning together however fragile or temporary. The stage is only accessible from the auditorium (only accessible from the city?) so the movement between the two is continuous, interrupting any notion that the audience seating is a refuge from the determination to tell stories that have been untold, stories that are always interrupted, stories that are best finished in the dark, in silence.*

The Recipes
"So how do you make the shows?"

The structure of the idea arrives very quickly and in fact it is usually born with the initial concept of the show – two seating banks facing each other / Susan and Darren's house / a table to share a meal at / a series of connected rooms / a ruby wedding party / a stage / a pool table. All these are situations that have in common the possibility for action and intervention. They are very 'real' settings or situations in the sense that they are, at the very least, recognisable and may also have very particular resonances, associations and memories for the spectators.

Of specific concern here is the tactile quality of the environments. The audience are always in physical contact with the 'set'. If my design work outside Quarantine principally feeds the eyes, here I have the challenge and pleasure of determining what it looks like, both on a macro and micro level, what the temperature to the touch should be (a concrete table or a wooden table); it matters what it feels like, even what it smells like. This extension of the audience's experience allows us to work with them both collectively and individually, allowing an element of choice that allows a variety of experiences to be drawn from the same evening.

However familiar and 'real' these environments might be, they are performance environments and do not pretend otherwise. It is in that contradiction that the design situates itself, tinkering with the reality of the familiar and positioned at its edges, looking for even the small spaces of ambiguity and tension between what we expect to happen and what might happen, an ambiguity that plays in the realm of the imagination.

Frank

See Saw

Eat Eat

Butterfly: *is made with three generations of a Glaswegian family. Each night they take us through a map of their lives and relationships. Each night the usual complications of family life manifest themselves within the performance. The situation is perhaps a family celebration of significance – the Tramway laid out with dance floor, surrounded by seating and tables for the guests, buffet tables with food for the interval, a bar at one end and the top table at the other. On the dance floor white balloons rebound amongst the dancers whilst, above their heads, the single mirror ball that still rotates forlornly after the party is over, becomes a cloud of 150 mirror balls floating over a parquet sea. The ceaseless meanderings of their refractions plotting a course to a thousand other celebrations. It is an investigation of our public and private worlds, of what we show and what we hide. It looks at ideas around family and belonging, at the* contradictions and the complications of those relationships that none of us ask for - at the accident of being born into a set of people that we're stuck with, one way or another, for life.

Eat Eat: The table is set, refugees to the UK offer their experiences in a performance which takes the form of a shared meal for performers and audience. A table and a room for a 'simple' supper, but a table (concrete, steel and rice) that needs to resonate beyond its immediate function to echo with the histories that are unfolding around it. Once seated, the view of the concrete table in the Tudor hall fades to be replaced by the sensation of the concrete on the palms of your hands, the sound of plates scraping across the surface as the food is served and the feel of the rice that traces a path up the centre of the table. This fades to be replaced by stories of loss, stories in song, stories in dance, stories told through photographs and official stamps, stories whispered in your ear, stories discovered in a parcel of herbs. This fades to be replaced by the conversation with your immediate and distant neighbours. The 'show' fades to be replaced by friends.

Rantsoen: A development of 'Eat Eat' in Ghent is in many ways a more aesthetically satisfying experience but does not function as well. Located in an old garage, a smaller walled and floored space is created, painted a deep red; within this a large, circular table with a perimeter band of warm wood and two tonnes of rice in the centre. The rice is raked and smoothed until a soft mound gives the table the sense of being pregnant with stories waiting to be born. However, the shape and scale of the table means that the guests are restricted to communicating with those within their arc of the table rather than, as previously, those across the long table. In this new environment, those on the opposite side of the table are only observed in the same way that the performance moments on the table become 'on stage'. Thus the shape and scale of the event denies the intimacy that fosters the shift from observing performance to becoming implicated in the event.

Table Linen
"Do you do the dresses as well?"

I think we have made one costume in the ten shows we've created and we rejected that at the dress rehearsal in favour of something found in the costume store that wouldn't quite do up at the back. The costumes are clothes belonging to those making the show, they are clothes that carry the biography of their owners, clothes that have the marks of idle hands and rainy days, mismatched threads and lost buttons, clothes whose elbows, knees and buttocks could only belong to one body. Clothes that carry the familiar smells of home cooking, grass cuttings, the remembered traces of cigarettes, cigars and pipes.

Washing Up
"Do we have to?"

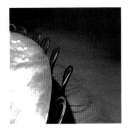 

Rantsoen

Butterfly

Have we started yet?

Transformation, interpolation, intervention

'Transformation is transformatory *Augusto Boal*'

One summer I am travelling in Greece and Turkey with very little money and even less reason to be there. I go to sleep at one end of a sandy beach. At the other end a group of young people sit around a fire and pitch tents for the night. I think about them; beautiful youth, innocent souls, and wonder whether they appreciate the beauty of the void above them; the fire and lights spoiling my shooting stars to whose sadness I am addicted. When I wake up it is really early, maybe five or six o'clock, and the beautiful ones are almost gone, tent and everything. I don't even remember what day it is; were they weekenders now off to work? There is a lady sleeping under a fur coat quite close to me.

She says she is from Budapest and the government has destroyed her pension. It's easier to be homeless in good weather on a beautiful beach.

That was a false start

An art student's experience in Soviet Russia: Liz Ascroft, wears her grandmother's old fur coat on a college trip because it was going to be cold. The coat was otherwise destined for the charity shop. She decided to explore beyond the usual tourist haunts and got off a train at its final destination. Empty shelves inside a corner supermarket and bleak communist housing. An elderly woman spits at her. There are verbal attacks, and she is harassed back to the train station. Only prostitutes wear fur coats in this neighbourhood.

That was a false start

In 2001, a newspaper prints an image of two sunbathers on a beach in Spain. Not far from them is a fully-clothed, middle-aged woman washed up on the beach, dead; a would-be migrant. In an exploratory workshop for Cardboard Citizens I watch actors recreate this image. Sylvia, who is so old that no one can guess her age, lies down on the grubby floor. She carefully positions her left arm with surprising accuracy in imitation of the dead body. Discussion and improvisations follow and Sylvia is still in her position, a constant *aide memoir*: image theatre.

Uncle Julian lives in Wiltshire. During the Second World War, he was stranded in North Africa waiting to cross the Mediterranean away from

The Beach

Mortuary

Snapshot

enemy fire. The rumour was that there were plenty of enemy forces waiting in Southern Italy, Sardinia and Sicily. A famous act of deception succeeded in allowing the safe crossing and landing of a great many troops into Sicily. Briefly, "Operation Mincemeat" involved the stranding of a body on a beach in Spain, carrying fake documents indicating a forthcoming landing in Sardinia. Enemy troops were moved to Sardinia and the Allied forces crossing to Sicily met with significantly reduced resistance. So who was the body on the beach this time?

Major Martin, as he had become known, was in fact a homeless man who had died of pneumonia after ingesting rat poison. His unclaimed body from Hackney Mortuary significantly changed the course of the war and saved many lives, perhaps even the life of Uncle Julian. Cardboard Citizens' production of *Mincemeat* reclaimed this story for the homeless man who was buried in Spain with full military honours.

Cardboard Citizens works with over 3,000 homeless people a year; 3,000 people who they can name. Homelessness in the United Kingdom is defined as living in bed and breakfast accommodation, a hostel or on the street; not in a house. The status of homelessness implies diminished citizenship. Addressing this perceived injustice Cardboard Citizens originated as a homeless people's theatre company but has more recently widenend its remit, as each week 250 refugees, displaced people, asylum seekers and homeless and ex-homeless people access the company's workshops. Each year Cardboard Citzizens provides over 400 weeks of paid employment to homeless actors.

Our experience of working with homeless and ex-homeless people, including refugees and asylum seekers, and our roots in forum theatre give our theatre a distinctive artistic voice. As our profile and reputation have grown, especially through touring to arts venues and mounting co-productions and site-specific projects, we have earned critical acclaim. A key feature of this work is the bringing together of mainstream and homeless audiences in a unique cultural partnership that develops new audiences for the future.

Audiences approaching Cardboard Citizens' work, perhaps for the first time, may have some preconceived expectations or even prejudice. The company endeavors to confront these expectations and collaboration with the Royal Shakespeare Theatre is one of the ways in which this takes place. Yet such a collaboration is quite natural, when we consider the Elizabethan period where 'rogues and vagabonds', 'sturdy beggars', actors who had had to develop their skills as a means of survival, were the normal purveyors of the dramatic art. Citz actors are no different, they have little if any training, they didn't go to drama school. It is often easy to be seduced by the notion that actors are somehow different or special, especially in this age of celebrity-obsessed culture. Kervork Malikyan, who played the older Pericles, is a regular RSC actor. He is a second generation refugee from the 1915 Armenian holocaust.

Cardboard Citizens mounted a small-scale, storytelling production of the play [Pericles] boiled down to one hour, with five actors and two stools, which we played to refugee groups around the capital - Afghans one night, Iraqis another, Kurds, Latin Americans, Africans, Albanians, Bosnians, as well as general audiences of homeless people (another kind of exile) and asylum seekers. The theatre became a meeting ground, a site of conversation; we told the story of Pericles and they told us stories back, by turns amazing, shocking, unbelievable, painful, normal. The famous recognition scene drew tears from audiences who could barely understand the words, but knew something about separation and sometimes reunion. Telling stories has that power...

Yes we have started

The Patron saint of actors is St Genesius. The 17th-century legend tells that he was so convincing in his role in a religious pageant that he was actually executed during the performance. Cardboard Citizens actors are playing themselves playing a role. Each actor's performance is marked as they play themselves in the role of actor, blurring the boundaries of real life and fiction. When a testimony or story is told, interwoven into Shakespeare's text, we might ask if it is the actors own experience he is sharing with us, or if is he speaking for someone else. When playing Timon in the woods, at what level do Madha's or Agron's life experiences as refugees and ex rough sleepers enhance the playing? This honest playing is a significantly influential factor in the design; there are no theatrical tricks or fake properties. In Woyzeck they declare themselves:

We are Cardboard Citizens and we are going to do a play called Woyzeck. We don't actually have enough actors to do this play so some of the actors here have brought along their pets. The rat will play the part of the performing horse and the goldfish play the drunks at the tavern. Sadly our oldest member of the company can't be with us as she is too decrepit, so the part of the Grandmother will be played by live video link to Sylvia. This is Sylvia...

a framed photo of Sylvia is passed round the audience. In fact, Sylvia was a projection on to one of the two moons that were part of the set that mirrored itself.

The company's performance style is derived from *The Theatre of the Oppressed* – an over-arching title given to the ensemble of techniques and approaches to theatre pioneered by the Brazilian theatre practitioner Augusto Boal. The common element to the various branches of Boal's work is that they all seek to make the power of theatre a force for change accessible to everyone, particularly those in oppressed situations. Citz use Forum Techniques to explore texts in depth, endeavouring to relate them to the lives of us all. Scenes are re-played at the audience's request and changes made to discover different outcomes. The facilitator of this improvisation is called the Joker. In *Woyzeck* the role of the Joker is expanded further, extending the idea of Boal's initial descriptors, often shifting between performers and stepping in and out of the action. The freedom inherent in a polymorphic style creates possibilities for different beginnings or false starts and opens the possibilities for interweaving of themes and images – a bricolage.

With each piece of work we try to find a group identity for the performers. In *Pericles* it was asylum seekers, in *Mincemeat* each actor was defined by their role at a funeral: officious undertaker, sensitive hearse driver, dispassionate pall bearer, token mourner; each role mirroring some characteristic of the performers themselves as well as relating to the characters in the play. Sylvia (rumour has it that one of her previous incarnations included an East-End madam) is a bumptious gruff mourner, who subsequently plays a belligerent Winston Churchill, her alopecia reflecting his baldness. In *Timon of Athens* we again accentuate the *inner* person. In this case the corporate trainer lurking within each actor grows from a stereotype identified within each performer. Character traits can then be visually portrayed through ideas for the subtle, or sometimes the less than subtle, attribution of costume. Few performers in any discipline, in any field, simply don the costume and repeat the lines. When we dress for work we assume our work character. Many actors in other companies prefer to not work with any of their own belongings in a performance as they feel that they may become distracted from engaging with their adopted character. For Citz performers it is quite the opposite. There are no special hair cuts, wigs or overt changes to the Citz performers. They may retain the use of some of their own clothes if they find it helpful, often their own favourite performing shoes.

Agron Biba

Redley Silva

Mincemeat

For a Shakespeare play, generally there are remarkably few items of clothing used to tell the story, change the characters, or to indicate status. This deliberate direction maintains the pace of the storytelling as no one is required to leave the performance space unnecessarily and the actors are trusted with maintaining the sense and the meaning of the words. Our own visual language is decided upon. Each performer has a set of clothes that in various layers and combinations give the audience enough images to allow them to adopt their own interpretation of the visual clues. In *Timon*, for example, when performers are playing servants they are seen wearing short sleeved shirts and name badges, when they play Lords they are transformed merely by the wearing of jackets and ties. These clothes are real clothes, there is nothing implicitly theatrical about them. Contrastingly, clothes are also able to assist with story telling in an entirely ambiguous fashion. In *Mincemeat*, was it jackets that the performers were shaking or fishing nets, in *Pericles*, was it socks or fish collected from the floor of the washing space?

Space is integral to the development of the work, never more significantly so than for the production of *Mincemeat*. With space in the capital at a premium the romantic notion of the site specific performance is in reality more than offset by the need to fight for permission to perform, additionally burdened by more legal requirements than one can imagine. Sites fertile for performance are also ripe for re-development. *Mincemeat* was written alongside the negotiated possibilities and limitations that the available space could offer. The old Hartley's Jam Factory had all the necessary qualities of industrial Victorian architecture. A vast upstairs warehouse was destined to become both Heaven's waiting room and a Bomb site, and the discovery of a tiled room inspired the writing of the Mortuary scenes. Broad, subtle strokes were used to intervene and manipulate the spaces. Modification rather than absolute change was an important principle as the building had its own visual language which was harnessed in order to create meaning and develop the potential for the audience to 'read' the spaces.

Working at this moderate scale there remained the opportunity to attend to the detail of each space. The intervention in the room which became the mortuary was to lay down a gloss white plastic floor covering with drainage plug holes at regular intervals. On the walls, there already existed a number of metal brackets, function unknown. More brackets were added to imply the possibility of shelving capable of storing bodies. Under each bracket, the addition of a plastic bucket filled with strange fluid, a glass fronted fridge containing

neatly folded empty body bags labelled 5ft - 5ft 6", 5 ft 6"-5 ft 10" and so on, evoked further, a sense of morbidity. The idea for a hanging row of leather belts came from an interview held with a mortician. I discovered that they use belts around the corpses when they wheel them about so that their arms don't fall off the trolley, getting in the way, and causing accidents.

For *Pericles* the vast spaces of the supermarket distribution warehouse posed different challenges, notably in terms of the sheer scale. Research into the Red Cross Centre at Sangatte informed the visual language up to a point but the improbability of Shakespeare's storyline required a development in the design that would support his fiction. Pericles is shipwrecked with improbable regularity and experiences a great many coincidental events all of which are shared by the audience as they promenade through and around the spaces. One bonus of having ten such enormous spaces was that the audience, cast as asylum seekers, were initially able to be placed at individual desks and confronted by a twenty page Home Office asylum application form and a pencil tied to the desk with string. More false starts. Shakespeare's *Pericles* takes us into a room inspired by a photograph showing the washing at Sangatte, hung out to dry on fencing. After two storms and two shipwrecks the later spaces on 'the journey' were blacked out allowing for significantly more scope in the use of lighting. (Earlier scenes having been exposed to daylight invading through the overhead skylights). The reunion scene at the Temple of Diana used theatre staging, blacks, gauze and lighting to unexpected magical effect. The sea of beds was traversed by the audience at one end of the room, in order that they might better appreciate the scale of the installation. The beds had no blankets. The blankets were stacked to one side. As the audience filed past they were given a blanket to sit on in the next room. This then became a location that might become inhabited. Perhaps it will be you who will sleep here tonight?

Space and Time were manipulated with the aid of video. In the reduced version of *Pericles* when the character of Thaissa is brought back to life having been buried at sea in a coffin, a frozen TV image held her face for the length of the scene until at last she opened her eyes and the actor stepped from behind the TV and the image faded. When this idea was transcribed to the large-scale production the iconic object of the shipping container became the ship, then the coffin. An image of Thaissa lying 'dead' inside the container was projected onto a slatted plastic screen at one end of the open container. The image zoomed in onto her face, her eyes opened and she stood and walked through the plastic screen. The Brothel was a two level

Portacabin with internal stairs. Selected audience were allowed to watch the 'rape' scene through peep holes in the windows. Two cameras placed inside the room allowed the rest of the audience to watch the scene projected onto the walls of the space.

My first professional job, many years ago, was as a Props ASM at the Royal Theatre, Northampton. Owing to unforeseen circumstances I found myself 'on the book', cueing a show. I remember being astonished and delighted to hear the audience applaud the set as the house curtain rose at my command. It was all going well when I mistook the telephone ringer button for the door bell; and I didn't stop ringing it. The actor, expecting to answer the door to let in the Vicar, eventually answered the telephone and began to have an improvised conversation with a completely fictional person. In the meantime, the actor waiting for his entrance, and hearing no doorbell, started knocking, then banging, unable to open the door from outside the set. There is always a thrill in the discovery of those objects that are embedded with the potential for intervention and invention.

In *Woyzeck* a running machine gave Woyzeck a place to be physically active at any time. In *Timon* the gold that he gives away and subsequently rediscovers is Ferrero Rocher chocolates, Benson and Hedges Cigarettes, and gold party poppers; the language of the conference world.
The chocolate is smeared on shirts as society begins to breakdown. When Timon goes mad in the woods he trashes the neat corporate world, having served up his own excrement at his final banquet, he then piles up staging, rips up carpet and builds himself a 'bash' from whatever is lying about.

By its very nature the context of the process is different with each piece. I am reluctant to make decisions until it is absolutely clear that I am making the right one. I sometimes regret that alternative solutions may not see light of day, and that different avenues are not explored. I look for the potential in each shooting star idea. Consequently resolutions may sometimes be late and working conditions stressful. I occasionally think that, as it is the actor, the audience and the space which orientate the design, so it is that I act merely as agent, representing all three. During the trials and tribulations of the design process I hang on to two pieces of advice: one, if in doubt do nothing, and two, if it's worth doing, it is at least worth doing badly.

Timon of Athens

Mortuary

Woyzeck

That was a false end

collaborators

Cardboard Citizens Theatre Company was formed in 1991 by Adrian Jackson and has forged a reputation for innovative, interactive, social theatre. Its roots and methodology stem from the work of the Brazilian theatre practitioner Augusto Boal and his work 'The Theatre of The Oppressed'. It is now recognised as a major contributor to the London theatre scene, providing many opportunities for cultural exploration to homeless and ex-homeless people, without compromising its integrity and its allegiance to the oppressed.

"Who can speak broader than he that has no house to put his head in? Such may rant against great buildings?" *(Timon of Athens Act III, sc IV)*

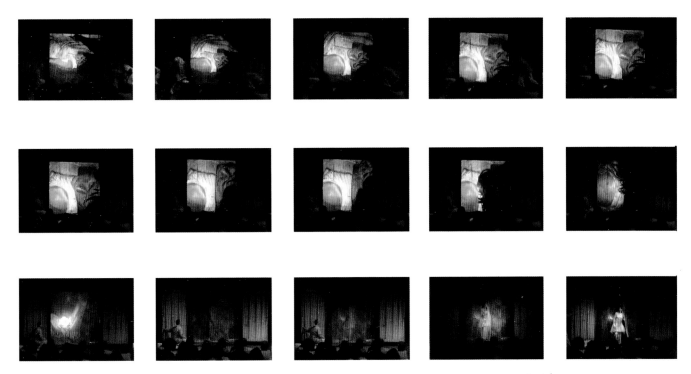

Pericles sequence

Listening shell
Credit: Dee Conway

Dody Nash
in discussion with a member
of the general public
Credit: Dee Conway

Demonstrating the art of
listening in 'counterpoint'
Credit: Dee Conway

futurespace

anyone who really loves music needs a practical relationship with it, as we can see from children, who are always very pragmatic, and begin to do things before they understand them

Luciano Berio

This is the Berio space.

A celebration of his music, his techniques, his culture, his visions for music technology, his love of musical instruments.

A man who sought to understand complexity of different cultures - past, present and future, with a passion for 'unmediated' and varied forms of communication.

A space celebrating Berio becomes a place for cultural exchange.

A vast and complex mix of social groups will use the space, and in doing so, learn about Berio. And so the mirror is turned towards themselves.

As such it becomes a 'music classroom for the future'.

The space is all inclusive. It welcomes all - the person who just wants to sit down, the fanatical musicologist, the daydreamer, the young person who is curious.

The space is there for creative responses in all their forms.

Space for private experience, social relaxation, public performance.

The space is a future expression of a futuristic past. It celebrates new technologies - audio-visual, digital, material.

The space embraces the Italian view that classicism lies hand in hand with the new.

A space to express the simple beauty of creativity.

collaborators

*Dody Nash is a designer who designs
specifically for music...*

*The Berio Lounge was commissioned for the Ballroom Foyer
by the South Bank Centre (SBC) and London Sinfonietta, to
celebrate the life and work of Luciano Berio (1925-2003).
It was part of the festival Omaggio;
A Celebration of Luciano Berio.*

*Over a six-month period, Dody was asked to develop
a concept based around the ideas of music, learning
and the future, and to coordinate the delivery of its physical
and technical aspects.*

*In it, she collaborated with a long list of people, including
public arts organisations, commercial design
manufacturers, educationalists, academics, translators,
museum directors, cultural attachés, product designers,
sound designers, web designers, filmmakers,
choreographers, school children, publishers, publicists,
graphic designers and printers.*

1 *You've mentioned that the job of creating the
Berio Lounge for the South Bank Centre was a
tender. How did this affect your relationship with
the client?*
It was a big surprise to be working in this way.
My ideal working scenario is that both client and
designer start off with more or less blank sheets of
paper and a contract. The education managers at
the South Bank Centre and London Sinfonietta
asked me to come up with a concept, based on an
ambition to create a futuristic music technology
installation. This would be used to exhibit the
several education projects and to hold live events,
with possible sponsorship in kind. I had to push the
boat out from the very beginning and squeeze the
basic research into a fortnight. During this period
I formulated a set of basic principles to be applied
to the exhibition content; I planned a diverse range
of sections to communicate to a kaleidoscope of
visitors and present many of Berio's principal
themes. Unwilling to write these down on paper,
I did not want to reveal or pin down my ideas.
So, I came up with two documents: *Future Space*,
and *Future Comment*. The first was a series of
sentences which described the ethos of the
installation, the second imagined visitor response
soundbites – a way of catching glimpses of the
various installation elements. I would describe
the beginning of this relationship as being slightly
'cat and mouse'. They were sufficiently intrigued.

2 *Did that change once you were under contract?*
Unusually, Neill Quinton (SBC Music Education)
told me that I had a free hand – the phrase he used
was that he would be 'hands off'. It was
remarkably free, trusting and very liberating.

Effectively, I was the creative director and project
manager for the installation, and Neill Quinton
managed all the education work and (together with
Fiona Lockwood of London Sinfonietta) assembled
music, films and copyright permissions. We wrote
the print material together, and collaborated on
any areas which needed work and on the overall
curation - be it in education, choice of films and
music, in the installation or in the planning of live
events. We co-commissioned a string of artists
together. This was an interesting process as some
were as a result of an animation competition,
and others were artists who we already admired.
The hardest part was bringing our areas together
in co-writing a good editorial for the catalogue
and exhibition signage, in a mood of obsessive
attention to detail and pre-first night nerves!

3 *Where were the problems?*
Given that the SBC is such a large organisation,
unanticipated problems were remarkably few.
Nearly all the sponsorship in-kind deals and
resulting publicity had to be handled by me, since
politically, the Development Department could only
be involved in direct financial sponsorship. As a
freelancer, that was a unique and responsible
position. It was essential to the success of the
project to be able to cement those relationships.
A second area was that I had not realised the
attendants looking after the installation were line
managed by people not as deeply involved in the
planning of it. In my opinion, the attendants are as
much a part of the ethos of an installation as
anything else. Once the installation had opened,
this made the inevitable troubleshooting a lot
harder as I found myself awkwardly asking for
permission to deal with the 'snagging'.
Lastly, it was the time when the Disability
Discrimination Act was about to come in, so senior
management seemed very jumpy about what
accessibility meant for them as an organisation.

4 *Much of the exhibition was made by design
manufacturers in Italy and USA. How did this come
about?*
For me, a 'Berio Lounge' should be an Italian
cultural space (complete with installation titles in
dual translation). A significant part of Italian culture
is design, particularly from Milan. The face of
contemporary music can be surprisingly fusty, so
I wanted to use classic design to create an
ambience in which any visitor would feel at ease.
The Ballroom Foyer has its own culture of visitors,
to whom it very much belongs. I thought hard about
the families, schools, concert goers, and people
who come for meetings or to socialise. The space
can be empty in the evenings, so I was pleased
that the ambience of lounging, reading, listening
and drinking carried on right up until closing time.
In the words of one visitor, it was a 'lifestyle', to

Media Tables Detail
Credit: Dee Conway

Media Tables
Credit: Dee Conway

"You are attracted to it because you can hear something curious and are unsure what it is - in order to engage with it, you have to be with it inside the shell for some time. It doesn't reveal itself immediately, but becomes an intimate experience, requiring time. It has a quiet tranquillity, with occasional surprises. The sound is like a watching clouds passing – you hear things in them you're not really sure you've heard, and you make up your own narrative."

which there were many return visitors.
People were able to learn about contemporary music in a relaxed way - a good example of accessibility and education!
Another aspect was the ambition of the installation to be a 'classroom of the future'. I visited a fair in Frankfurt called *Material Vision*. There were two material technologies particularly suitable: one was CorianTM - a plastic-like material made from aluminium-tri-hydrate and acrylic resins, the other was Sentryglas®ExpressionsTM. This is decorative glass consisting of a polmer sheet, printed with images, laminated between two sheets of toughened glass. Both were manufactured by the international company, DuPont.
The third reason was that there was no chance that a future technology environment could be paid for within the budget. The strategy had to be to approach companies who would be interested in working with us on a sponsorship basis.

5 *How did you negotiate sponsorship?*
Future Space and *Future Comment* texts formed the basis of my approaches to design manufacturers. I created new texts for each company, envisaging a perhaps imaginary product within the lounge environment. For DuPont, both projects were new creative explorations of their technology. For Italian companies (Unifor, Cabas & Montina) it was good to be part of an Italian cultural event revolving around a legendary figure, and people were interested in what was happening culturally in London. It was also a beautiful and genuine project which they contributed to in a gesture of kindness. The Italian Cultural Institute and industry contacts endorsed
my proposals. Big names like Zanotta (beanbags) and Apple (computers), are constantly besieged with requests, and I repeatedly made the case for their involvement. With an impressive list, it became easier to negotiate with other companies. The English carpet makers, Ryalux, wove 16 square metres of long shagpile in a bespoke colour. Publishers, record labels and booksellers were also involved. Very much a one-off project!

6 *One of the projects, the Media Tables involved several different manufacturers. What did that involve?*
The installation needed a way of including viewing screens for films. I thought about how film is used in public spaces, and how both glass and whiteness affects where we focus and how we think.
The Ballroom Foyer is like a swimming pool and I wanted to keep its calm feeling by designing horizontal elements for the installation. I was also looking for an application for Sentryglas®ExpressionsTM. I came up with a printed glass table which would contain plasma screens. Visually, it was a collage of live and

printed images - a collection of score material,
photographs of Berio, Italy, and enlarged pencil
drawings representing 'linear journeyings'
or landscapes recalling musical lines and life
journeys. The underside of the glass would be
frosted, except for a small rectangle exposing the
plasma screen.

I had two project managers at DuPont, in Geneva
and Milan. The Photoshop files had to be couriered
to Washington DC to be printed, and then shipped
back to London for lamination at Fusion Glass.
After false starts, a solution for the table structure
(in beauty, structure and budget) came in the form
of an office table with a very elegant frame which
was manufactured by a company called Unifor.

7 *This table frame was quite special. Can you tell
me more about it?*
The beauty of the frame was that it was made from
sections of hollow, triangular, extruded aluminium,
and hence the section contained the structural
triangulation. The shallow depth of the plasma
screens and wiring could be contained within
the thickness of the frame.

The glass was cut at a 45° chamfer and sat within
the triangular frame. A 45° cut on laminated,
toughened glass was hard to achieve, and there
were several conference calls between
Washington, London and Milan. In the end I told
Unifor, via my contact via fax (everything was
translated) that we were having problems.
Extraordinarily, Unifor applied new tooling to the
extruding process, and produced the same frame,
but with a small ledge which would take the glass
with a standard 90° cut. They also offered to
design an undercarriage to hold the plasma
screen. I went through the specifications of the
screen with Pioneer, and these were relayed to
both Unifor and Fusion Glass (responsible for the
frosting). This then left the question of tolerances.
Unifor's glass/frame tolerance was tiny at +1/-1.
With no room for mistake, I needed guarantees
from Fusion Glass. Both frames and glass were
stunning when they arrived, and the effect was one
of images floating in water in a shallow surface,
a dreamspace.

8 *You worked with product designer Julian Brown,
on the design of the Listening Shells.
Can you tell me something about that?*
I've known Julian for many years, and we know
each other's strengths and weaknesses as
designers. We often cast an eye on each other's
work. Where I turn out prop designs in a day, he'll
spend months designing a coffee pot. Julian's real
forte is shape. This comes from a very deep
conceptual understanding of what he is trying to
create. Julian has tended to grow a design from a
pure idea, where I have looked to assimilate from
complexity. Influences rub off and I have started to

*Product designer Julian
Brown, with the design of the
Listening Shells*

create more abstract performance spaces, with more direct parallels between visual and musical forms. I wanted to bring that to the design of the *Listening Shells*, which was the Berio Lounge's most ambitious piece, from a conceptual and technical point of view.

9 *How did you come up with the design?*
The Berio Lounge needed a signature piece to reflect the composer as an iconic figure who was bold, avant garde, and experimented with sound. We wanted something which might have been thought of in the 1960s, but was waiting for 21st-century technology. It was about privacy and listening. The practical starting point was that you sat in something which had speakers near your ear, transmitting barely perceptible sounds, as if from a day dream. You would need to listen very, very carefully.

'Piling in'
Credit: Dee Conway

We talked about eggs, pods, stems, shells, trumpet speakers and musical instruments. We knew it should be made from white Corian, which feels like a shell, is cool to touch and reminds me of *2001: A Space Odyssey*. Normally used as a cladding material, it is thermoformable, so we thought it theoretically possible to create an integral 3D structure with interesting acoustic properties.
We chose a shape which felt original, centring around the simple form of a 'stick' which fed sound to a 'sphere'. In design terms, it operated on many levels: there was a common sound throughout the microenvironment of the shell; it was a designed thing, almost a piece of furniture, embuing a listening experience with a physical experience of being inside a shell. It had the physical and spiritual quality of a musical instrument which you became part of. The striking appearance of the tail or stick, which provided structural support, gave it both an expression of stance and otherworldliness. It's also where the sound came from - like an organic stem feeding a seed pod, it fed sound to an 'audio pearl' in the centre of the sphere.

'The Room of Folk Songs'
Credit: Dee Conway

10 *You've mentioned that it was technically very challenging. Can you tell me about the manufacturing process?*
The *Listening Shells* were project-managed by Steve Ball (DuPont Corian) and fabricated by Richard Marwood Interiors. According to them, neither had attempted anything like this before. Engineering, physical strength, ingenuity, patience and belief – all were put to the test over a three-month period, during which we visited the factory to work on the design.
There was a period of experimenting and load testing in order to find the right process.
The hardest part was the sphere. It needed an accurate female and male jig. Corian sheets were cut into eight leaves, individually heated and then formed and left to cool on the jig. A routing jig was

'Noise Shaping'
Credit: Dee Conway

made to trim the leaves into the exact geometric shape. Four leaves were put on the male jig and glued together to form one half. This required a strong clamping device. Clamping the two halves together was more challenging since each weighed 110kgs. The opening was cut using a second routing jig and strengthened with a thin disc. Between the sphere and the stick was an interlinking 'trumpet' section. We produced several drawings, since it contained the audio element and was the structural connecting point: Corian was formed on a female jig placed inside a vacuum bag press, then trimmed and seamed to the sphere. The joint between the trumpet and the stick was internally connected with a steel component. The stick was formed around a steel tube, with a female jig to hold it in place, and tipped with a sculpted block of Corian. The entire piece was sanded for several days, throughout the assembly process.

A. 'Lounge Circle' by Nash
Site for many of the live performances.
'Audio Landscape' by Sound Intermedia
Berio's music drifted through recordings of Florence by the Centro Tempo Reale (founded by Berio).

B. 1968:'Sinfonia' and the 'Sacco'
BBC Symphony Orchestra/21st Century Classroom 'Sinfonia' project; 'Sacco' by Zanotta; beanbags by Dalmain Primary School/Cloth of Gold; ZigZag by Nash for DuPont Corian
'Sinfonia' was a great early work which combined playful free-thinking and technological advancements and influenced a generation. I found parallels in the iconic 1968 'Sacco' beanbag and led a design project, which asked "How do we sit? How do we listen?" Sitting on the beanbags at the 'ZigZag' headphone trees, you could listen to 'Sinfonia', alongside music and thoughts by student composers.

C. Computer Information Zone website by Nash/Sound Intermedia/Sibelius/various; 'Naòs' tables by Unifor; computers by Apple; 'Loop' chair (RFH edition) by Julian Brown for Cabas. For music students, festival followers, and new listeners, I commissioned a website to provide a biography, list of works, discography, bibliography, musical excerpts and festival programme notes. On suggestion of musicologist David Osmond-Smith, I explored literary connections with a number of extracts by Berio himself and other writers whom he worked with on librettos, including Calvino, Eco and Sanguinetti, some in new translation. Installation films and projects were included and a complete list of credits.

D. 'Noise Shaping' by Sound Intermedia
"Use the graphics tablet to compose your own piece using noise. As you move the stylus across the tablet, listen to how the apparently chaotic hiss of the noise can be transformed to a musical pitch, and how stillness can become a rhythm. Play for a while and when you are ready, record your performance. Listen and watch a graphic animation generated by your music." Sound Intermedia

E. 'Media tables', Glass tops by Nash/DuPont/Fusion Glass; 'Naòs' table frames by Unifor; screens by Pioneer; film installation by Sound Intermedia/various.
In addition to much archive material, new commissions included: documentary by Deborah May; 'Making New Sequenzas' by Royal Academy of Music/London Sinfonietta/ Deborah May ; 'Voices' by London Sinfonietta/Connect/Oblong; 'Linking to Berio' by Philharmonia Orchestra Schools Link/Claudia Lee; animations by Oblong/Elina Roditou/Pete Gomes.

F. 'Exploding Soundscape' by Sound Intermedia
In response to my brief to recreate the action and drama of Rebecca Horn's exploding piano, Sound Intermedia used four channels to explode, interrupt the tranquillity of the lounge with bursts of spatialised sound, using musical fragments and reflecting a genre pioneered by electronic sound.

G. 'Listening Shells' by Nash/Brown for DuPont Corian/Sound Intermedia

H. Book Lounge
'Eidelweiss' carpet by Ryalux; books supplied by Italian Bookshop/various; 'Romeo Moon' by Philippe Starcke for Flos and 'Dan' table by Jürgen Müller for DePadova supplied by Coexistence
Lounging on decadent white shagpile, you could read in Italian or English, scores, books and magazines on Berio, the orchestra, world music, opera, contemporary music and electronic sound; Italian novels, educational theories, children's books, 50s/60s photography, design, architecture, fashion magazines and dictionaries - reflecting both specific and general connections which I had used, discovered, or felt would help visitors to explore the subject matter in whatever way was suitable to them.

I. 'Room of Folk Songs'
'Folk Songs Project' by London Sinfonietta/Creative Partnerships/ Sound Intermedia; 'Magnetic World Map' and 'Viola Carpet' by Nash; 'Folk Cushions' by Cloth of Gold/Dalmain Primary School; games for babies and small children (Nash/Timms).
On a map of the world you could trace your origins: The project was to create recorded compositions using folk songs from students' origin countries and Berio's 'Motettu de Tristura'.
I suggested they photograph objects which were of importance to their family history and write a text. We printed stories from around the world and paired them with recordings of native songs. Visitors discovered it was fun to listen to two songs at once. Other students created textiles for cushions using family objects and 'musical response' artwork. I invited visitors to write where they came from and their favourite songs and post in a perspex box or attach to the map with a magnet person.

J. 'Lounge Furniture'
'Leopoldo' tables and 'Leopolda' chairs by Konstantin Grcic for Montina; 'Glo Ball F' by Jasper Morrison for Flos supplied by Coexistence

a landscape
of possibilities

by Greer Crawley

Forkbeard Fantasy was formed, in 1974, by Chris and Tim
Britton. Penny Saunders became the third artistic director in
1980. They were later joined by Ed Jobling, who performs as
well as operating sound and film projection and Robin
Thorburn, lighting director and cinematographer. Forkbeard's
pioneering performance work, which has played an important
role in shaping new directions in theatre and developing new
audiences, has its roots in pursuing innovative possibilities
with science and technology. Noted for its experiments with
film, animation, mechanical props and interactive
installations, the company has always revelled in breaking
rules, creating the unexpected and mixing different media and
art forms. The approach has always been: 'What if we tried
this?' and 'why not?' - because anything is possible.

Collaboration within both the design and the devising /
rehearsal processes is very important to Forkbeard.
Chris Britton has described how 'all of us tend to get involved
in all aspects of creating the show. We are more related to
artists' style of expression than that of the theatrical culture
when we devise the work. Many ideas and experiments
we might spend ages working on get shelved for developing
at a later date, or never see the light of day.'

This experimental approach requires a great deal of trust.
For Penny Saunders, 'it's like jumping into the dark, but it does
allow individual thought patterns to grow to a decent size,
before they have to combine with other imaginations.'
The company members see themselves as equal contributors,
with each other's interests at heart. This equality is
empowering. 'The more you allow another's creativity,' says
Penny, 'the more they'll allow yours, but you also have to fight
your corner and be prepared to lose. The resulting dialogue
is a negotiation. This may sound chaotic but there is a point
when the cohesion happens, so that our intention will be clear
to an (imaginative) audience.'

collaborators

The Forkbeard collaborations take place in their studios, at Waterslade in the Devon. Here are the laboratories where 'imaginative possibilities' are explored through workshops and experiments. Among the assortment of buildings, 'Penny's barn' has a magical status. A place for metamorphosis and invention, it is crowded with her creations, spare parts, objects and materials in the process of being, or waiting to be, transformed. This is a familiar environment for the designer who grew up surrounded by the inventive efforts of her father, a frustrated engineer who delighted in DIY and making her toys. His influence, together with her lack of a conventional training in theatre design, is responsible for the idiosyncratic approach she takes to set design.

'My sewing machine table is next to the welding bay. I love making things from the very small and soft to the heavy and slow-to-make. In theatre culture, the work of the designer is often separate from that of the set builder and costume maker. I find that the nature, shape and look of a part of the set or costume grow as I make them. I use a very wide range of materials in a single piece - metal, latex, fabric, timber, and automation - and it is often when one is right in the structure of something that one realises the potential for a radical change in the convention of what one is making.'

At first, the mechanisms she used were simple adaptations of parts from domestic equipment such as washing machines, food mixers and vacuum cleaners. Then, as she became more familiar with the mechanics and wiring, she grew more ambitious and specific about the effects she wanted to achieve and has regularly sought out specialist advice on 'how things work, things like the different tensions on the inside and outside of a spring, the variation in air pressure inside an inflatable with a variable shape, electrical circuits, switch and trigger mechanisms, on and on, gradually adding a little more to the whole.'

When looking for an explanation of a new process or for technical information, her research often begins with studying trade magazines and following up leads in telephone or internet directories. Her sets and props have been operated by remote sensing, a wide variety of motors, gearing systems and drive belts, electronic circuits, solenoids, timing systems, light sensors and specially engineered parts made to a high specification to survive the heavy usage in Forkbeard's shows and exhibitions.

The problems of structural engineering present as much of a challenge as those of mechanical engineering. One of her most ambitious projects is to create a full-size, glass temple that moves in the wind. She describes its as 'an earthquake upside down'. To achieve her aim, she is collaborating with students and staff from Bristol University's Civil Engineering Department, which specialises in earthquake technology. A prototype has been made and experiments have been undertaken in wind tunnels.

'I've always wanted to make a snail, to get to know the structure inside, how the shell is made.'

Penny is equally happy experimenting with structures involving string and candlewax. She values the different natures of fabrics, exploring the possibilities, for instance, of combining heat-absorbent paper with different laminates, nappy liners with latex, bicarbonate of soda with switches. The barn is full of evidence of her wide-ranging research and design process. Shelves are loaded with high and low-tech materials, piles of trade catalogues for industrial plasters, plastics, laboratory glassware and many other materials and resources with potential for producing new effects.

Details, however, have to say something to be pertinent. In order to construct Leonardo's Time Ship for *The India Rubber Zoom Lens*, a Forkbeard touring show in 1995, she studied sailing technology, delighting in the 'fitness for purpose' of sailing ships and the variety of equipment available from chandlers. 'If Leonardo had built a time machine,' she reflects, 'it is quite likely to have been a form of ship and I was attracted by the idea of a very large, fan-shaped sail being a film screen. I built the ship structure on to springs, so it could sway back and forth. With film of a high sea projected on to the billowing sails, the journey started.'

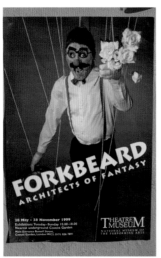

Because Forkbeard shows mix live performance and film, many of the experiments involve projection screens. An extraordinary variety of materials have been used for projection, including car airbag material, balloons, sails, tubes, washing up liquid with glycerine and many different textures and shapes. 'Film space is an environment you have to break into and explore,' she says. 'What screens are when film is not on them is important in crossing the celluloid divide'. Penny sees a screen as part of the narrative; it must never be a dead area of white, never a vacuum. A favourite device is to puncture the screens in exact alignment with the film image. This she describes as providing 'great potential for magic, enabling objects to be passed from stage to screen and vice versa'.

The position of the projectors, both in and out of the set and often visible to the audience, is equally important. As well as using traditional forms of celluloid and digital projection, Forkbeard has developed the Pedagyroscopic-Ektachronophotoscope, a cycle-powered projector; the Rotundatrope - a revolving projector; and the Liquid Film Projector. Penny uses projection to create sets within sets, animation and lighting effects. In order to see how they work, she will sit in the audience and work out the relationship of props and performers and what and who is upstaging whom. 'Props can hang around too long on stage, especially if they are extraordinary. They make an immediate impact that can delight the audience, because they cannot understand how they were done, but leave them there too long and you betray that delight. Ordinary props can stay longer as they work differently on the imagination. They can mellow, be forgotten and then sometimes do something shocking because they have become so familiar'.

Each prop is a character in its own right. It 'lives' on stage. Sometimes the stage is in a theatre, sometimes a gallery, sometimes outdoors, and the different settings require a

different type of performance. The props, which may be
mechanized, string-operated, or sensor-triggered, are
adapted to the space. Miss Moody, for example, a weeping
old lady on stage, becomes reinvented as a doddery,
giggling, old dear in the gallery, triggered by a pressure mat
which operates a timed sequence of her shaking chair and
looped giggles. Anthony, a full-sized string puppet, who has
been in exhibitions for many years after leaving a production,
now sports a disguise of false nose and moustache. He isn't
real, but still he's trying to disguise himself. 'These are objects
constructed to withstand considerable battering,' Penny
explains, 'because there is nothing as destructive as an
adrenaline-burning performer!' and in an exhibition, their
toughness and worn demeanour invite visitors to touch them
and operate them.

Many of Forkbeard's puppets and costumes are three-
dimensional realisations of Tim Britton's cartoons.
Penny adapts them to suit the performer. While wishing to
retain the intention of the original design, she is concerned
with how the performer manipulates the costume and the
relationship of inside and outside.
'The outside is easy, it is the interior that is challenging,'
she says. She describes the interiors in ways that make them
seem as magical as the exterior. She spends hours working
inside costumes, for example, a nine-foot teddy bear, and is
very aware of the hard work the performer has to do once
inside them. 'It is important to reduce the strain as much as
possible both while in it and getting in and out of it. The most
difficult resistance I have had to one of my costumes was from
three actors who felt silly singing in a mashed potato costume,
but that was vanity rather than discomfort!'

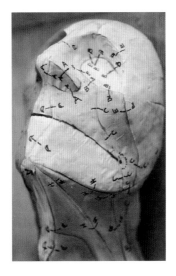

When making figures, she sometimes works initially in clay to
explore the expression, proportions and character. 'A paper
pattern is then built on the damp clay surface and an exact
pattern of the total surface is created with darts, seam markers
and structural notes. The paper patterns are then scaled up to
the final size.' These paper patterns are themselves works of
art, as are many of her maquettes and models.

Penny has become adept at overcoming the restrictions of
touring and is inspired by having to tailor ideas, scenes and
set changes for portability and a quick get-in. These skills were
fully tested when Forkbeard was commissioned to create a
piece for the Royal Shakespeare Company's *Complete Works
Festival* in 2006. The RSC had already decided to build a
large, fabric-walled cube in the auditorium of the theatre, in
which several companies could perform during the festival.
Forkbeard was asked to challenge the status quo – to be a
'Trojan Horse'. It decided to create a promenade
performance, starting in the foyer, progressing into the
auditorium, then into the cube and finally on to the main stage.
The production *Rough Magyck*, was based on the premise that
a wormhole had opened up during the rebuilding of the
theatre – a creative forcefield that released the 400 centuries-
suppressed inhabitants of Faerieland on to the stage, which is
still the one place where they have a tenuous toehold. It was
an ideal subject for Forkbeard, concerned as it was with the
magical, mythical and the untoward. 'Many of our shows have

been concerned with human vanity constructing its own ultimate comeuppance,' Penny explains, 'man-made creations running wildly out of control, the unknown engulfing the known, tinkerings and tamperings with the natural order of things.'

In the past, this meddling has produced a rabbit eight feet tall, the giant teddy, an oversized Elizabethan turkey, and a toxically-enlarged crow. The question now was, how would Forkbeard's magic compare with Shakespeare's? Ideas were written down rather than storyboarded. Research was collaborative, with everyone adding notes, drawings and found material to scrapbooks, which were referred to during the devising process. Penny visited the theatre space numerous times to discuss liberties that could be taken with the foyer, possibilities in the disturbed auditorium, how the cube would relate to the main stage, when it came to audience movement and the team to be involved in the installation. A complex sound system was installed, both to create sound effects of disaster and faerie mayhem and for the band, which was to perform in three different locations. 'With so much uncertainty, someone has to be certain.'

'There is lots of potential in a horse.'

Penny took photographs of everything, built a model box and produced a comprehensive set of plans and drawings. In order to place the installation within the existing spaces, measurements were checked and re-checked and health and safety restrictions discussed with RSC staff. The staging of *Rough Magyck* involved a variety of materials and construction methods. Penny had decided to use a Kabuki drop at the front of the cube but, because it was too expensive to buy or hire an electrically-operated system, she devised her own version. 'I made a ten-metre-long version of a Kabuki drop, probably as they were first made. It just involved hinges and string-release systems, but ten metres was a bit much to handle in my barn – I learned to be a limbo dancer!

A number of Forkbeard's creations made a return to the stage for the production, including the 12-foot caryatids that originally appeared in *The Fall of the House of Usherettes* in 1996. They stood motionless on either side of a water projection screen until the very end of the production, when they crashed to the ground, controlled by a complex pulley system manipulated by concealed performers. A similar system was used for the life-size, white horse, which made a spectacular entrance on to the main stage. It was based on a smaller white mare made for the Forkbeard exhibition, *Horsing About*, at the Cheltenham Museum and Art Gallery in summer 2006.

The construction of both horses was approached as an engineering problem that needed to be solved through research and experiment. To make the horses' movement as authentic as possible, she consulted veterinary textbooks, studying the structural composition of the horse, the interconnection of muscle, bone and tendon. She has described in the *BrUNIMA Puppet Notebook* how her work 'connects with puppetry, in the sense of trying to capture movement. I am fascinated by how many choices are involved in making a puppet and by how the movement is affected by decisions about which parts should be stiff and which loose.' Her full-scale horse hangs within a robust steel frame so that it can take the weight of a performer and be animated as a string puppet.

Rough Magyck brought together the essential Forkbeard elements: the illusions created through manipulating scale and perspective, the relationships between stage and screen and between audience and performer. As well as the visual spectacle there was the 'felt' presence of performers and props. According to Paschale Straiton, a performer in the production, one of the design features Penny was most pleased with were the small flags which stuck up from the shoulders of the tour guides at the beginning of the show. These characters interacted with the audience at the beginning of the show and later emerged as fairies who had been in disguise. 'The flags not only marked out the tour guides with comic effect, but also alluded to fairy wings (a detail that I heard a couple of audience members comment on). In such a way, her work reflects the comedy and poetry inherent in the substance of the show itself.'

In a question and answer session after one of the shows at the RSC, Penny was asked about the symbiosis of design and performance in the development of Forkbeard shows. Was the design dictated by concepts for the show or the other way around? She acknowledged that there is often a tricky relationship between design and devising but stressed that the almost constant sharing of ideas within the company had, over time, led to an ironing out of many of these problems. "They are reading from the same song sheet" to such an extent that they can make bold decisions months before a project starts. For instance, with *Rough Magyck* they knew they would need a life-size puppet of a horse for the Queen of the Faeries or another character to ride and so, Penny could just go ahead and make it. Regular funding and a brilliant creative space, at Waterslade, facilitate the making of these kinds of decisions but the way the company works together is all-important.

As with many of Penny's creations, the *Rough Magyck* horse will have an after life. The Department of Environment Food and Rural Affairs has commissioned Forkbeard to create a show about climate change. *Invisible Bonfires* will be about the history of humanity's love affair with carbon and the 'white mare' will once again have a supporting role. For Penny, 'the horse - as a way to get around, a working horse, origin of the term horsepower - is a symbol of a period of clean existence on earth, before we started to depend on carbon.'

Forkbeard's summer schools are supported by the Esmée Fairbairn Foundation and workshops for artists and teachers have, this year, been funded by the Paul Hamlyn Foundation. The company members are generous teachers, willing to reveal the secrets of their techniques and working practices. 'Workshops remain very inspiring for us, as much through the fact we can teach methods and media that we have years of experience of working in, as well as through being able to continue our love of experimenting by working with new

people and collaborating in ideas.'
At Waterslade, the evidence of 'the Forkbeard effect' is pinned to the walls in the form of invitations and images sent by former students of their own work. Some come back to help with Forkbeard's productions. 'We enjoy this quality of contact with people interested in our work, compared to the more obscure relationship with the faces in the dark during the show,' says Penny. Watched over by The Paranoids, Penny's automated figures operated by intelligent lighting mechanisms and dmx control systems, the students learn from a highly original navigator how to explore the 'landscape of possibilities'.

www.forkbeardfantasy.co.uk
Forkbeard are funded by Arts Council England

Edited by Sophie Jump

Craft With A Bit Of A Gob On

a ridiculous thing to want to do

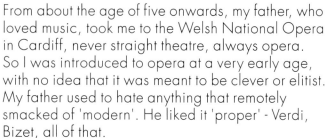

From about the age of five onwards, my father, who loved music, took me to the Welsh National Opera in Cardiff, never straight theatre, always opera. So I was introduced to opera at a very early age, with no idea that it was meant to be clever or elitist. My father used to hate anything that remotely smacked of 'modern'. He liked it 'proper' - Verdi, Bizet, all of that.

I was in my mid-teens in rural Wales when I decided that I wanted to be a theatre designer, or actually a stage manager. I didn't understand how it worked. I did school shows where the stage manager painted the set, and that's what I wanted to do. The music teacher laughed openly when I told him, as if that was a ridiculous thing to want to be doing. My father, who had no experience of this way of life, wrote to a careers page in a daily newspaper saying his son wanted to be a theatre designer, and the reply said, "I think this is a bad idea. It's a precarious profession."

I took a year off between school and university and I did various jobs, one of which was working at the Sherman Theatre in Cardiff, where I basically did a lot of cleaning! While I was there I explained what I wanted to do and was told, "Well, don't go and learn how to do it. Grow up. Go out and learn about life and then come back," which I think was wonderful advice. I had four years doing an MA at St Andrews, in English. It was a marvellous growing up period of my life (although some of it was rather regressive as well!). We did student drama in our spare time and nobody told us how. It was about inventing it for yourself, which was a great way to learn. And in those days the government paid for you to be educated; it was enlightened. Towards the end of my time there the university even employed an outside professional director, Malcolm Edwards, who came and worked with students of history, physics, biology, maths and so on. He brought the professional world to our amateurism. It was a marvellous and very creative period. I took some advice from the father of a student friend of mine, who happened to be the playwright Keith Dewhurst. He knew Hayden Griffin and suggested that I apply for a postgrad course: Bristol Old Vic or Motley, (which was then based at Riverside Studios). I nearly didn't go to Motley because I'm slightly dyslexic and I'd put Rotherhithe instead of Riverside on the letter, but the post office sent it back.

collaborators

your own attitude to the piece

Right from the start, Percy Harris (the founder of Motley) was an extraordinary person for me. I arrived with a bit of arrogance and a lot of ignorance. I didn't know how it all worked, I didn't know what the rules were, but I knew what I thought, and she encouraged that. She also taught me some humility. You learnt that nothing you were doing was new, it was all just the same thing, sold in a different way. I don't know how it is now, but then the course was not necessarily about tying you down to the rules of how to do it, more about letting you fly so that you could do it; coming up with an attitude towards the piece, rather than presenting a 'framework' of how to do the piece. And that's what was fostered there for me, and I loved it.

On the Motley course you were one of ten designers working with a single director, so the important relationship was between you and the piece. The poor director had to work on ten different productions, so you found you had to make decisions without collaboration. But, if you don't have an attitude to the piece that is yours, then what are you doing, what's your job? Simply decorating the director's ideas? Well you don't want to be doing that!

I got two jobs out of the exhibition at the end of the course. One was with Christopher Fettis, at the Drama Centre and the other was with Anne Pennington, at the Sir Richard Steele pub theatre. I did three plays for her and out of those I got work at the Royal Court, eventually doing *Road* by Jim Cartwright at the Theatre Upstairs. *Road* started out with a two hundred pound budget and ended up with Kevin Bacon in New York with lots of money thrown at it. The original production remained my favourite, for its raw energy if nothing else. Through that, I got an agent who arranged interviews with some directors, one of whom was Graham Vick. That was in 1987. He was just finishing in Scotland and was about to set up his own company in Birmingham. Our first production was *Falstaff*. It had a one-in-three rake, with 36 trap doors and women in medieval costume with two feet of extra fabric in the front - lethal really! Nanetta appeared on the first night with a broken arm. I was very irritated because she'd actually broken it outside the rehearsal space but it did look, given that it was a one-in-three precipitous drop, that I'd pushed the leading lady over the edge. Since then, however, I've done 30 odd shows with Graham.

Eating off the same table

I've only worked with very few directors, Graham Vick and Jonathan Kent mainly. I've been lucky with those I've worked with. If the director's a fool, the production is sunk, because they can't be a weak link. They're the strainer through which everything goes. A good relationship with a director is a very open relationship in which you can express your feelings about everything – the great and good emotions as well as the nasty, twisted, perverse things that are in most of us. Graham Vick and Jonathan Kent work in very different ways.
With one of them you plot exactly where people enter and what they do, so you have a framework, which is a point of departure. It's not what the production ends up looking like but it is all very worked out.

With the other one, it's more about slabs of images that are then developed in rehearsal in a much more freeform way. Sometimes you can be working on a show which is going to be done in two, three or even four years time, and you have to make the directors responsible for the design as well.
You have to extract out of them something that commits them to the piece. When you know a director very well you need to be careful that you don't start 'short-handing'. Even if you know what they are thinking, you can't leave the other people, the audience, out of the equation. You must have proper conversations each time about the piece and about the place. So it's not just: "What shall we do this time?" You have to presume that this is the first time the audience have seen either the piece or your work. You shouldn't have to communicate through other productions or through programme notes. It needs to stand on it's own.
You have to reinvent yourself all the time.
Working with a director is about collaboration. You both need to be working towards one aim. With Graham and Jonathan we always start with talking, and it obviously varies who brings most to the table, but you have to be eating off the same table. Similarly, it's always worth having the courage to throw ideas out. It's important not to get attached. and that is a state of mind you need to get into when you are creating a piece. You need to leave your options open because you have to have the courage to throw it out. The process is an exercise in self-discipline.

Nothing but a way of getting the production on

With models for example: some are very beautiful but they are not ends in themselves. It might be a lovely 1:25 chair, but it isn't valid in itself: I've never thought of it as ruthless to put something that an assistant has made into a bin. I think that discarding is a necessary process. I've been lucky with assistants. I worked with Ros Coombes for a long time and now I work with Luis Carvalho, and discarding is never an issue with either of them. That is part of how it goes - you have to destroy, you have to discard. You can't just put in your first idea, or maybe you can, if you've proved it. Percy was very clear in that respect. The model and the costume drawings are nothing but a way of getting the production on. You do nice models or you do nice costume drawings to convey your ideas clearly. They are a lot of effort for me, but they are an attempt to gain some sort of control of the situation. Everyone's time is wasted if you don't know what you're doing or what you're trying to create, and a good costume drawing helps. Sometimes, with a show where costumes are bought rather than made, you'll do some drawings of a theoretical 'world', but these drawings are not exactly what the costume eventually looks like. Sometimes you have to defend your drawings, insist that this is what the costumes are, at other times it is important to be fluid and organic. The process is never the same twice. You meet the actor and they're a completely different shape to the one you imagined, or the character develops in a different direction during rehearsals and you respond accordingly.

It can work that way with sets as well. I recently did a production of *Don Giovanni* in Birmingham and we didn't have a confirmed, found space, in which to perform the piece until a week before we started rehearsals. We had located some very nice caverns underneath New Street Station car park in the middle of Birmingham and it seemed possible to do the sort of production where a woman in a big frock, drags a chandelier through the mud, lit by bonfires - that sort of world. We had also been looking for a church for a long time, which seemed to be quite a good place to do a *Don Giovanni*, since it's a piece which deals with blasphemy, in a world where there is divine intervention. We couldn't find one of those, but came across this Bank, which was very good. Banks are nearly as good as churches - temples for money and power and all that. Eventually the cold marble promenade space was littered with coffins The most interesting thing was the audience's relationship to the piece; they were forced to sit on coffins! It's amazing how many people don't want to do that!

*communicating to a whole load
of people we don't know*

I think you can take audiences out of their comfort zone. When they are sitting in the dark en masse with the lights out in a comfy chair it can be harder for them to commit or engage. That production of *Don Giovanni* in bright light was rewarding because you can see the audience's response and, in fact, the event became their response. The skill that we have as designers is very hard to define and perhaps that may tempt us to hide behind beautifully made models and nice costume drawings. But I don't think that this is what our job is. Our job is to communicate emotionally through visual things to a whole load of people we don't know. However, unless it's a devised piece, a designer is not actually creating from scratch. We're using somebody else's view of the world. The job lives within somebody else's framework. It's not like a blank canvas.

One of the most exciting things for me recently, was to do the same piece with the same director a month apart, in two different venues. Luckily *Die Zauberflöte* is a piece that can be interpreted in thousands of different ways. In this case, one fundamental difference was the audience: one was in Salzburg where they "own" Mozart, and the other was the Bolshoi where they haven't done the piece since 1920. There was something, however, about the one in Moscow which I liked more, because it was raw. I think the piece responded much better to being vulgar and dirty and slightly ugly and human. It smelt a bit, and I think that at Salzburg the audience can deify Mozart a little too much.

the space informs what you do as much as the piece

Finding Gainsborough Studios for the Almeida was a happy accident. It looked great from the outside but the inside was initially characterless. So we distressed it, stripped out the intermediate floor and needle-gunned and burnt the walls, threw yogurt at it, made a big crack the full height of the building and gave it a history. For the audience the journey to Shoreditch then, contributed to the show, because it wasn't familiar territory – no pre or post-theatre restaurants. It can create a good dynamic with an audience if they are slightly unsettled. They're more receptive I think. For me, found spaces like the Gainsborough Studios or Kings Cross Almeida are not that different to somewhere like Drottningholm Palace Theatre. There you've got an intact, eighteenth century theatre with an auditorium which has a quality that is quite extraordinary - there are only two seats where the perspective works, everyone else is looking at something from *Doctor Caligari*! So it informs what you do. Yes, you can strip it all back and do something odd and strange, but on the whole, (and when I've worked there I've done eighteenth century shows), the space has informed the piece as much as a warehouse in the East End or King's Cross would do.

collaborators

great beauty and crass vulgarity

Arena Di Verona works the same way, it is obviously not a neutral black box. We did *La Traviata* there. In a huge space like Verona you have to do things in a different way because you have to signal to 22,000 people. At the beginning of performances at Verona the audience all light their candles, so it seemed to be very vigil-like. Marguerite Gaultier at the time of her death was the most famous woman in Paris, and her funeral was an extraordinary popular public event, apparently. So that's where we started. Our idea was that she started off as a Princess Diana figure, a famous glamorous woman who died young. I think it is quite a vulgar piece. It has great beauty, but crass vulgarity as well. The opening of act one is rasping and vulgar, a party, hence the quilted heart and the grotesque pink doll. Then the flowers were stripped away and there is a lawn of printed dollars, an image of a bought arcadia.

In act three Alfredo disgraces Violetta by pulling her wig off at Flora's party, to reveal her balding scalp. In a world where so much emphasis is placed on glamour and youth; disease, death and decay are real taboos. The Princess Diana shrine idea came very suddenly as I was riding the bike going down to Hastings. I nearly crashed because I got so excited about it. For certain things, you know that if you put in four hours work you will get four hours back, but coming up with ideas is completely out of your control. It's why we wake up out of fear! In Verona half the audience cheered and half booed. It was quite bestial all those people screaming. You do get used to it. You just try to be honest and if they don't like it you go on and you learn from it. Working abroad is good for that - you get asked back to a country about every six years - they forget. You just keep moving in an easterly direction around the globe and you're fine!

When I first started off, Percy pointed out that you don't have to focus everything on the piece. It has to be a response to the work, rather than you bringing in personal baggage. Invariably, your life is in chaos and you're utterly miserable and you're given a comedy to do. I'm happy now and my life is good and what I get is shows where women die or Ethiopia is humiliated.

*moving from a little box
to something three dimensional.*

For me the job is quite clearly divided.
There's sitting downstairs with Luis creating models
and doing costume designs, that's one process,
which takes it to a certain point. Then there's the
second process of communicating and trying to
inspire and excite the people who are making your
production. That collaboration is hugely important:
firing people up and exciting them or
communicating with them, or however you do it,
but ultimately moving from a little box and flat
drawings to something three dimensional.
It is something I enjoy but trying to engage all the
people that are working on the show is very hard.
I know at Covent Garden they did twenty two new
productions last year, an enormous work load, and
because of that your production can become
relegated to a file number. You've got to make your
show stand out, so that they'll invest the time and
energy and emotion. That's part of the job,
communicating, and inspiring and exciting people
to do your thing, because believe me, if it was left
to me to cut the costumes or make the wigs or
engineer the hydraulics the show would be a fiasco.

you need that collaboration

You really do need those people to do their best
work. Although there are some fantastic makers in
this country there is also the thrill of going into a
completely alien world where you know nobody.
It's very educational working in Russia,
for example, where they slide a glass of milk
towards you if you are dealing with toxic materials,
as if that will make it all alright. Health and Safety
is not an issue. There are people paid tiny sums of
money to knot rope but similarly you wouldn't get
the same quality of embroidery anywhere else
I know. Then the painters in Italy are extraordinary.
As long as you cry publicly early on in a rehearsal
period there, as long as they've broken you, they'll
give you whatever you want and they really give
you beautiful stuff, but only at the end, when you've
sweated.

As a contrast, Santa Fe Opera is energised by the
apprentice system they employ there. Students staff
the costume, prop and carpentry shops, and that's
a wonderful experience. The workshops have
a level of enthusiasm and energy that is quite
humbling, reminding you of where we all started.
Seeing somebody mastering a technique for the
first time! You can almost physically see something
different happening in that breakthrough moment.
Seeing that happen is a great payback.

it has to be different every time

When it comes to process, I think that if there's
a formula, then there is a problem. It has to be
different every time. It's about the piece and the
space. How do you convey this material to that
number of people, in that environment? That's the
job - the difference between Verona and
Birmingham - the difference between 22,000
and 200 people. That variety is what's great.
Otherwise it would just be routine, which might
be less frightening but would certainly be less
interesting. We're all interested in putting on the
show. That's the main thing. How do you get a
better show? How do you make the event
worthwhile for the people turning up to see it?
It's a craft. But it's a craft with a bit of a gob on.

collaborators

A RESPONSE TO...

"But its all collaboration"
This first section acknowledges the above statement as the instinctive response of many designers to our title.
The statement below by designer Jean-Marc Puissant is the reflection that follows:

"Thinking systematically about collaboration brings me back to specific cases, people or events. Apart from the fact that it is the most crucial aspect of any project, there seems to be nothing generic or universal about my experience of it so far. Even with the same person, each collaboration ends up being about something else, articulated in different ways. In my mind, the word itself refers to a context, not a definition; it does not stand alone. I think of a fruitful collaboration, an ongoing collaboration, a lack of collaboration, a rewarding collaboration, a will to collaborate.

Inevitably, from concept to production, theatre is interactive. The nature and scale of the work produced requires team effort at each phase and performing it involves an audience.
But interaction alone doesn't necessarily amount to collaboration, and vice versa. There seems to be a specific mind to collaborating, - an acknowledgement. The taste for collaboration was a key element of my training at Motley and its become fundamental, if not central, to my work ever since.

I like the fact that some aspects of collaboration remain slightly mysterious. I see no real pattern to what could make it successful other than consistently making it the priority at every stage of my process." (Jean-Marc Puissant September 2006)

Perhaps the key component in the work that follows is an insistence on the centrality of the performance material - text, music, dance - to which designers respond and have ultimate loyalty. This may seem obvious, but with ever increasing visual and performance possibilities and choices, the core material can sometimes seem to be less important in realisation. Useful maybe to remember that even the most apparently extreme visual solution originates in a response to...

Elroy Ashmore

The Canterville Ghost
Shaun Prendergast (2004)

*The Haymarket Theatre, Basingstoke
December (2004)*

Elroy Ashmore: 'All theatre is about
collaboration - in this case, writer,
director, designer, musical director,
actor, musicians, lighting designer and
sound engineer all contributed to making
this a successful Christmas show. Based
on an Oscar Wilde short story about an
American family and a ghost who needs
to find eternal rest, the script had many
complex locations in and around
Canterville Chase. We decided to set
everything on one giant staircase which
zig-zagged in a crazy nightmare from
deep in the orchestra pit to way high up
stage. Only in one magical moment did
the staircase move, when it split wide
open to reveal a land of ice and snow.'

*Director: John Adams
Set and Costume Designer:
Elroy Ashmore
Lighting Designer: Simon Hutchings
Sound Designer: John Greet
Choreographer: Lorelei Lynn
Musical Director: Trevor Allan Davies*

David Burrows

The Dinner
Leah Vitali (1998)

*Skala Theatre Company
Municipal Theatre, Larnaka, Cyprus
February 2003*

David Burrows: 'A return to Cyprus
after designing *Tartuffe*, in Nicosia in
1997, with Alkis Kritikos. The designs
were sent via email, a temporary web
page and fax before my only visit, a
week before the show opened. Happily
the same workshop team which had built
the set for *Tartuffe* was responsible for
The Dinner and it all fell into place
smoothly enough. I enjoyed designing
the furniture, particularly the three-
legged chairs with the serpent tails and
zebra skin seats. The Perspex table top,
with its frosted centre, allowed for
dramatic up-lighting through the debris
of glasses at the play's tragic
conclusion.'

*Director: Alkis Kritikos
Set and Costume Designer:
David Burrows
Lighting Designer: David Burrows*

collaborators

Colin Falconer

Endgame
Samuel Beckett (1958)

Theatr Genedlaethol Cymru
Tour
October 2006

Colin Falconer: 'Hamm is blind and incapacitated in the centre of the room. Clov looks after him but cannot tease. We wanted to achieve a sense of the characters existing in a recognisably Welsh domestic space. The room itself has been stripped bare of decoration. Only the most basic elements remain, leaving an imprint of what was once there. The world outside traps them in a desolate void, showing no sign of life.'

Director: Judith Roberts
Set and Costume Designer:
Colin Falconer
Lighting Designer: Jenny Kagan

The Tunnel of Obsession
Ernesto Sabato (Novel 1948)

Contemporary Stage Company
Warehouse Theatre, Croydon
November 2003

David Burrows: 'A simple setting of blue-painted flattage and a central, floor-to-grid, mirrored, slatted blind. White and blue painted furniture. Costumes in tones of cream and white. A mercury vapour floodlight provided a flat field of intense blue light throughout the show, coupled with a constant veil of mist (using a hazer). The lighting, the conceptual heart of the design, was intended to underscore the play's structure of a first-person narrative, the action of which is a series of memories. The photographs here accurately capture the quality of the prevailing atmosphere.'

Director: David Graham-Young
Set Designer: David Burrows
Costume Designer: Chrystine Bennett
Lighting Designer: David Burrows

Patrick Connellan

This Lime Tree Bower
Connor McPherson (1995)

Belgrade Theatre Company and Richard Jordan Productions
Reconfigured Belgrade Theatre, Coventry and Assembly Rooms, Edinburgh
June and August 2003

Patrick Connellan: 'Three characters inhabit the space. Each has their own story, yet their stories relate to each other's. Their tales are spoken in monologue, except for one small exchange. The design is a simple exercise in relationships in juxtaposition to each other, their stories and related memories. The chairs become a metaphor for the jumble of stories and memories that we all share.'

Director: Patrick Connellan
Set and Costume Designer:
Patrick Connellan
Lighting Designer: James Farncombe
Photographer: James Farncombe

The Resistible Rise Of Arturo Ui
Bertolt Brecht (1941)

The Mercury Theatre, Colchester
April 2005

Patrick Connellan: 'Ui's gangsters
have just killed Roma, Ui's right-hand
man. They inhabit a skeletal structure
that, in this case, represents a
dilapidated garage. The structure also
has a metaphorical resonance. In its
general form, it represents capitalism in
crisis and decay, it is collapsing into the
floor waiting to be revived by a "great
man" such as the Hitler-like Ui.
The structure was inspired by Tatlin's
Tower which, unlike this one, was a
eulogy to the Russian Revolution.'

Scene 11 The Killing Of Roma

Director: Janice Dunn
Set and Costume Designer:
Patrick Connellan
Lighting Designer: Helen Morely
Photographer: Robert Day

Sophia Lovell Smith

The House of Bernarda Alba
Federico Garcia Lorca (1936)
David Hare (2005)

Mountview Academy of Theatre Arts –
postgraduate showcase
New Players Theatre, London
August 2006

Sophia Lovell Smith: '*The House of Bernarda Alba* entombs the fate of three generations of women and their servants.
The design defines the claustrophobia with vertically enclosing walls. The outside world enters only through tight apertures. Pale streaked walls are played with in the lighting design to suggest the changing colours of morning, afternoon and night.'

Dick Bird

By the Bog of Cats (Am Katzenmoor)
Marina Carr (1998)

Theater Heilbronn, Germany
March 2004

Dick Bird: 'Marina Carr's beautiful reworking of *Medea* takes place around a frozen bog. We didn't want to disturb the stark simplicity of this landscape with many scene changes, and so realised Hester's farm and caravan around a sunken shipping container. In the middle of the play there is a terrifying bourgeois wedding with five women in white vying for the groom. For this, the container lurched up out of the mud to provide the wedding table, sinking back at the end of the scene to leave us with the desolation of the moor.'

Director: Patricia Benecke
Set and Costume Designer: Dick Bird
Lighting Designer: Ralf Baars

In the costume, the carapace of black funeral lace is stripped by Act 3 to vulnerable white, as the characters' desires are exposed. At the last, the play is a tragedy. Lorca consigns all ambition to the ever present earth, from husband's funeral to daughter's suicide.'

Director: Margarete Forsyth
Set and Costume Designer:
Sophia Lovell Smith
Lighting Designer: Matt Prentice
Sound Designer: Chris James
Photographer: Rowan O'Duffy

The Gambler (De Speler)
Sergei Prokofiev (1929)

Opera Zuid
Theater aan het Vrijthof, Maastricht
October 2005

Dick Bird: 'Three quarters of *The Gambler* is about people waiting; languidly in the hotel lobby for the rich, old grandmother to die and leave them her money, or desperately, outside the casino, while inside she loses her entire fortune in one evening. In the last act, in which the hero Alexei breaks the bank, Prokofiev generates the excitement through a series of filmic, musical close ups. We projected each spinning number on to the large, mirrored ball that hung above the space like a chandelier. The players placed their bets on a table, the perspective of which allowed the audience to follow the game. As the scene moved to long shot, the table turned round to become a mirrored ceiling over another roulette wheel, and the players clustered round, so that the audience could watch the game, as it were, from behind.'

Act 1 The Grand Hotel Roulettenberg
Act 3 The Casino

Director: Dalia Ibelhauptaite
Set Designer: Dick Bird
Costume Designer: Anita Yavich
Lighting Designer: Giuseppe Di Orio
Choreographer: Arthur Pita

David Cockayne

Don Giovanni
Mozart/Da Ponte (1787)

*Royal Northern College of Music,
Manchester
March 2003*

David Cockayne: 'A flexible set of huge doors pivoting on steel columns. These were covered with images of women's faces, encased in panels. The door created multiple spaces leading to a fully enclosed chamber. The Commendatore's statue was a full-size puppet operated by a team of five people. The set was deconstructed by the company, looking for Don Giovanni.'

*Director: Stefan Janski
Set and Costume Designer:
David Cockayne
Lighting Designer: Richard G. Jones
Choreographer: Bethan Rhys Wiliam
Conductor: Mark Shana*

David Collis

'Maria de Buenos Aires'

Brothel Keeper

Maria de Buenos Aires
Astor Piazzolla (1968)

*Dartington Summer School
Barn Theatre, Dartington
August 2004*

David Collis: 'The piece is extremely opaque as to time, location and even characters, e.g. "Men Who Come Back From Mystery" and "Voice of That Sunday". It was therefore open season as far as the director and I were concerned, and it ended up as a louche Latin cabaret on a stripped stage, with highly atmospheric lighting.'

*Director: Richard Williams
Set and Costume Designer: David Collis
Lighting Designer: Ninian Harding
Photographer: CPNC*

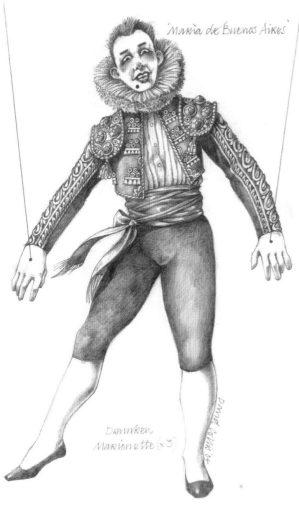

Madeleine Boyd

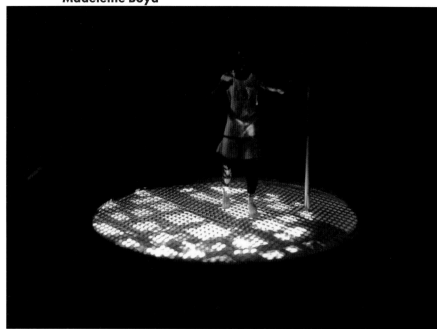

Rhymes, Reasons and Bombass Beatz
Harold Finley (2006)

Harold Finley
The Studio Space, Oval House Theatre
London 2006

Madeleine Boyd: 'One man plays 11 very different characters in this monologue piece. The storytelling flows from scene to scene, and it was important that the set, lighting, projections and sound all moved smoothly around it. Music and rhythm were an integral part of the performance, so collaboration and timing were paramount.'

Director: Chris Goode
Set and Costume Designer:
Madeleine Boyd
Lighting Designer: Peter Harrison
Sound Designer:Chris Goode
Video Artist: Jemma Pardo

Sean Crowley

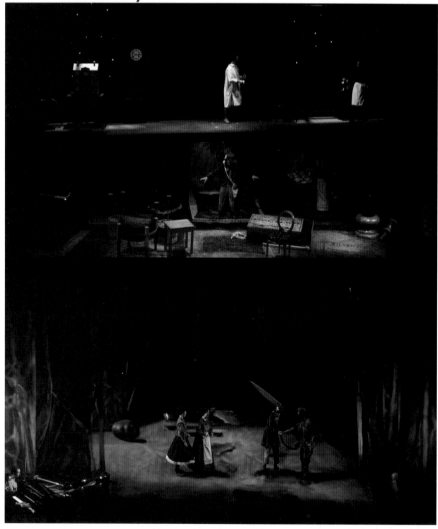

The Borrowers
Charles Way - from Mary Norton's book (1999)

Sherman Theatre, Cardiff
November 2003

Sean Crowley: 'The Sherman's Christmas show has involved the same creative collaborative team for over seven years, producing large-scale children's theatre with small design budgets stretched to the maximum by a dedicated in-house production team. *The Borrowers* presented enormous challenges in scale both in the creation of the split-level world of Humans and Borrowers within the house in Act 1 and the landscape of the garden and countryside as seen through the Borrowers' eyes in Act 2. Through puppets and live projection and the skills of the design realisation team, the worlds became completely tangible for the audience.'

Director: Phil Clark
Set and Costume Designer:
Sean Crowley
Lighting Designer: Ceri James
Sound Designer: Mike Beer
Photographer: Ceri James

Helen Fownes-Davies

Satin 'n' Steel
Amanda Whittington (2005)

Co-production between Nottingham Playhouse and Bolton Octagon February 2005

Helen Fownes-Davies: 'As this was a new play, there was a great opportunity for the creative team to come together at the early stages and help visualise aspects of the show with the writer. The main challenge was a musical montage in Act 1, through which a variety of song and dance routines show the progression of the working men's club duo going from strength to strength. It needed to emulate various locations, changing style as their professionalism grew over a number of years. By the end, they are top-notch cabaret singers at a Butlin's Holiday Camp. The entire creative team were involved in working out carefully timed changes through the use of props, movement, songs, lighting, set and costume changes, all happening over a matter of minutes.'

Beginning of the montage scene - small club act

*Director: Esther Richardson
Set and Costume Designer:
Helen Fownes-Davies
Lighting Designer: Richard G Jones
Musical Director and Composer:
Stuart Briner
Choreographer: Claire Maurer
Photographer: Robert Day*

A Who's Who of Flapland
David Halliwell (2005)

Lakeside Arts Centre, Nottingham April 2005

Helen Fownes-Davies: 'Written originally for radio (1967), the story relies on the elaborate accusations of swindling both men make. Fusing a surreal, filmic backdrop, authentic styling, subtle shifts in sound and lighting and exaggerated movement helped us accentuate this darkly comic play.'

*Director: Matt Aston
Set and Costume Designer:
Helen Fownes-Davies
Lighting Designer: James Farncombe
Sound Designer: Paul Stear
Musical Director and Composer:
Stuart Briner
Choreographer: Charlotte Vincent
Film- maker: Mark Bushnell
Photographer: Usula Kelly – Fluk
Photography*

Simon Holdsworth

Messiah
Steven Berkoff (2000)

East Productions
Old Vic, London
December 2003

Simon Holdsworth: *'Messiah is a take on the story of the crucifixion. With much of the location, time and action mimed by the performers, the set and costumes needed to be simple statements about the play. The floor was a large, raised, cross, wedged between the proscenium arch. The backdrop was a painted hand, which became pierced by a large nail. The actor playing Christ mimed crucifixion by stretching another large nail across his arms and back.'*

Director: Steven Berkoff
Set and Costume Designer:
Simon Holdsworth
Lighting Designer: David Edwards
Photographer: Nobby Clark

screwmachine/eyecandy or: How I Learned to Stop Worrying and Love Big Bob
C J Hopkins (2005)

Scamp Theatre
Assembly Rooms, Edinburgh
August 2005

Simon Holdsworth:
'screwmachine/eyecandy, is set on an American TV game show where contestants do anything to win prizes. As the presenter, Big Bob pillories the Midwest contestants, cruelty takes over and Dan is tragically clubbed to death with prizes. As the show was supposedly being beamed into living rooms across the world, we decided to do the set as a mock living room. A psychedelic TV lit up the background, the two contestants podiums were the backs of sofas and the lamps either side lit up when contestants hit their buzzers. As chaos, ensued the set buzzed and flashed.'

Director: John Clancy
Set Designer: Simon Holdsworth
Costume Designer: Ronnie Dorsey
Lighting Designer: James Bartrum
Photographer: Louise Callow

Mark Jonathan

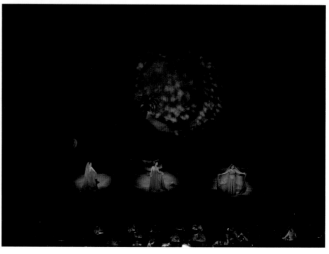

collaborators

Les Liaisons Dangereuses
Christopher Hampton (1985)

Theatre by The Lake, Keswick
June 2005

Martin Johns: *'Les Liaisons
Dangereuses is a multi-locational play in
which the action has to move swiftly from
one salon to another. The director and I
decided to set the play in a fragmented
world of Versailles mirrors and Boucher
paintings to reflect the characters'
obsession with outward appearance
and the lavish opulence of the society
they inhabited. The different locations
were achieved by simple furniture moves
by liveried servants, who were integral
to the action, and by the lighting
designer's use of a variety of directional
gobos and colour washes to change the
scale and atmosphere of the permanent
setting.'*

Director: Ian Forrest
Set and Costume Designer: Martin Johns
Lighting Designer: Nick Beadle
Sound Designer: Andy Bolton
Fight Director: Kate Waters
Photographer: Keith Pattison

Ariadne auf Naxos
Composer Richard Strauss (1911)
Libretto Hugo Von Hofmannsthal

Los Angeles Opera
Dorothy Chandler Pavilion, Los Angeles
June 2005

Mark Jonathan: *'Mark Jonathan:
'This was an extraordinary collaboration
led by William Friedkin (director of
The Exorcist), who sets the opera in the
house of the richest man in Hollywood.
"Make me a 'horror-movie' of a storm",
he asked for Act 2. For me, the
collaboration extends in many
directions: the relationship between the
piece dramatically and musically; the
story that we need to tell; the director's
approach; the designs; the singers'
needs; and the capability of the theatre.
While lighting is a major part in
transporting the audience and telling the
story, it is only for the duration of the
performance that you can appreciate the
overall collaboration.'*

Director: William Friedkin
Set Designer: Edwin Chan
Costume Designer: Sam Fleming
Lighting Designer: Mark Jonathan
Puppetry Design: Michael Currie
Photographer: Maiko Nezu

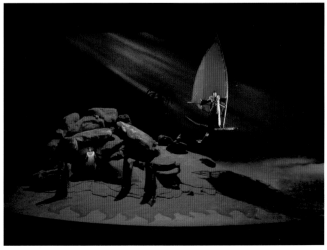

Simon Kenny

True or Falsetto?
Lucy Powell (2003)

Drill Hall, London
September 2003

Simon Kenny: 'Part lecture, part satirical cabaret, *True or Falsetto?* and *The Veiled Screen* are the first two pieces in a series of performances uncovering hidden aspects of the arts and contemporary culture. Each part of the cycle has visual echoes of the others, while colour is used to give each piece its own identity - the red and the gold of baroque opera, the black and silver of silent movies. A series of gauzes and curtains emerge from the darkness to continually evolve the space, while the set and costumes become

Bridget Kimak

Il Tabarro and Gianni Schicchi
Giacomo Puccini (1918)

Guildhall School of Music and Drama
June 2006

Bridget Kimak: 'I love being surprised by my collaborators. It's like being presented with unexpected gifts. After weeks working with the model box, the first sight of the set under lights is invigorating, the lighting transforming the space through time. It can be like seeing a very familiar design for the first time. Then the stage and piano rehearsals; singers arrive and animate the space bringing new meaning, and adding depth to the narrative. Finally the band! Everyone is revitalised by the first stage and orchestral rehearsal. Suddenly all the pieces are there. Opera is the place where music, drama and visuals can combine to make a whole that is greater than its parts. The challenge is to leave enough room for each discipline to breathe, and for each member of the team to be creative. This layering of creative energies is one of the things that gives opera the power to move us deeply.'

Director: Martin Lloyd-Evans
Set and Costume Designer:
Bridget Kimak
Lighting Designer: Simon Corder
Conductor: Clive Timms
Photographer: John Reading

interchangeable velvet drapes turning into period dresses, gauzes act as veils, chandeliers become crowns, clothing is used in place of projection screens.'

Director: Amit Lahav
Set Designer: Simon Kenny
Costume Designer: Ilona Karas
Lighting Designer: Adrian Croton
Sound Designer: Toru Yoshioka
Musical Director: Stephen Robinson

Le Nozze di Figaro
Wolfgang Amadeus Mozart (1786)

Theatre Company, Royal Scottish Academy of Music and Drama
New Athenaeum Theatre, Glasgow and The Edinburgh Festival Theatre
January 2004

Bridget Kimak: 'It was in the pub after the first stage rehearsal with the piano that Colin said to me, "Shame we didn't think of it before now, but wouldn't it be great to have two identical chandeliers, one downstage of the wall and one upstage, visible through the window to cross fly for the transformation from indoors to outdoors?" A drink or two later and I said, half jokingly to Davey, the production manager, "Any chance of a pair of chandeliers?" Thanks to Kate McGeary, our very persistent stage manager, and to the goodwill of Scottish Opera and our crew, we had the chandelier and its double installed in time for the first dress rehearsal.'

Act 4 Finale, The rape of the Countess, (disguised as Susanna) by her husband, the Count Almaviva.

Director: Martin Lloyd-Evans
Set and Costume Designer: Bridget Kimak
Lighting Designer: Colin Grenfell
Production Manager: David O'Neill
Student Stage Manager: Kate McGeary

Count Almaviva
Act 3

Byron Watson

Ruari Murchison

The David Hare Trilogy-Racing Demon, Murmuring Judges, The Absence Of War
David Hare

Birmingham Repertory Theatre
March-April 2003

Ruari Murchison: 'The trilogy requires 38 different locations; from urban and rural exteriors, to offices and official spaces, legal, constitutional and parliamentary. Presenting all three pieces on some performance days, required a design that was flexible enough to accommodate all these locations. A huge revolving underlit floor representing a Union Jack formed the focus of the design. Sections could be illuminated by underlighting strips in the floor to create 'light walls'. When some strips were illuminated, they created a giant cruciform corridor leading players to the centre of the space. Surrounding the space was a gigantic, curved, panelled wall signifying the enduring historic and architectural nature of the institutions which could split four ways, vertically and horizontally. Its colour - blue - hinted at the essential conservatism of the state, church and judiciary. This was counter-balanced by

Adrian Linford

Betrayal
Harold Pinter (1978)

Mercury Theatre Company
Mercury Theatre, Colchester
June 2006

Adrian Linford: 'The play's action is told in reverse; a long-term and secret love affair between a husband, his wife and his best friend. Both the director, Sue Lefton and I wanted to push the action right out and up close to the audience, so they became almost part of the room, building into the auditorium from the proscenium arch. The harsh white and steel of the abstract space left the cast with nowhere to hide and confrontation was inevitable.'

Director: Sue Lefton
Set and Costume Designer:
Adrian Linford
Lighting Designer: Tony Simpson

a large, red breezeblock wall upstage, sometimes seen when the panelled wall split. A white cyclorama provided the third colour of the Union Jack and a visual political neutrality. With two directors and a company of 26 playing in all three pieces, this production amounted to a collaboration of the closest form.'

Directors: Jonathan Church and Rachel Kavanaugh
Set and Costume Designer: Ruari Murchison
Lighting Designer: Nick Beadle
Composer: Matthew Scott

The Vanishing Bridegroom
Judith Weir (1990)

Royal Scottish Academy of Music and Drama
Space New Athenaeum Theatre
June 2005

Adrian Linford: 'Bridegroom is based on three 19th-century folk tales that interlink. Lee Blakeley and I wanted the piece to appear timeless, using the full stage and the chorus to interact more with the principal singers. People and few props moved the action from internal to external spaces. The space and characters needed to be mystical, spirited, macabre and witty, all at once.'

Director: Lee Blakeley
Set and Costume Designer: Adrian Linford
Lighting Designer: Mary Fisher
Conductor: Timothy Dean

Adrian Vaux

Oliver
(Lionel Bart 1960)
Produced by Networks USA
in association with
Cameron Mackintosh Ltd
US tour
2002

Adrian Vaux: 'This is called "a bus and truck tour" of the United States, which set out in November 2004 from Denver. Apart from the usual parameters of touring, i.e. ease of handling and damage proof, the show had to fit into six trucks, be set up in eight hours and struck in six. In addition to meeting the demands of the show itself (which are considerable), one had to satisfy the producers' demands for very high standards, both visual and technical. I loved the show and I loved the process of seeing it through.'

Director: Graham Gill
Set and Costume Designer: Adrian Vaux
Lighting Designer: Jenny Kagan
Choreographer: Geoff Garret

Colin Richmond

Guys & Dolls
Frank Loeser (1950)

*Theatre Bet Lessin, Tel Aviv
March 2006*

Adrian Vaux: 'This was a rare occasion when the whole process of design and execution went exactly according to plan. It was a combination of a clear picture in my mind coming to fruition, together with the director's wishes. I also enjoyed seeing the backdrops and front gauzes being printed on huge digital print machines. Amazing stuff! Also all the signs for Times Square digitally printed on to panaflex and stretched on to light boxes making a huge work relatively simple. No neon tubes, which are so fragile. One of the best moments in the show itself was, for me, when the whole of Times Square slowly began to lift off into the grid to make way for Havana to assemble onstage.'

*Director and Choreographer:
Ken Oldfield
Set Designer: Adrian Vaux
Costume Designer: Yosi Ben Ari
Lighting Designer: Hillick Orgal*

Twelfth Night
William Shakespeare (1601)

*West Yorkshire Playhouse
Quarry Theatre, Leeds
September 2005*

Colin Richmond: 'As Feste the clown croons his final song, the storm cloud that has been brewing over Illyria's strange world finally breaks to rain on love's happy parade. Set on a derelict bandstand, Ian Brown's production alluded to the halcyon days of 1930s seaside to illustrate Illyria's strange and forgotten world. Two moving, concentric rings of cracked boardwalks and slung festoons hang precariously above the slumped floor, itself buried in a vast dune of sand. An entire visual metaphor for a lost and fragile world, full of bittersweet emotions and speaking achingly of the torture of love.'

*Director: Ian Brown
Set and Costume Designer:
Colin Richmond
Lighting Designer: Chris Davey
Sound Designer: Mic Pool
Composer: Richard Taylor
Photographer: Keith Pattison*

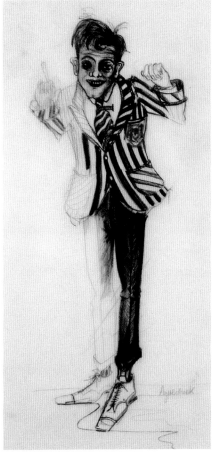

Conor Murphy

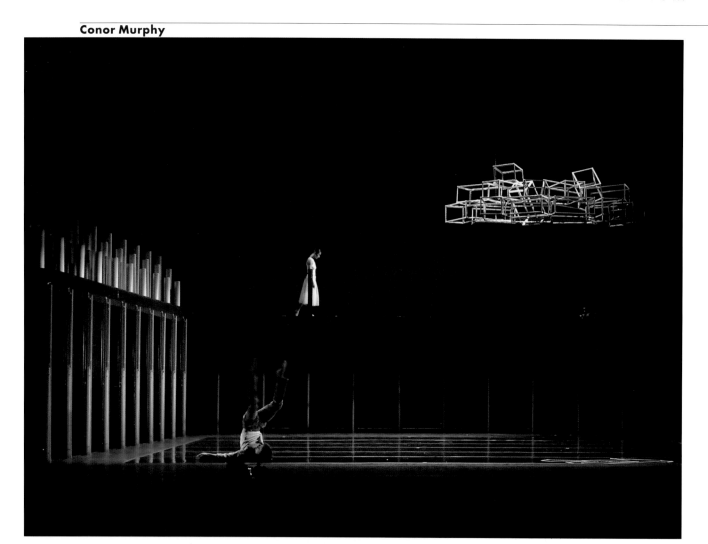

Giselle Reloaded
Donlon Dance Company (2006)

*Donlon Dance Company, Saarbrücken
Saarländisches Staatstheater,
Saarbrücken
January 2006*

Conor Murphy: 'This is a
contemporary version of *Giselle,* which
moves from a rural Irish first half to a
mystical underworld in the second.
The music was an eclectic mix of
traditional Irish, contemporary
soundscape, live percussion and a
fragment of the original Adolphe Adam
ballet music. We started the piece with
"real" elements on stage such as
haystacks, stable doors and grass.
For the underworld, the colour was
drained from the stage and the real
elements became identical outlines
in light. The image (above) shows the
moment in the second half when
Albrecht has realised that Giselle is
dead.'

*Director: Marguerite Donlon
Set Designer: Conor Murphy
Costume Designer: Marcus Maas
Lighting Designer: Lutz Deppe
Sound Designer: Sam Auinger
and Claas Willeke
Choreographer: Marguerite Donlon*

Salome
*Richard Strauss/Anton Marriotte
(Strauss 1905, Marriotte 1908)*

*Opéra National de Montpellier
Le Corum, Opera Berlioz, Montpellier
November 2005*

Conor Murphy: 'This was a double bill
of *Salome*, the familiar Strauss opera
and a version by Marriotte, played on
alternate evenings. All the action takes
place in one setting and we decided
that the set should be identical for both
operas so the two pieces could be easily
compared. The set consisted of
a staircase, a sandy floor, a moon and
a cistern that reflected the shape of the
moon with Salome, the moon and
Jokanaan being almost interchangeable
symbols. The costumes and lighting were
opulent and brightly coloured for the
Strauss and monotone for the Marriotte
to enhance its more sombre mood.'

Herodias, Herod and the Jews (top)

*Director: Carlos Wagner
Set and Costume Designer:
Conor Murphy
Lighting Designer: Peter van Praat
Choreographer: Ana Garcia
Photographer: Marc Ginot*

Neil Murray

Homage to Catalonia
Allan J Barker (2003)

*Northern Stage with West Yorkshire
Playhouse. Theatre Romea, Barcelona.
Mc Bobingny'93, Paris
Northern Stage
2003 - 2004*

Neil Murray: '*Homage to Catalonia*
was conceived as a surreal nightmare
with little concern for naturalism. Its focus
was towards generating the atmospheric
essence of what it was to be lost in the
centre of the Civil War. In Act 1, the
streets of Barcelona are filled with the
stink of war and the facts of life: people
still fall in love, cook, eat, shit, have sex,
give birth and die. Throughout it all,
archive footage of the war, much of it
deeply upsetting, plays out hugely on the
metal wall behind the action.
In Act 2, we moved into the gruesomely
macabre and decadent world of the
bourgeoisie, trapped indoors at the
Continental Hotel. Jovet, a young man
suspected of membership with the Boum
party is dragged from the streets and
interrogated by the Communists.
The boy entertains, in drag, before
being shot while Manolo, eats fried
eggs with garlic.
Charlie Chan, a vigorously humorous
and disturbing character from popular
entertainment, representing the
communists Stalin and Mussolini,
introduces us to the world of the
bourgeoisie. While the streets outside
are crammed with the decaying remains
of slaughtered people and horses, some
semblance of middle-class existence
carries on bizarrely behind closed
doors.'

*Director: Josep Galindo
Set and Costume Designer: Neil Murray
Lighting Designer: Malcolm Rippeth
Sound Designer: Mic Pool
Dramaturg: Pablo Ley
Film Maker: Carles Caparros*

Charles Cusick Smith

Cavalleria Rusticana / I Pagliacchi
Pietro Mascagni / Ruggero Leoncavallo (1890)

*Gut Immling Opernfestival
Indoor riding arena, Gut Immling,
Germany
July 2005*

Charles Cusick Smith: 'Santuzza's personal space is invaded by the populace chorus. They rejoice in marriage and love. Santuzza sits, anxious where her lover is and with whom. The stage is 20 metres wide and five metres deep. The two operas were performed in the same space, with an internal box room serving as the house of Santuzza and of Pagliacchi's performance space.'

Costume designs for the Commedia team

Pagliacchi, Beppe and Nedda improvise while Taddeo introduces the prologue

*Director: Stefan Tilch
Set and Costume Designer:
Charles Cusick Smith
Lighting Designer: Arnd Sellenten
Photographer: Peter Litvai*

Francisco Rodriguez-Weil

Alice in Wonderland
*Lyrics by Coot van Doesbourg
Music by Ton Scherpenzeel*

*OpusOne
National tour, Netherlands
September 2005*

Francisco Rodriguez-Weil: 'The director wanted an Alice that most girls could identify with, modern and fresh, so rather than a mirror, we used a computer as a window into Wonderland. Our Alice receives an email from the Red Queen and sees the White Rabbit come out of her bed. Together they go through the walls of the bedroom, landing on a gigantic laptop in Wonderland. We are now inside Alice's desk, and all of its contents, books, pencils etc. are transformed into the doors, furniture and props of this absurd world. The books, furniture, and the Mad Hatter's table were printed, all the complicated designs, being generated, as a scanned and enlarged image would have become pixilated on such a large scale.'

*Director: John Yost
Set and Costume Designer:
Francisco Rodriguez-Weil
Lighting Designer: John Valkering
Graphic Generation: Adam Horwood
Video Designer: Tjeerd Belien*

Spiel Im Berg
Felix Mitterer (October 2005)

Young Actors Theatre, London
October 2005

Francisco Rodriguez-Weil:
'I developed what I considered to be the essence of a salt mine in shape and form, creating a structure out of fabric. This allowed for thematic projections, which differed for each character and illustrated their various hallucinations. The set could be varied by back lighting and front projection, creating different moods and providing indications about the nature of the characters on stage.'

Director: Andrew Harries
Set and Costume Designer:
Francisco Rodriguez-Weil
Lighting Designer: Sally Ferguson
Projections: Andrew Savage

George Souglides

Barbe-Bleue
Jacques Offenbach (1866)

Bregenz Festival
August 2006

George Souglides: '*Bluebeard* is a story of intrigue, of Princes in disguise and Princesses lost and found; of horrible King Bobeche and his nymphomaniac Queen Clementine; of predatory serial monogamist Bluebeard, who thinks he is a serial killer but is not; where the women finally get their revenge. In our version, he becomes a predatory shark but also a Bond baddie. Our references were the Bond movies, *Thunderbirds, Young Frankestein* but also Brigitte Bardot and the 60s. This is the first time I have used Photoshop to create collages of the costume drawings. It seemed, somehow, to be the right style for this mad but beautiful piece.'

Director: Stephen Langridge
Set and Costume Designer:
George Souglides
Lighting Designer: Chris Davey
Choreographer William Tuckett

Maria Stuarda
Gaetano Donizetti (1834)

Grange Park Opera House
August 2006

George Souglides: 'For this
production, a collaboration with
Stephen Langridge and Chris Davey,
we attempted to pare down the emotions
of the piece and to concentrate on the
psychology of the characters, especially
the journey Elizabeth has to take: from
her grand entrance to her court in Act 1,
to shedding her elaborate costume to
reveal a more vulnerable human being
underneath, to her Act 3 appearance,
without her wig and in a modern dress.
Mary ascends to the heavens, an echo
of the religious martyr she almost
became. The set and lighting tried to
evoke the emotions of the characters and
the claustrophobia of their world.'

Director: Stephen Langridge
Set and Costume Designer:
George Souglides
Lighting Designer: Chris Davey
Choreographer William Tuckett

Keith Lodwick

Ruthless!
Book and Lyrics by Joal Paley
Music by Marvin Laird

The Okai Collier Company
Stratford Circus, London
October 2002

Keith Lodwick: Ginger del Marco
(Louise Hollamby) confronts her Agent /
Mother, Sylvia St. Croix (Paul L. Martin)
in the final scene of *Ruthless!* The musical
is a parody of films such as *Gypsy,
Valley of the Dolls, All About Eve* and
The Bad Seed. Collaborating with the
director and the lighting designer,
we created a saturated 'Technicolor'
palette of pinks, lemons and turquoise
in homage to the cinematic world of
Douglas Sirk and Pedro Almodovar.

The intense colours in the costumes, set
and lighting reflected the heightened
emotions of the characters and their
drive for ultimate stardom.'

Director: Omar F. Okai
Set and Costume Designer:
Keith Lodwick
Lighting Designer: Flick Ansell
Sound Designer: Chris Whelan
Choreographer: Omar F. Okai

Nancy Surman

Barbarians
Maxim Gorky (1906)

Salisbury Playhouse
May 2003

Nancy Surman: 'In *Barbarians*, Gorky is exploring the moral struggle between industrial capitalism and the petty bourgeoisie in the changing world of Tsarist Russia on the eve of revolution. The play opens in the vast landscape of provincial Russia at the height of summer, full of optimism and expectation but, as relationships deteriorate, so the stage becomes darker and more threatening, until the ultimate tragic unravelling in the tense, brooding atmosphere of the final scene.
The design is an empathetic response rather than a naturalistic one.
Heightened colours blend the familiar

Simon Wilkinson

Mary's Wedding
Stephen Massicotte

Byre Theatre of St Andrews
Perth Theatre
February 2005

Simon Wilkinson: 'Mary's Wedding is a dream play which flits between the expansive plains of Canada, the claustrophobic trenches of World War 1 France, and the tranquillity of a country barn. Punctuated with thunderstorms and artillery bombardments, these location shifts were achieved on a simple skeletal set. The same cast and creative team had presented a production of the play in the Byre Theatre's Studio the previous year, and the existing relationships led to a streamlined rehearsal and production process for this enlarged version of the show.'

Fiona Watt

Outlying Islands
David Greig (2002)

Traverse Theatre, Edinburgh
July 2002

Fiona Watt: 'The island of David's writing was based on a combination of St Kilda and North Rona, the remotest island off the coast of Britain.
The fearlessness with which actor Lesley Hart launched herself down the spiral of turf took us on an instant journey from one environment to the other, giving life to the island of our imaginings.'

Director: Philip Howard
Set and Costume Designer: Fiona Watt
Lighting Designer: Chahine Yavroyan
Sound Designer: Gavin Marwick
Other creative collaborator: Lesley Hart
Photographer: Douglas Robertson

with the expressionistic to underpin the emotional journey of the play.'

Act one: Waiting for the Railway
Engineers
Act 3: The wife and the mistress

Director: Joanna Read
Set and Costume Designer:
Nancy Surman
Lighting Designer: Jim Simmons
Music and sound: Matthew Bugg
Photographer: Jim Simmons

Director: Rita Henderson
Set and Costume Designer:
Karen Tennent
Lighting Designer: Simon Wilkinson
Sound Designer: Tobin Stokes

Further than the Furthest Thing
Zinnie Harris

Prime Productions
Byre Theatre St Andrews and Tour
February 2006

Fiona Watt: 'In this opening sequence our combined skills created the image and sound of an old man diving into water, seeking resolution. The slash of light across the space later symbolised the cracking of the earth, the division between land and sky, and the distance of the island from the "civilised" world.'

Director: Ben Twist
Set and Costume Designer: Fiona Watt
Lighting Designer: Andrew Coulton
Sound Designer: Dave Fennessy
Actor: Jonathan Battersby
Photographer: Marc Marni

Mark Bailey

Melody on the Move
Finalé
Words and music by various artists

English National Ballet
Sadler's Wells, London
July 2003

Mark Bailey: 'Creating a new ballet must be one of the most collaborative processes for a designer. To start with only a piece of music and then finish with a full piece of dance theatre was a challenge and a thrill. Michael, the choreographer and I began with music of the 30s and 40s, devising scenarios and characters, which I realised visually and Michael realised in movement, to create a series of witty divertissements. An affectionate look at an England that existed only through the wireless.'

Director: Michael Corder
Set and Costume Designer: Mark Bailey
Lighting Designer: Paul Pyant
Choreographer: Michael Corder

One Flew Over the Cuckoo's Nest
Dale Wasserman (1963)

Anthony Hopkins Theatre,
Clwyd Theatr Cymru
February 2004

Mark Bailey: 'A technical collaboration to realise an artistic one. The director and I decided we needed a visual coup to match the intensity of the final moments of the play, a stunning collapse of the nurse's workstation. The excellent construction manager and workshop team made it happen, on cue, every time.'

Director: Terry Hands
Set and Costume Designer: Mark Bailey
Lighting Designer: Terry Hands
Sound Designer: Kevin Heyes

collaborators

DIRECTOR · DESIGNER

Where and how are these partnerships made? With almost the entire theatre, opera and dance landscape employing freelance designers, there are very few building-based or touring companies in which designers are resident. It is true that a handful of companies have retained their design positions and others are beginning to re-evaluate this situation. The RSC, New Vic at Newcastle-under-Lyme, Theatre by the Lake in Keswick and Northern Stage are amongst those with Head of Design, Resident, or designer as Associate Director positions included here. Some community and TIE companies also have regular rather than resident designers. While variety in conceptual and aesthetic approaches may be achieved within a company's work by working with 'freelancers', these SBTD exhibitions demonstrate the significant contributions designers can make within a company, as well as within the community of a city or region, working with other collaborators, including directors.

Long-term designer / director partnerships, with both being freelance, do produce some remarkable work. Their productions may be identifiable and highly valued because of shared aesthetics, coherence and rigour, demonstrated in a particular body of opera, musicals, political plays, site-specific productions, or children's theatre. A designer may move through a relatively small number of such partnerships, taking occasional projects with other directors as one or other of the team seek the creative buzz elsewhere.

In this apparently happenstance, word-of-mouth, personal contacts, scouting-for-award-winners world, it becomes increasingly important for emerging designers to make the most of their student placements, to network with other design, performance, or directing students / graduates, to learn to make funding applications for their own work, anything but wait for the phone call. Small wonder that a kind of revolution has been happening. With no career prospects, as such, designers have been taking things into their own hands and making their own projects, sometimes in partnership with directors, but also by becoming directors. For many, the scenographic ideal - that of participating equally in the process of creating a stage work - is stimulating enough. For others, conceiving of the project and developing it through to performance in every aspect becomes paramount. Perhaps the ultimate act of the scenographer is to become a director.

Paul Brown

Lucio Silla
Wolfgang Amadeus Mozart (1772)

Santa Fe Opera
July 2005

Paul Brown: 'In this Opera Seria, elaborate and over-sized costumes resulted in repressed emotions and unnatural, artificial behaviour.'

Director: Jonathan Kent
Set and Costume Designer: Paul Brown
Associate Designer: Luis Carvalho
Lighting Designer: Duane Schuler
Photographer: Ken Howard

Paul Brown

Lez Brotherston

collaborators

Les Liaisons Dangereuses

Adam Cooper/ Lez Brotherston
(2005/2006)

Adam Cooper Company
Newport Hall, Japan/Sadler's Wells,
London
January 2005

Lez Brotherston: 'Adam Cooper and I, in looking for a project to collaborate on, landed on the Laclos novel. We set about co-writing and co-directing a dance theatre version of *The Dangerous Liaisons* with Adam responsible for the movement and I for the visuals.
We directed and developed the piece for Adam's own company.'

Directors: Adam Cooper and
Lez Brotherston
Set and Costume Designer:
Lez Brotherston
Lighting Designer: Paul Constable
Sound Designer: Adam Pink
Choreographer: Adam Cooper
Composer: Philip Feeney

Edward Scissorhands

Mathew Bourne/Danny Elfman
(Dec 2005)

New Adventures
Sadler's Wells, London
December 2005

Lez Brotherston: 'Edward's costume was developed in collaboration with the costume maker Phil Reynolds and prop maker Robert Allsop. Phil's expertise with dance costumes allowed us to prototype versions using leather, lycra power net and elastic to create an "anatomical", leather Edward. Robert developed the hands using vac formed, plated plastic - prototypes that were constructed for balance and weight.'

Director: Mathew Bourne
Set and Costume Designer:
Lez Brotherston
Lighting Designer: Howard Harrison
Sound Designer: Pete Rice
Choreographer: Mathew Bourne

Es Devlin

Kevin Knight

Tannhauser
Richard Wagner

Teatro La Scala, Milan
February 2005

Kevin Knight: 'Wagner's epic piece,
fronted by the Venusburg ballet, needed
a clear physical and psychological
language to give it a strong sense of time
and place. We worked closely together
to evolve a sensual, theatrical language
that examined the tension between the
natural and constructed worlds.
We wanted the danced contribution to
be integrated into the narrative and as a
creative team, worked closely to blur the
edges of what was ballet and what was
opera. In part we did this by bringing
the dancers into the chorus of the second
act, to react physically.'

collaborators

Orphée
Jean Cocteau/Philip Glass (May 2005)

Theatre Company, ROH 2
Linbury Studio, Royal Opera House,
London
May 2005

Es Devlin: 'The Linbury Studio has a
central orchestral pit that descends two
metres underground. The director and
I were led by this architectural feature to
conceive an additional lift to continue
our protagonist's journey through the
underworld.
Miraculously, the ROH approved and
achieved the installation of a 12m x 1m,
arrow-shaped, Perspex-clad beam that
raised two apparently unsecured opera
singers 7m off the ground. One of them
was the exquisite and intrepid soprano
Ha Young Lee. I collaborated with her
again the following year at Hamburg
Staatsoper – this time at 5m off the
ground, strapped to a bed full of
projected snakes.'

*Orphée's journey through the
underworld*

Director: Francisco Negrin
Set and Costume Designer: Es Devlin
Lighting Designer: Bruno Poet
Production Manager: Carl Root

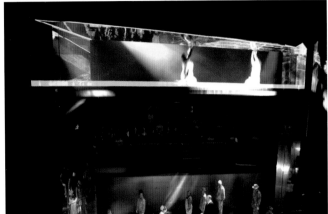

Director: Paul Curran
Set and Costume Designer: Kevin Knight
Lighting Designer: David Jacques
Choreographer: Andrew George

Paul Edwards

Eva
Josef Foerster (1899)

Theatre Royal, Wexford.
October 2004

Paul Edwards: 'The first act of the
opera is located "On The Edge of
The Village". The director and I
discussed that this would be where the
rolling wheat fields of the Slovak
countryside began. To make this idea of
vastness collaborate with what is quite
a small stage, I decided to make the sky
the same colour as the wheat field,
which was shaped in perspective,
to create a sense of rural infinity.'

Act 1

Director: Paul Curran
Set and Costume Designer:
Paul Edwards
Lighting Designer: Giuseppe Di Iorio
Photographer: Derek Speirs

Jonathan Fensom

Twelfth Night
William Shakespeare (1601)

Background
Albery (now the Coward)
July-September 2004

Jonathan Fensom: 'We decided to
transpose the play from Illyria to
a contemporary Indian setting.
A monsoon on the Arabian sea wrecks
the ship that washes Viola and
Sebastian ashore.
With its honour codes, the rules of
marriage, holy men, beliefs and the
significance of the festival, the Indian
setting was intended to find a fresh,
contemporary relevance for the world
of the play.
Everything we discovered in India
seemed to make sense of the play.
Its vibrancy, its passion, its cruelty, the
irreverent humour that informs every
interaction, the public nature of people's
emotional lives and the social
delineation of the characters, often
through the way they speak the verse.
Shakespeare might have recognised a
great deal - not least the unsentimental
way people approach what's thrown
at them.'

Viola and the Sea Captain washed
ashore in the monsoon
Malvolio and Olivia

Chérubin
Jules Massenet (1905)

*Teatro Lirico di Cagliari
January 2006*

Paul Edwards: 'Massenet wrote *Chérubin* as a homage to Mozart's *The Marriage of Figaro*, but very much in the contemporary style of his day. I followed the composer's lead and created a world drawn from a modern audience's knowledge of the 18th century, one informed by movies. The director and I called this look "Hollywood Rococo". The costumes where based on the 18th century but through a 1930s aesthetic.'

Act 2 – The Countess and the Baroness

*Director: Paul Curran
Set and Costume Designer:
Paul Edwards
Lighting Designer: David Jacques*

Steven Beresford
'Modern people in a modern setting but living in a culture that's rooted in its past, mysterious, religious and magical; a place where attitudes to sex, love and death are frank and realistic, but where women might veil themselves in front of strangers; a world of shrines and marriage settlements, where ancient music and ritual are a part of daily life… Once India had suggested itself, the solutions followed. Feste becomes a Baul singer, a Bengali tradition of nomadic minstrels and soothsayers. If Shakespeare were to be dropped into modern day Mumbai and then London, he would definitely feel more at home in Mumbai. Moving the play nearly 4,000 miles and setting it in India brings it closer to the spirit in which it was first written.'

*Director: Stephen Beresford
Set and Costume Designer:
Jonathan Fensom
Lighting Designer: Jason Taylor
Sound Designer: Fergus O'Hare
Choreographer: Chix Chandara*

Richard Hudson

RHINEGOLD

1. Alberich and a Rhinemaiden Scene 1

2. Mime in Nibelheim Scene 3

3. Alberich and Wotan Scene 4

The Ring of the Nibelung
Richard Wagner (1848-1874)

*English National Opera
Coliseum Theatre, London
2004/2005*

Richard Hudson: 'Designing the four operas of the Ring Cycle is the ultimate act of collaboration. I worked with Phyllida for over three years, often meeting twice a week. It was a very challenging and inspiring experience.'

*Director: Phyllida Lloyd
Set and Costume Designer:
Richard Hudson
Lighting Designers: Simon Mills,
Mark Henderson, Adam Silverman,
Paule Constable
Photographer: Robert Workman*

VALKYRIE

1. Siegmund and Sieglinda in Hunding's Hut Act 1

2. Wotan, Hunding, Siegmund and Sieglinde Act 2

3. Wotan, the Valkyrie and Heroes Act 3

Richard Hudson

SIEGFRIED

*1. Mime in his
cave Act 1*

*2. Siegfried
forging the sword
Act 1*

*3. Siegfried and
Mime outside
Fafner's cave
Act 2*

*TWILIGHT OF
THE GODS*

*1. Hall of the
Gibichungs Act 1
Scene 1*

*2. Brunnhilde's
Rock Act 1 Scene 2*

*3. The Flooding of
the Rhine Act 3
Scene 2*

Marie-Jeanne Lecca

The Dwarf (Der Zwerg)
Alexander Zemlinsky, libretto Georg C. Klaren (1919/21)

*Opera North
Grand Theatre, Leeds and touring
April 2004*

Marie-Jeanne Lecca: 'Based on Oscar Wilde's story *The Birthday of the Infanta*, the opera centres on the tragedy of the individual different to those around him, the "ugly man" in love with the unattainable Princess. At the Spanish court, the Dwarf is used, mocked and ruthlessly destroyed by the beautiful, spoilt Infanta and her sycophantic retinue.
David's brief to me was very inspirational: "You should create a punk-Velasquez look". His vision was that of a cruel and grotesque court, of a hideous and destructive childlike retinue, the "in" crowd, stuck in the formality of their synthetic fashion, in contrast with the heart and soul of the "little man" and his romantic songs and chivalrous poetry. In order to give this feeling of vulnerable and aggressive, naive and nasty, superficial and worthless world, I used semi-transparent, plastics, lots of them cut out, cobweb like, everything light and airy and held together with metal studs and eyelets.
Some of the outfits were decorated with over-sized butterflies and bows, in

Penny Saunders

Rough Magyck
Forkbeard Fantasy (September 2006)

*Forkbeard Fantasy
October 2006*

Penny Saunders: 'I work with Tim and Chris Britton in Forkbeard Fantasy on the designing and building of sets and props. I didn't train in theatre design and our work is quite idiosyncratic; we create the contents of the show together. The purpose of a part of the set is as likely to have an effect on the final script as the other way around. This equality does make one feel empowered, as does the importance of the standard of what is made.
The aim in *Rough Magyck*, which was commissioned by the RSC for their Complete Shakespeare season, was to make a life-size horse that would "enhance the beauty of horsiness" and move very well. It hangs within a steel frame, so that it can take the weight of a performer as well as be animated as a string puppet. Horses have awe-inspiring bone structures and muscle design. Their bones are beautiful shapes so I copied them and tried to duplicate the movement of the joints.'

Life-sized horse puppet.

*Directors: The Company and Andy Hay
Set Designer: Penny Saunders
Lighting Designer: Marcus Bartlett
Sound Designer: Joe Bone, Dom Schirrer and the Company
Choreographer: Liz Rankin
Costume Supervisor: Ellie Kurtz*

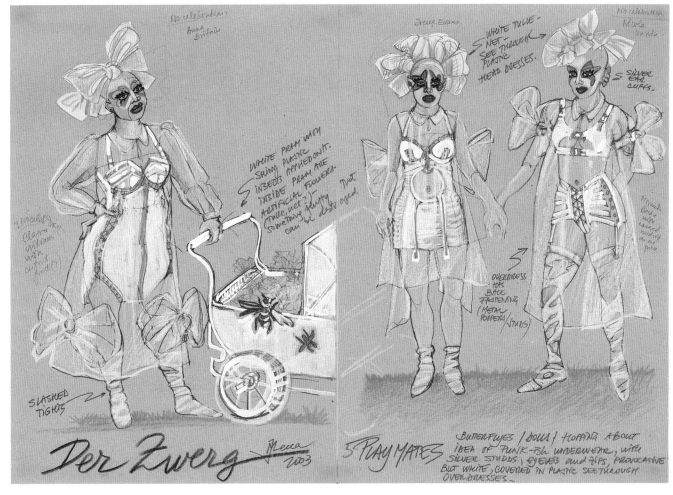

innocent, girlie style.
The Infanta's costume followed the Velasquez silhouette, culminating with her headdress, realised by Robert Allsopp. His input was a perfect combination of creativity and technical expertise.'

Director: David Pountney
Set Designer: Johan Engels
Costume Designer: Marie-Jeanne Lecca
Lighting Designer: Adam Silverman
Conductor: David Parry
Costume props and headdresses:
Robert Allsopp
Photographer: Laurie Lewis

Macbeth

William Shakespeare (between 1604 and 1606)

Heartbreak Productions
Outdoor Touring Theatre
June 2004

Paul Barrett: 'Since 2003 I have designed a series of outdoor Shakespearean shows for the director Peter Mimack and his touring theatre company, Heartbreak Productions. We collaborate from the outset, designer and director working together to overcome the usual issues faced by any outdoor touring company; committed to the view that budget should not limit creativity. By using a flexible, modular stage I am able to create a landscape that supports the main themes addressed by the performance.

For *Macbeth*, the stage represents the architecture of the castle, bleak countryside and an ever present Hell mouth. The throne is carved into the rock face, a constant part of the land rather than a piece of furniture.'

Director: Peter Mimack
Set and Costume Designer: Paul Barrett
Sound Designer: Darren Scott
Choreographers:
Geoffrey Buckley (Movement)
Marc Vance: (Fight sequences)

Paul Barrett

Phil Newman

The Playground
Beverley Naidoo (September 2004)

*Polka Theatre, Wimbledon
September 2004*

Phil Newman: 'My second collaboration with director Olusola Oyeleye, *The Playground* explored racial conflict and the crossing of boundaries during 12 pivotal years in South Africa. I felt the harsh realities of the story needed to play out against a naturally beautiful backdrop (as they had originally done), and visited Johannesburg for the first time in order to get a truer sense of place.
With numerous diverse locations, it was important to create a flexible performance space. The two main houses opened out from opposite sides, whilst the main stage could be redefined using a series of folding, rusted wire mesh screens.'

*Director: Olusola Oyeleye
Set and Costume Designer: Phil Newman
Sound Designer: Simon McCorry
Choreographer: Prudence Mampe*

Nick Moran

A Masked Ball (Un Ballo Maschera)
Giuseppe Verdi, Antonio Somma (1859)

*English National Opera
London Coliseum
February 2002*

'When it came to developing a new lighting design for *A Masked Ball* in London, I wanted to ensure the strongly contemporary visual aesthetic was free of any "old fashioned" connotations, including the de-naturalising follow spots which had originally been used in Act 2. Working closely with Joan Anton, the assistant director, both in the rehearsal room and during stage rehearsals, we came up with blocking that would allow us to dispense with the follow spots in favour of directed light from the pit rail. Working with the lighting team during stage rehearsals, and with the co-operation of the orchestra and the principal performers, we experimented with placement, focus, colour and level of just four Source 4 profiles, two from each side of the pit. These were the principal "face light" for the scene, set on waste ground outside the city where betrayal and disguise are key. The only other major light source was a large

Christopher Oram

Evita
Andrew Lloyd Webber and Tim Rice

Really Useful Group
Adelphi Theatre, Strand, London
21 June 2006

Christopher Oram: 'A classic and iconic moment - Eva Peron's *debut* on the balcony in front of the Descamisados, the ''shirtless'' workers of Argentina - was staged and lit to emphasise her ascendance to the ultimate position in Buenos Aires society. Dressed in a shimmering Dior gown (made by Carol Molyneux and hand-beaded by Tansy Blaik) she is radiant against the dark splendour of the presidential palace as she sings the anthemic *Don't Cry for Me Argentina* to her people silhouetted beneath her.'

On the balcony of the Casa Rosada
Act 2 Scene 1

Director: Michael Grandage
Set and Costume Designer:
Christopher Oram
Lighting Designer: Paule Constable
Sound Designer: Mick Potter
Choreographer: Rob Ashford
Assistant designer: Morgan Large
Photographer: Johan Persson

HMI as a backlight for the whole stage. This would have been a high-risk strategy were it not for the collaboration of all involved; the assistant director understanding the need to keep diagonal lines clear to prevent one performer casting shadows on another at a key moment, the orchestra members for putting up with our constant tweaking of lamps above their heads during rehearsals, the lighting team for sticking with it, and the performers for going with a rejection of follow spots.'

Director: Calixto Bieito
Assistant Director: Joan Anton Rechi
Set Designer: Alfons Flores
Costume Designer: Merce Paloma
Lighting Designer: Nick Moran
Conductors: Andrew Litton
and Alex Ingram
Photographer: Neil Libbert

Lili Rogué

Aesop's Fables
Mike Kenny (2002)

*Nottingham Playhouse Roundabout
Nottingham Playhouse Studio and
touring
October 2005*

Lili Rogué: *'Aesop's Fables is a fun,
modern adaptation of timeless stories,
aimed at 4 - 7 year olds.
The storytellers, who also double as
musicians, transform into numerous
animals, telling some of the most popular
fables. With a short production period,
the design process had to be
condensed. It was made possible by
the director and I spending an afternoon
making crucial decisions about the
production. We decided to create an
environment that would immerse the
children in the universe of the
performers. The resulting set and
costume designs are a metaphor for
the oral tradition. The actors become
travellers from a faraway land, who
welcome us in their colourful tent and
proceed to tell stories with the use of
a transformable coat, hats and a double
stepladder.'*

*Director: Andrew Breakwell
Set and Costume Designer: Lili Rogué
Composer: Matt Marks
Photographer: Robert Day*

Transformable Coat

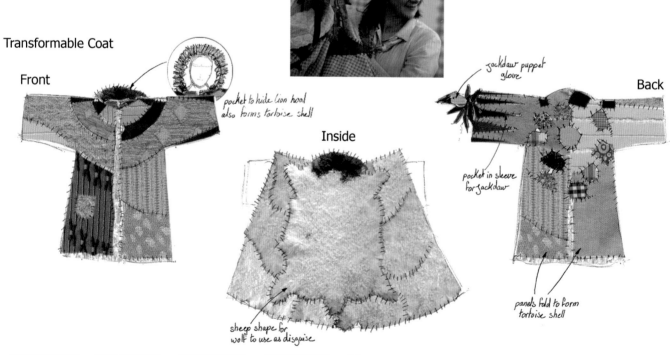

Front

pocket to hide lion head
also forms tortoise shell

Inside

sheep shape for
wolf to use as disguise

jackdaw puppet
glove

Back

pocket in sleeve
for jackdaw

panels fold to form
tortoise shell

Eyecatcher
Richard Hurford (October 2005)

Sheffield Theatres Creative Development Programme
Sheffield Theatres studio and touring February 2006

Lili Rogué: 'Hanging on the edge of the human world, in a surrealistic, deserted landscape... a cave, high up in a cliff face, a refuge, jerry-built out of the flotsam and jetsam of the human world, amassed over thousands of years. Shelter to the Graeae and their secret prisoner, the den reflects both the lifestyle of the three mythological creatures and their individual character. *Eyecatcher* is a new version of the Greek myth of Perseus' encounter with the Gorgon Medusa. Concentrating on the unknown side of the story, the visual was created through an ongoing collaboration between designer, writer and director. Design and script evolved together, interpreting and informing each other throughout the design period. The resulting set and costumes were highly detailed, with a timeless quality, creating a base for the actors to expand the identity of their obscure characters.'

Director: Karen Simpson
Set and Costume Designer: Lili Rogué
Lighting Designer: Gary Longfield
Composer: Luke Carver Goss
Photographer: Chris Saunders

The Graeae

Gru   Grim   Gris

Ben Stones

Paradise Lost
*John Milton adapted by Ben Power
(April 2006)*

*Oxford Stage Company
National tour
April 2006*

Ben Stones: 'In this redesigned production, the director and I got to revisit our discussions about what were Hell and Eden. After many meetings we eventually started talking about inversion. If Hell was a bare, burnt out room in which we introduced sculptural forms to change the space as Satan journeys through Hell and into the universe, then Eden was the exact opposite. And so Eden became a stark, white, plaster restoration of the Hell set, where lighting was used to suggest atmosphere. We also made the decision to use no foliage in Eden and that architectural pillars would form our forest.'

*Director: Rupert Goold
Set and Costume Designer: Ben Stones
Lighting Designer: Mark Jonathan
Composer: Adam Cork
Choreographers: Georgina Lamb
and Liam Steel
Projection Design: Lorna Heavey
Photographer: Robert Day*

Daphne Stevens-Pascucci

Pompeo Magno
Francesco Cavalli (1666)

*Varazdin Baroque Evenings Festival
Varazdin State Opera House Croatia
September 2002*

Daphne Stevens-Pascucci: 'For this world premiere, the English director wished to find visual inspiration from Roman artefacts and the French 17th-century court where the opera was commissioned. I was particularly fascinated by a royal family portrait by Jean Nocret as they were dressed in classical robes from antiquity, together with full-bottomed, curly wigs of the Baroque at the same time! Two-tone silks in rich colours expressed the opulent music.'

*Director: Tom Hawkes
Set Designer: Dinka Jericevic
Costume Designer:
Daphne Stevens-Pascucci*

Beautiful Thing
Jonathan Harvey

Neil Laidlaw for NML Productions
Sound Theatre, Leicester Square
January 2006

Ben Stones: *'Beautiful Thing* is set on the balcony of a council estate in Thamesmead, South London, during the hot summer of 1993. We wanted to evoke the architecture of Thamesmead, which felt very textural, oppressive, and colourless. We used the full length of the space to accentuate this. The bedroom scenes were placed within the architecture of the balcony as this felt the heart of the piece. The final moment of Jonathan Harvey's play demands the designer to make concrete beautiful, and in our production the estate fades away, revealing the two couples dancing on a starry sky.'

Director: Rupert Goold
Set and Costume Designer: Ben Stones
Lighting Designer: Mark Jonathan
Composer: Adam Cork
Choreographer: Georgina Lamb
and Liam Steel
Projection Design: Lorna Heavey
Photographer: Robert Day

Juliet Shillingford

The School for Wives
Arnolphe's House
Derek Mahon after Molière

Nuffield Theatre Company
Nuffield Theatre, Southampton
14 April 2005

Juliet Shillingford: 'My collaboration with Patrick Sandford has developed over several years and many productions. What I enjoy is how our ideas meet and become inseparable. For *The School for Wives* we began with images of cells by Louise Bourgeois and then experimented with the way a paper lampshade folded flat. Agnes is imprisoned by Arnolphe in order to mould her into the perfect wife. She sits beneath a cage formed by her handmade trousseau, enclosing a spiral staircase, leading to nowhere. At the end of the play, when she is rescued by her lover, the cage falls to the ground.'

Director: Patrick Sandford
Set and Costume Designer:
Juliet Shillingford
Lighting Designer: David W. Kidd
Photographer: Mike Eddowes

Louise Ann Wilson

Mulgrave, a journey
Writer and co-creator: Amanda Dalton
Composer and co-creator:
Hugh Nankivell

wilson+wilson
Mulgrave Woods, Sands End,
Nr Whitby, North Yorkshire
May-June 2005

Louise Ann Wilson: *'Mulgrave was a live theatre performance inspired by and performed in Mulgrave Woods. Travelling both on foot and by buggy, audiences were taken from the shores of the sea, into the woods, and back to the sea again. Their journey emulated the sweep of a great wave which brought with it characters and stories past, present and future, real and mythic: A boy running like a river from the sea, Land-Rover-bound huntsmen tracking a feral girl, the Maharajah Duleep Singh and his beloved elephants, landscaper Humphrey Repton painting his Red Book, a horse-drawn carriage conveying botanist Joseph Banks and prize specimen Omai, a washed-up tree-top boat, shoals of driftwood fish, a tattooed traveller singing to the trees.... '*

Conceived and co-created by:
Wils Wilson
Conceived, co-created and designed
by: Louise Ann Wilson
Photographer: Dominic Ibbotson

collaborators

ART · CRAFT · DESIGN

Establishing strong creative relationships with other visual artists such as projection or lighting designers and increasingly with digital artists on a project can be highlights of the process. Similarly, finding a scene painter, costumier or costume supervisor, prop maker or set sculptor / builder with an instinct for empathetic interpretation can make all the difference to what the designs aspire to. Marie-Jeanne Lecca, Kandis Cook and others have found in Robert Allsopp, a brilliant costume-prop maker, whose imagination and craftsmanship fleshes drawings out into fabulous monsters and sculptural costumes, while fruitful collaborations with lighting designers Paule Constable and David Howe are commented upon by Tanya McCallin and Becs Andrews.

This creative input of lighting and projection designers is now one of the most fundamental in the realisation of almost any performance design. The advances in both luminaire design and their control systems have offered designers more input into how any moment is seen and interpreted than ever before. Inclusion of digital imagery and effects is now accessible to even low budget productions and the influences of lighting , projection and digital media in both contemporary fine art and of the music industry have been completely incorporated into theatre and even opera. While the specialisms of the lighting designer are to be celebrated, designers are increasingly considering the interpretation of form through light and the interaction of projection and surface(s) in their set and costume designs. Projected imagery and sequences have been a choice for designers within very controlled light conditions for many years. But we are now seeing projection and display technologies used even in daylight conditions and they can be considered as a component of the design in the same way as textile and paint.

This complete interdependence of form and light is ironically both the ultimate reason why design for performance is such an ephemeral art form, dependent on the lit moment to reveal or conceal its possibilities, as well as being the major factor in the making of arresting and significant photographs which appear to capture the essence of the moment for ever.

Becs Andrews

Orestes 2.0
Charles L. Mee (1992)

*Guildhall School of Music and Drama
Guildhall Theatre, Barbican, London
January 2005*

Becs Andrews:'A ruined homeland
sinking in oil greets the veterans as they
return from an unjust war abroad.
Helen's oil-spill train contains the greed
of capitalist culture, her war veterans
appear like wounded sea-birds, tarred
and feathered.
The "no-build" condition of the design
brief was solved by close integration
of set and lighting design, using stock
reflective dance floor as "oil" and
illuminating a tallscope to represent an
oil well. Furniture jutting at angles and
black feet reinforced the effect.
The dramatic ending of the oil running
out was achieved by flying strips of the
floor to reveal the "blood" underneath.'

*State Visit by Menelaus
Helen's Death and The End of Oil*

*Director: Daniel Kramer
Set and Costume Designer:
Becs Andrews
Lighting Designer: David Howe
Choreographer: Ann Yee
Photographer: Nobby Clark*

David Howe

Orestes 2:0
The Trial
Charles Mee

*Guildhall Scool
of Music and Drama
Guildhall Theatre, London
January 2005*

*Director: Daniel Kramer
Set and Costume Designer:
Becs Andrews
Lighting Designer: David Howe
Choreographer: Ann Yee
Photographer: Nobby Clarke*

David Howe:'As a creative team
we all felt that clean "beautiful and
brutal" beams of light were essential in
the "capturing" of the various
characters. *The Trial* is where each
group of characters explain their
motivation, all contained in their own
worlds. One actor is shown standing on
a metal hospital stretcher with a 5kw
Fresnel looming over his head, the unit
was chosen for its pure size and
dominating quality.'

Liz Ascroft

The Rise and Fall of Little Voice
Jim Cartwright

*The Royal Exchange Theatre,
Manchester
January-February 2002*

Liz Ascroft: 'I concentrated on creating the space from Little Voice's agoraphobic point of view. Everything is laid wide open and exposed. Little Voice's precise journeys around the house are her way of controlling some of her fears and feelings of exposure. She abides compulsively by the rules of the laid out house while others freak her out by walking freely throughout the house.'

Paul Burgess

Selfish
Devised (May 2003)

*Daedalus Theatre Company
The Arches, Glasgow
May 2003*

Paul Burgess: '*Selfish* was a devised exploration of identity and the persistence of myth. Bringing together performance and video installation, it was created from research into the theories, myths and metaphors that have been used to describe what it feels like to know that you exist. Much of the visual material, which included pre-recorded and live-feed video, models, slides and temporary installations, was largely visual. The performers operated the technical equipment from onstage and adapted the set, creating a degree of flexibility that led to a continual evolution of the performance.'

*Director/Designer: Paul Burgess
The Company: Graeme Mackay,
Onur Orkut, Susan Swanick*

Pete Rice
How we collaborated

The House
'Collaborating with Liz on this show created a few challenges. On a practical level, because of the way the house was split and laid out, naturalistic sounds like door knocks, stones thrown against windows and cars approaching needed to come from underneath the stage behind the relevant places in the floor. Even though the actors entered through the normal entrances, this was a way of reinforcing the original design concepts with sound and combining our artistic goals.'

The Medley
'The record revolve in the centre of the stage not only helped reinforce the musical themes of the piece but in sound terms gave a me a position to localize the recorded soundtrack of the medley that LV sings too. Making one complete revolution over the five-minute medley meant that Liz, by designing the revolve, assisted me in making sure all the audience experienced the same listening perspective at some point during the song. A normally near impossible thing to achieve with sound in the round.'

The Fire
'As the fire ignited along 7 individual telegraph lines, one to each side of the theatre, rather than just up the pole, I was also able to deal with each side of the theatre individually and match the rate of ignition of the fire with a sound. Working together to maximize the design potential of the effect.'

Director: Sarah Frankom
Set and Costume Designer: Liz Ascroft
Lighting Designer: Richard Owen
Sound Designer: Pete Rice
Choreographer: Beverley Edmunds
Musical Director: Richard Atkinson

Donatella Barbieri

Rigoletto
Giuseppe Verdi (1851)

Opera Holland Park
Holland Park
20th July 2006

Donatella Barbieri : 'During the overture, Rigoletto - Olafur Sigurdarson - enters, in his civilian clothes, dragging a hessian sack containing his jester outfit, which he dons on stage. He forces the sack into the back of his doublet, creating the hunch, his deformity, a clearly constructed part of his hated "work uniform". This same hessian sack, which sits as a weight on his shoulder in the court scenes, is later used by the chorus to kidnap Gilda, and, again, by Sparafucile, to carry the dying daughter back to a devastated Rigoletto.'

Director: John La Bouchardière
Set Designer: Jamie Vartan
Costume Designer: Donatella Barbieri
Lighting Designer: Colin Grenfell
Choreographer: Isabel Mortimer
Conductor: Peter Robinson
Rigoletto: Olafur Sigurdarson
Photographer: Fritz Curzon

Chris de Wilde

Il Trovatore
Giuseppe Verdi (1853)

Tbilisi Opera
Tbilisi Opera & Ballet Theatre, Georgia
June 2006

Chris de Wilde: 'Setting *Il Trovatore* during the Spanish Civil War, with its iconic images of freedom fighters, refugees and internment camps, created access to the heart of a complex libretto. The naturalistic props and costumes of the acting space were juxtaposed with stylised backcloth images.
These backcloths both provided context for the story and commented on the action. I selected a number of photographs and posters of the period, which I then manipulated and collaged on my computer. The resulting images were scanned on to poster hoarding fabrics by a local company, deliberately emphasising the mechanical reproduction process and creating a Modernist feel.'

Director: Vernon Mound
Designer: Chris de Wilde
Lighting Designer: Amiran Ananiashvili

Imogen Cloet

Noir
Peter Straughan (2002)

Co-production between Northern Stage Ensemble and Live Theatre
Newcastle Playhouse
March 2002

Imogen Cloet: 'A large cinema screen made up of a series of sliding black screens on two levels. This enabled the non-linear action of the play to move swiftly and seamlessly, cutting between time and place and opening to reveal the various locations - woods, a casino, a psychiatrist's office, an all-night diner to name but a few. Central to the success of this production was the simple use of key objects, visual motifs - illuminated signs, clocks, neon and Malcolm Rippeth's atmospheric lighting, all of which echoed the cinematic style of the Noir genre and gave the production its Hopperesque quality.'

collaborators

David W Kidd

Die Walküre
Richard Wagner (1856)

*Den Ny Opera
Esbjerg Musikhuset
September 2005*

David W Kidd: 'Roy Bell's set and
costume design for *Die Walküre* were
gargantuan and timeless. The set
contained many textures specifically
with lighting in mind. These textures
include the Act 1 trunk and tree covering
Hunding's house, the vast monoliths and
desolate landscapes of Act 2 and in Act
3, here performed amid rising volcanic
pillars, the famous *Ride of the Valkeries*.
In the final image of the opera, we see
Brünnhilde surrounded by fire,
the textures of the transluscent pillars
and rocky precipice turning into molten,
undulating lava.'

Brünnhilde finale

*Director: Troels Kold
Set and Costume Designer: Roy Bell
Lighting Designer: David W Kidd
Photographers: Den Ny Opera and
Roy Bell*

Malcolm Rippeth: 'We researched
film noir, and lit the piece almost as
much with shadow as with light –
dramatic shadows sculpting faces and
dominating the backgrounds.
We motivated the light for almost every
scene with practical units – desk lamps,
pendant shades, fluorescent tubes, neon
signs – lending the atmospheric
chiaroscuro a believable reality.
The scenic design and use of video also
necessitated keying many scenes with
sidelight, a happy coincidence which
lent depth of focus and encouraged
strong contrast, both key values in the
film noir aesthetic.'

*Director: Max Roberts
Set and Costume Designer:
Imogen Cloet
Lighting Designer: Malcolm Rippeth
Photographer: Keith Pattinson*

Liam Doona

collaborators

The White Album
Michael Pinchbeck (2005)

Nottingham Playhouse
2005

Liam Doona: 'Miles, an obsessive
Beatles fan, chooses to commit suicide
to the soundtrack of the The White
Album. As he dies, each track triggers
combinations of memory and fantasy,
replaying his love affairs and the stories
underpinning or contextualising the
songs on the album.
Each scene, inspired by a track on
the album, ran to the same sequence
and generally speaking lasted for as
long as the song. Each operated visually
in a similar way to the aural one, having
its own context, intention and style. The
overlaying projection aimed to create a
fluid, changing environment – each
scene/song fading away to reveal the
next.
The space was engineered to facilitate
a series of simple but important
movements. The main wall presented
the album cover, pivoting to reveal new
episodes in the story, finally the white
box/gallery/hospital of the final act.
Simple linear columns, stage right,
allowed the entrance of trucked
scenery – emerging like the record from
the sleeve.
The modular division of the design into
squares reinforced the idea of the record
cover but also implied soundproofing
in the recording studio and gave us
doorways through which events could
spill out. Projection was used to create
portals suggesting worlds beyond – tight
framing to the squares, echoing 1960s
split screen cinematography.'

Director: Giles Croft
Set and Costume Designer: Liam Doona
Lighting Designer: Richard G. Jones
Video Projection: Arnim Friess
Design Assistant: Lili Rogué

Lis Evans

Amadeus
Peter Shaffer (1979)

New Vic Theatre with the Phoenix Singers
New Vic Theatre, Newcastle-under-Lyme
May 2004

Lis Evans: 'In response to the "precocious youngster" Mozart's musical genius, Salieri struggles with his conscience and makes a deal with God. As the main focus of the audience's point of view in the round, the elaborately painted floor cloth, inspired by Borromini's St. Ivo della Sapienza in Rome and the ceiling of the Sistine Chapel, represented the society in which the play is set, and Salieri's state of mind.'

Director: Chris Monk
Set and Costume Designer: Lis Evans
Lighting Designer: Daniella Beattie
Choreographer: Beverley Edmunds
Scenic Artists: Michael Roberts, Laura Clarkeson, Denise Hogan

Rick Fisher

Billy Elliot - The Musical
Music by Elton John, book and lyrics by Lee Hall (2005)

Victoria Palace Theatre, London
May 2005

Rick Fisher: '*Billy Elliot* is a musical that has a very unmusical setting, the miners' strike during the 1980s. It charts the parallel stories of a boy who yearns to be a ballet dancer and the community under intense pressure as the strike continues. Finding a theatrical language that was true to the characters and the setting and satisfying to the audience was a great challenge for us all. At times the stage becomes empty and light helps to define an emotional landscape as Billy struggles against the prejudices of the community to express himself through powerful dance.'

Director: Stephen Daldry
Set Designer: Ian MacNeil
Costume Designer: Nicky Gillibrand
Lighting Designer: Rick Fisher
Sound Designer: Paul Arditti
Choreographer: Peter Darling
Photographer: David Scheinmann

collaborators

Wai Yin Kwok

The Mona Lisas
Brigitte Louveaux

Theatre Mélange in association with the Romanian Company Theatul Municipal Ariel
Touring the UK, including The Brewhouse Theatre and Riverside Studio 2, London September/October 2006

Wai Yin Kwok: 'Placed in a damp, abandoned warehouse, art is dead and locked away. A desecrated world where six Mona Lisa lost souls, from the painting of Leonardo da Vinci, are trapped and want to escape from the isolated world.They take the audience on a surreal journey through a transition of visual art, with rotating columns and objects to create the landscapes.'

Act 1 Scene 3
Impressionism, Edgar Manet: "Le Dejeuner Sur L'Herbe"

Director: Sandy Maberley
Set Designer: Wai Yin Kwok
Costume Designer: Julie Bowles
Lighting Designer: Geraint Pughe

Phil R. Daniels

Cliff The Musical
Mike Read / Trevor Payne

Producers: Derek Block,
Stuart Littlewood and Colin Rozee
Prince of Wales Theatre and tour
March 2003

Phil R. Daniels: 'The challenge was to create a set that could function in both conventional theatrical performance spaces and also concert venues.
The show used both traditional theatrical settings, utilising gauzes and trucks and more contemporary video and concert technology. The narrative moved from interiors, through concert and fantasy segments spanning several decades.
The set design incorporated seven video screens, a rock band on two levels, a full lighting rig and computer-operated light boxes.'

Cliff The Musical (full set, Act 1)

Director: Trevor Payne
Set and Costume Co-designers: Phil R Daniels and Charles Cusick Smith
Lighting Designers: Graham J. McLusky and Simon Johnson
Sound Designer: Ken Hampton
Choreographer: Simon Shelton

Stefanos Lazaridis   *Das Rheingold*

Siegfried

See over page for production credits

Die Walküre

Götterdämmerung

Marie-Jeanne Lecca

The Ring Cycle (Das Rheingold , Die Walküre, Siegfried, Götterdämmerung)
Richard Wagner (1874)

*Royal Opera House, London
December 2004*

Marie-Jeanne Lecca: 'I tried to convey the familiarity and closeness of the everyday and the distance of the myth – and operate on a metaphorical level, but grounded in reality. This meant going for costumes cut as ordinary clothes, but giving them additional depth by creating special fabrics.

On Wotan's coat, the Opera House's dye department printed my own photograph of tree branches, onto which, Webb Costumiers embroidered strips of velvet and shredded satin ribbon.

Over basic dresses the Norns have a knitted layer of "cobweb", made by the textile artist Trevor Collins, with a luminous cable woven in the knitted fabric itself.

For the Walküre, blood and bone seemed to be the right image.

Their breast plates, made by Robert Allsopp, suggested bleached bone, and their dresses, dyed by the Royal Opera House's costume department, appeared to be caked in blood'

Director: Keith Warner
Set Designer: Stefanos Lazaridis
Costume Designer: Marie-Jeanne Lecca
Lighting Designer: Wolfgang Göbbel
Conductor: Antonio Pappano
Video Design: Mic Pool
Costume props and headdresses:
Robert Allsopp
Photographer: Johan Persson
Previous pages (104, 105)
Photographer: Clive Barda

Marie-Jeanne Lecca

Die Zauberflöte
Wolfgang Amadeus Mozart (1791)

Vienna Volksoper
December 2005

Marie-Jeanne Lecca: 'Once the idea was established that the animals did not belong to the cute-cuddly world, but to the one of nightmares and strange creatures, I decided to develop threatening silhouettes, in blacks and silvers, with sharp, angular lines, keeping the period feel. For the costume-prop elements, Robert Allsopp was the obvious choice. Having worked with him several times before, I knew how far, and nearly limitless, I could let my imagination travel, and how brilliantly he would transform into reality my designs.'

Director: Helmuth Lohner
Set Designer: Johan Engels
Costume Designer: Marie-Jeanne Lecca
Lighting Designer: Friedrich Rom
Conductor: Leopold Hager
Costume props and headdresses: Robert Allsopp

Le nozze di Figaro
Wolfgang Amadeus Mozart (1788)

*The Royal Opera House, Covent
Garden, London
January 2006*

Tanya McCallin: 'All theatre
practitioners are collaborative artists,
working together to produce a complete
work of art. The success of any
production depends entirely upon this
joint effort to support and signify the
story in time and space. After the
composer, director and performers, the
most important collaborator for me is my
lighting designer. Paule Constable here
uses the architecture of the set to define
time and place by flooding the space
with the dramatic side light of dawn,
illuminating the previously shuttered
chateau and seeking out the household
servants preparing, with excitement, for
Figaro's wedding later that day.'

*Overture preset: the chateau with
household servants - early morning*

*Director: David McVicar
Set and Costume Designer:
Tanya McCallin
Lighting Designer: Paule Constable
Choreographer: Leah Hausman
Photographer: Bill Cooper*

David Howe

Cabaret
Music: John Kander, Lyrics: Fred Ebb,
Book: Joe Masteroff

English Speaking Theatre, Frankfurt
Esbjerg Musikhuset
December 2004

David Howe: 'Bob Bailey's skeletal set, on a shallow stage, meant that lighting had to work hard to keep the various tight areas separate from each other and yet blend together for the slightly surreal musical numbers. Colour played a huge part by seeping into the characters' minimal reality and exploding into the big production sequences. With the aid of haze, the black box surrounding the skeletal set became a second canvas to paint on.'

End of Act 1 "Tomorrow Belongs to Me"

Director: Matthew White
Set and Costume Designer: Bob Bailey
Lighting Designer: David Howe

Miranda Melville

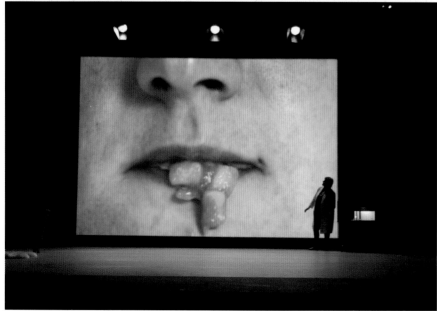

How to Live
Bobby Baker (2004)

Daily Life Theatre
Barbican Theatre
November 2004

Miranda Melville: 'Fill the Barbican stage with peas and make them sing and dance, was Bobby Baker's brief. Primarily a performance artist, Bobby Baker conceived this sci-art project in consultation with psychologist Richard Hallam. It was developed through collaborative workshops, often producing totally absurd ideas, but always underlined by the seriousness of the subject of mental health.
The framework was of an imposing conference, presenting a new therapy

Fiddler on the Roof
*Music: Jerry Bock, Lyrics: Sheldon
Harnick, Book: Joseph Stein*

*UK Productions
UK tour
February 2003*

David Howe: 'The nightmare sequence
when ghosts of dead family members
come back to haunt Tevye and Golda in
a dream. The choreography had a
nightmarish rhythmic counterpoint to it
and the lighting flowed around the live
characters, transporting them from one
scenario to another. Bursts of white light
gave the sequence an unreal energy.'

The Dream Sequence

*Director: Julian Woolford
Designer: Charles Camm
Lighting Designer: David Howe
Choreographer: Chris Hocking
Photographer: Robert Workman*

for mental illness, illustrated through
Bobby's chosen patient, a pea. To make
the pea visible, video playback
inevitably became integral to the show,
along with her powerpoint presentation.
The finale was a specially composed
chorale performed by the dancing
peas.'

*Director: Paloma Baloh Brown
Artist, Deviser, Performer: Bobby Baker
Designer: Miranda Melville
Lighting Designer: Chahine Yavroyan
Composer: Jocely Pook
Video and Graphics: Deborah May
Engineer and Set Builder: Simon York
Production Manager: Steve Wald
Photographer: Andrew Whittuck*

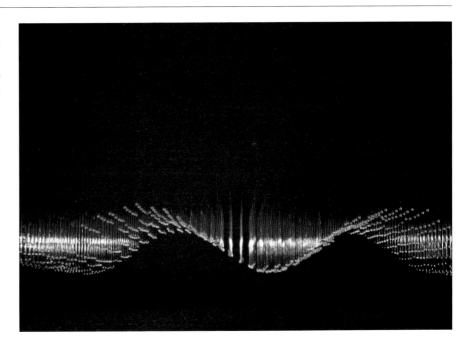

Pamela Howard

Three Fragments from " The Marriage "

Chamber Opera by Bohuslav Martinu after Nikolai Gogol

A professional production supported by Purnell Centre for the Arts, Carnegie Mellon University, Pittsbugh, USA Regina Miller Gouger Gallery of Contemporary Art, Purnell Centre for the Arts, Pittsburg, USA Installation and performance October - November 2006

Pamela Howard: 'The installation *Martinu in America*, in which *Three Fragments* is performed, is a collaborative venture between visual artists, musicians, architectural lighting specialists and myself - a theatre maker. The aim was to interrogate chamber opera, exploring ways of using the space so that the musicians are integrated into the action, creating an environment that can exist and tell the story of the world it depicts, even when there is no performance. Seventy two assorted empty chairs wait expectantly for the spectators, who receive a brown paper bag programme as they enter a dark room on the ground floor. An elevator brings them into New York in 1953, and the lives of Russian émigrés living in the New World, as if they were still in The Old Country.'

Director: Original creation by Pamela Howard Lighting Designer: Cindy Limauro (USA) Music Director Nizan Leibovich (Israel) Pianist: Katie Palumbo (USA) Fine Artist: Susana Amudarain (Venezuela) Created/installed/Spoken and Sung by a group of visual artists and directors Photographer: Louis Stein (USA) TC Schwindling (USA)

The Greek Passion
Bohuslav Martinu/ Nikos Kazantzakis (1957)

*Opera of Thessaloniki (National Theatre of Northern Greece)
June 2005*

Pamela Howard: 'When Henk van der Geest and I began to collaborate, we carefully went through the score and the original book, looking at the huge model of the site made by Sakis Kolalas and imagining how the production might be out of doors, at night. We could only use light to change the scenes and simple props and furniture. Henk worried that the moon and stars in my drawings might not always be exactly as drawn. I drew as we talked and by the end, we had a structure with which to work. The staging concentrates on placing the 'larger than life' characters in the space. Many of the scenes have only two people, and a priority was to be able to see and hear their stories very clearly. The village of Lycovrissi is indicated by the large wall and staircase, stage right, and the Sarakina Mountain by the wall, stage left. The Church is in the centre and the constructed stage becomes both the village square with the café, and the refugees' mountain camp, clarified by lighting changes.'

*Director, Set and Costume Designer: Pamela Howard
Lighting Designer: Henk van der Geest
Sound Designer:
Geogos Papanikolaov
Choreographer: Melpo Vassilikou
Greek Translation: Ioanna Manoledaki
Photographer: Henk van der Geest*

Gary McCann

Promised Land
Mark Dougherty (2006)

*Canterbury Festival Productions
Marlowe Theatre Canterbury and UK tour
October 2006*

Gary McCann: '*Promised Land,
a large-scale community opera,
chronicles the heyday and demise of
two of Kent's indigenous industries, hop
farming and mining. The design,
a fusion of natural and industrial motifs,
was inspired by the landscape paintings
of Samuel Palmer and Anselm Kiefer.
Given that the opera depicts 30 different
scenes over the course of 50 years,
the members of the 120-strong
community chorus were very much
involved in the sourcing of period
costume, props and furniture.*'

*The Beach /Barn Interior/The Field of
Hops / The Pit Head*

*Director: Syd Ralph
Set and Costume Designer:
Gary McCann
Lighting Designer: Colin Grenfell
Choreographer: Paul Madden*

The Government Inspector
Nikolai Gogol (1836)

R.A.D.A
The Vanbrugh Theatre, R.A.D.A
June 2004

Gary McCann: 'Gogol's satire depicts a decadent society teetering on the brink of moral collapse. Correspondingly, the design - a crumbling, gilded Rococo ceiling decorated with allegorical figures - appears close to caving in on the performers and the audience, who are seated around the space in a horseshoe thrust. Careful collaboration was required with the lighting designer, finding unorthodox lighting positions on the floor, galleries and in the rig, behind holes in ceiling, from which to light the piece.'

Model Photograph.

Director: Indhu Rubasingham
Set and Costume Designer:
Gary McCann
Lighting Designer: Felix Brown

Martin Morley

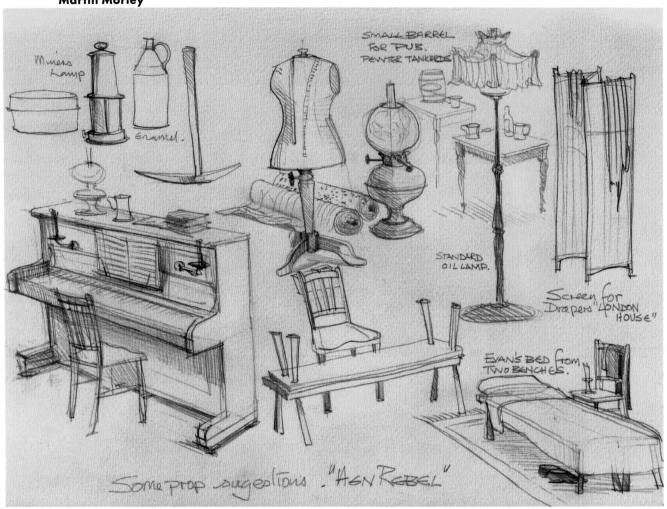

Some prop suggestions "Ash Rebel"

Pippa Nissen

A Midsummer Night's Dream
Benjamin Britten (1960)

Royal Scottish Academy of Music and Drama, Glasgow
June 2004

Pippa Nissen: 'There are three suspended screens across the stage. Two are back projected on to plastic, forming the background to the action; the larger screen is gauze at the front of the stage. Light boxes, both in the sky and on the ground, change colour throughout the piece, as banks of landscape and the edges of architecture.
Colour goes through the costumes, light boxes and film. This mirrors both the emotions of the music and follows whoever is on stage; the mechanicals (brighter colours), the lovers (red), or the fairies (green). The textures and colours of a magical forest dominate the film, the sparse lines of a building, created in light, form the last scenes in the palace.'

Director: Cathie Boyd
Set and Costume Designer: Pippa Nissen
Lighting Designer: Colin Bell
and Cathie Boyd
Choreographer: Kally Lloyd-Jones

Hen Rebel
Valmai Jones (November 2005)

Theatr Genedlaethol Cymru
National tour of main stages in Wales
November 2005

Martin Morley: 'Hen Rebel was commissioned by Theatr Genedlaethol Cymru, and told the story of the Religious Revival in Wales (1904-5). The collaboration between the writer, director and designer was close and began with a meeting in April 2005, when the first draft was ready and we planned the general feel and look of the production. The set and costumes were to tie the drama to a specific time and place but the layout and simplicity of the scene changes allowed the action to move speedily. A great deal of the collaboration was carried out through the wonder of email.
Most of the characters were working or middle class, either miners or pillars of the local community. The props and furniture had to be simple, specific and robust. Many items, for example benches and chairs, were used from scene to scene. Rather than a written prop list, I did a pictorial list.

I find this a clearer and easier way of communicating with stage management who are key collaborators on any production. I had a very constructive collaboration with my computer. For the first time I produced a simple computer model using Turbo CAD. Needless to say I also still had a working relationship with card, balsa wood and glue, but I did the computer model to prove to myself that I could do it. The print-outs of different views, including plans, proved very useful. Each scene, with its furniture, was on a different layer so all the different combinations could easily be shown. A CD is also considerably easier to transport than a model box.'

Act 2, Scene 9, Llion Williams as Robin and Maldwyn John as Stokes

Director: Cefin Roberts
Set and Costume Designer: Martin Morley
Lighting Designer: Ace McCarron
Sound Designer: Sion William

"Hen Rebel"
Theatr Genedlaethol Cymru
Scanned print out of model generated using TurboCAD v9 standard

Breaking the Code
Hugh Whitemore

Royal and Derngate Company
Royal Theatre Northampton
November 2003

Pippa Nissen: 'The set uses two 6m-wide screens at an angle to each other, suspended over the actors on the stage. Below is a naturalistic, reduced set of each scene, with carefully chosen furniture from each place and time. The play goes backwards and forwards in time, from the 1920s to the 1950s and 60s, between Turing's memory and the present day. This is represented in the set, film and costumes through colour and texture. Early childhood is filmed in super 8mm, focused on a still image, the fragile quality of his family life echoed in the film quality and saturated colours. Present day is a mixture of black, white and red, like the graphic techniques from the time. There is also a gradual shift in the film images from naturalistic to abstract, as Turing's world disintegrates, until his suicide at the end of the play.'

Director: Philip Wilson
Set and Costume Designer: Pippa Nissen
Lighting Designer: Oliver Fenwick

Yannis Thavoris

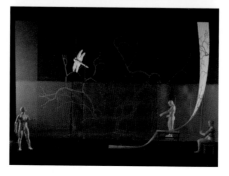

A Night at the Chinese Opera
Judith Weir (1988)

Royal Academy of Music
Sir Jack Lyons Theatre, London
June 2006

Yannis Thavoris: 'Working closely with our production manager we arrived at a design, including two half-height, flown gauzes in what is essentially a non-flying house. These enabled us to change the space fluidly for the many scenes of the opera and also became the canvas for light-generated visual compositions. The main image of the set, a tree-like formation of blood vessels, is an open metaphor springing from the themes of the opera, evocative of place and period, but avoiding descriptive chinoiserie. Movement around balancing chairs, toy tanks and excavators, kites, lanterns, tapes etc. played with scale, mood, cultural stereotypes and performance styles.'

Act 1 Scene 3 'Chao Lin's childhood'
Act 1 Scene 1 'The Night-watchman and the Mongolian Army invasion'
Model Storyboard

Director: Jo Davies
Set and Costume Designer:
Yannis Thavoris
Lighting Designer: Chris Davey
Choreographer: Kay Shepherd
Production Manager: Ted Murphy

Così Fan Tutte
Wolfgang Amadeus Mozart (1789)

*Opéra National du Rhin, Strasbourg
December 2005*

Yannis Thavoris: 'The opera demands swift transitions. From the smoke-filled interior of a gentlemen's club to the luminous exterior of a villa perched "at the edge of the world", overlooking an expanse of sea and precipitous rocks, loosely based on the landscape of Capri. The side walls unfold in view (by an expert stage crew) to take us in and out of the fragile, crackled, porcelain-like interior of the villa. For the seduction scene nature invades in surreally phosphorescent blues, purples and turquoises (that we achieved by using UV sensitive paint). At the end, the couples face their choices against the rocks, frozen in mid-explosion.'

*Director: David McVicar
Set Designer: Yannis Thavoris
Costume Designer: Tanya McCallin
Lighting Designer: Paule Constable
Choreographer: Leah Hausmann*

Jenny Tiramani

Measure for Measure
William Shakespeare (1604)

Shakespeare's Globe Theatre, London
October 2005

Jenny Tiramani: 'A suit of clothes such as these, worn to play a high-ranking, European aristocrat, demonstrates the collaboration of a large group of craftspeople: milliner, glover, cordwainer, embroiderer, weavers, lacemaker, jeweller, tailor and sewer - and ultimately the collaboration of the actor to wear the clothes appropriately.'

Director: John Dove
Set and Costume Designer:
Jenny Tiramani
Choreographer: Siân Williams
Director of Music: Claire Van Kampen
Photographer: John Tramper

Jamie Vartan

Carmen
George Bizet (1875)

Teatro Lirico di Cagliari
July 2005

Jamie Vartan: 'Capturing the movement of a huge, angry bull was the inspiration for the gauze painting. It dissolves with the arrival of a propeller plane (image 1), the blades of the propeller echoing the banderillas that hit the bull. The painted, wounded bull image returns, frozen on the external walls of the arena (image 3) .
The movement of the flamenco-inspired female chorus is set against the stillness of the men (image 2). This painted image from the storyboard was also used on all the posters, leaflets and the programme cover, representing, in a single image, the ideas of the show.'

Ian Westbrook

Seaside Special 2006 Variety show

Openwide International Ltd
Pavilion Theatre, Cromer Pier, Norfolk
June 2006

Ian Westbrook: 'Light entertainment and variety shows often lack high production standards, but there are exceptions. On a smart Victorian pier in Cromer, a seaside entertainment has some of the highest and is renowned for its high-quality sets, costumes and performance. I have designed these shows since the mid 1980s and a strong collaboration between the director and designer are essential. The director and I normally only meet once, in February, to share design ideas and again in March to finalise them. The rest is done over the telephone and by me sending 30 or more drawings through the post.

The Winter's Tale
William Shakespeare (1611)

*Shakespeare's Globe Theatre, London
August 2005*

Jenny Tiramani: 'As this image shows, the Globe audience are fully visible in the afternoon performances and are active collaborators in the playing of the story. The actors all wear handmade Jacobean clothing created for this production from materials available to Shakespeare and his fellow actors 400 years ago.'

*Director: John Dove
Set and Costume Designer:
Jenny Tiramani
Choreographer: Siân Williams
Director of Music: Claire Van Kampen
Photographer: Andy Bradshaw*

*Director: Stephen Medcalf
Set and Costume Designer:
Jamie Vartan
Lighting Designer: Simon Corder
Choreographer: Maxine Braham
Photographer: Paolo Calanchini*

Illustrated is an Oriental theme on a more contempary feel but with a traditional style *Singing in the Rain* finale, complete with a hot water rain curtain for 12 dancers to perform under, which always brings the house down. Creating up to 30 visually exciting sets each year on a tiny stage space is part of the challenge (if only not to repeat your designs).'

*Director/Choreographer: Di Cooke
Set Designer: Ian Westbrook
Costume Designer: Sue Simmerling
Lighting Designer: Amanda Hill
and Ian Westbrook
Sound Designer: Amanda Hill
Scenic Artist: Mark Keen
Photographer: Eric Brickes Photo
Services*

Libby Watson

Three Sisters
Mustapha Matura (2006)

*Eclipse (Birmingham Rep, Wolsey,
Nottingham Playhouse)
Birmingham Repertory Theatre
and UK tour
February 2006*

Libby Watson: 'Mustapha's
adaptation of Chekov's *Three Sisters*
was transposed to the heat and humidity
of Trinidad in the 40s. After a visit to
Port of Spain, with the director, we found
many examples of colonialism in the
architecture and interiors of the grand
houses. We chose to use a plantation
house with its many shutters and
high-ceiling grandeur. Working closely
with James Farncombe at the design
stage, we positioned the set to maximise
the possibilities of the intense heat and
light of the exterior breaking into
the interior. This emphasised the
oppressiveness of the characters'
apparent captivity.'

*Director: Paulette Randall
Set and Costume Designer:
Libby Watson
Lighting Designer: James Farncombe
Choreographer: Omar Okai
Other creative collaborator:
Susannah Henry
Photographer: James Farncombe*

collaborators

OTHER ART FORMS

As indicated earlier, designers - or perhaps we should say artists-in-performance - are seeking direct collaboration with other art form artists. Teaming up directly with choreographers, writers, composers and poets, has produced some of the UK's most innovative performance work.

The stimulus of working with artists of different disciplines is celebrated here. In particular, working closely with choreographers and performers in dance and ballet companies offers a very immediate collaboration. Clearly, costume and movement are, or should be, integrated. Integration with dance space is a far more abstract concept with, traditionally, elements of set kept out of the way, defining the perimeters of useable space. Both dance and design for dance have changed and now frequently negotiate each other, using both plastic and digital media in various forms of interaction.

Responding to music, sounds and narrative with artwork is one of our earliest educational activities. There is no room here for a treatise on imagery in music or writing, but it is common for writers and composers to need to picture a scene, or moment, in order to write it, or to be inspired by a visual experience. Similarly, a glimpse into the essence of, the shape of, the possibilities of a piece of music or writing or movement is essential to the designer's giving back a visual response, which will, with dialogue, craft and tenacity become a design for the presentation of that original material to others.

When we see a performance, it is embodied ideas and emotions. An established play, opera, ballet has achieved a weight, a history, a context. It has been envisioned, realised, it has become flesh, so to speak. How does a new piece of writing or music achieve visible form? What is the designer responding to? Much contemporary playwriting is hugely influenced by screen drama and images, and working with it is often about reaching out beyond the screen into a 3D world. Working directly with poets, composers, dancers, musicians is... the glimpse, the groping for meaning, the tentative drawing, the rough models, the rehearsal room experiments... the craft.

Helen Fownes-Davies

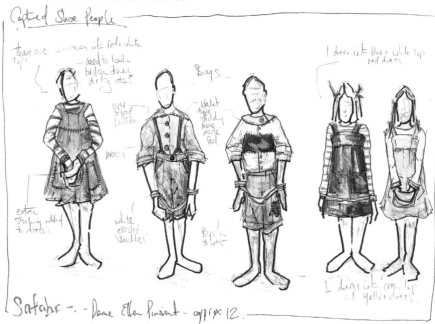

Safahr - Telling Tales of a Journey
*Dinos Aristidou and Therese Collins
(2004)*

*Birmingham Royal Ballet
The Birmingham Hippodrome
February 2004*

Helen Fownes-Davies: 'The production was a result of a one-month collaboration between Creative Partnerships and Birmingham Royal Ballet. Over 500 young people and community members from six schools were involved as researchers, writers, composers, designers, and dancers, all working alongside professional artists. The story of *Safahr* intended to bring together different cultures and communities and would reflect the interests, ideas and concerns of the creators. Its final conclusion culminated

Bob Frith

In The Shadow of Trees
Bob Frith (2005)

*Horse + Bamboo Theatre
Royal Exchange Theatre, Manchester
(Studio)
December 2005*

Bob Frith: 'Horse + Bamboo normally work with teams of creative collaborators, but the commission for *In the Shadow of Trees* by the Royal Exchange Theatre offered an unusual opportunity to engage with an expanded technical team. In this non-verbal production, the story being told through movement, image and music, the design was integral to the narrative momentum. Writing and design, became two sides of the same process.'

Keith Baker

Sweetpeter
John Retallack and Usifu Jalloh (2004)

*Company of Angels and Polka Theatre
Polka Theatre and tour
March 2004*

Keith Baker: 'The play explored 200 years of the colonial experience in West Africa. Because John Retallack needed the floor kept free for Landing Mane's movement, I created a large "light box" of etched panels, with a series of backdrops behind, that could be changed to place, date and reflect the action on stage.'

*Director: John Retallack
Set and Costume Designer: Keith Baker
Lighting Designer: Ian Scott
Choreographer: Landing Mane
Musical Director: Usifu Jalloh*

in a spectacular piece of live theatre where the performers told a story about dance through dance. A direct, creative response was the key to capturing the essence and style of the participants' own ideas, at the same time maintaining a high level of production values for both set and costume.'

Original costume drawing for 'The captured shoe people' Finale 'The Captured Shoe People ' Dame Elle Pinsent School.

Director: Dinos Aristidou
Set and Costume Designer: Helen Fownes- Davies
Lighting Designer: Nick Ware
Choreographers: Dominic Antonucci, David Bintley, Lee Fisher, Kit Holder, Jonathon Payn and Alexander Whitley

Director: Alison Duddle
Set Designer: Bob Frith
Mask and Puppet Design: Alison Duddle, Bob Frith, Jonny Quick, Alison Duddle, Vanessa Card, Tracy Dunk
Lighting Designers: Richard Owen and Helen Tsingos
Sound Designers: Chris Davies and Claire Windsor
Choreographers: Shobna Gulati
Musical Director: Chris Davies
Other creative collaborators: Jonny Quick, Claire Windsor, Mark Whitaker, Kathy Bradley, Morag Cross, Joana Mendes, Catarina de Matos Goncalves, Keith Broom, Cheila Lima, and the Royal Exchange Theatre Workshop.
Photographers: Bob Frith and Alison Duddle

Hansel and Gretel
Carl Miller (2005)

Theatre Royal, Bury St Edmunds February 2005

Keith Baker: 'This was to be the Hansel and Gretel with no gingerbread. We didn't shy away from the unpleasant aspects of the story. The family were starving, did abandon their children and children were eaten. I wanted a magic house that was dangerously seductive. Inspired by burger bars, kebab shops and Soho chip joints, the design was both gaudy and appealing.'

Director: Collin Blumeneau and Sue Rosser
Set and Costume Designer: Keith Baker
Lighting Designer: John Bramley
Choreographer: Bronja Novak

Simon Daw

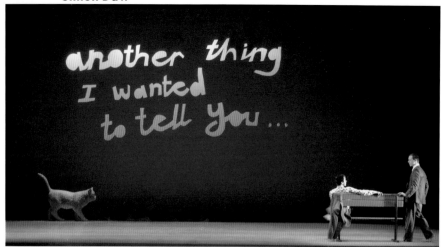

bloom
Aletta Collins (2006)

Rambert Dance Company
Sadler's Wells, London
May 2006

Simon Daw: 'In *bloom*, 16 dancers crash in and out of focus as they search for the perfect romantic moment. Inspired by the 1970s romantic poster, a front cloth image of a giant ginger kitten saying "I Love You" opens to reveal a wall with letters cut out, a front door and a bench. With all the ingredients of a romantic rendezvous in place, the onstage lounge band delivers the final element – a large bunch of roses lowered in on a rope…'

Director and choreographer:
Aletta Collins
Set and Costume Designer: Simon Daw
Lighting Designer: Charles Balfour
Costume Supervisor: Caroline Hagley

Richard Andrzejewski

Waltz #6
Sonia's Realisation
Nelson Rodrigues (1951)

Stonecrabs
Greenwich Playhouse, London
June 2005

Richard Andrzejewski:
'A collaboration with the Stonecrabs, a Brazilian company working with the methodology of Boal and Kantor. The fragmented nature of the text, influenced the design; the pale, naked body of a young woman lies on a stage strewn with lilies and overshadowed by the entrails of an old piano. As the strains of Chopin's Waltz No.6 are heard in the distance, the body painfully animates in a ballet of awakening and self discovery, conjuring the taut, elegant atmosphere of 1950s Rio and creating an image of both birth and death.'

Director: Franko Figueiredo
Set Designer: Richard Andrzejewski
Costume Designer: Lu Firth
Lighting Designer: Lucy Hansom
Sound Designer: Dinah Mullen
Choreographers: Estelle Ricoux
and Briony Plant
Associate Director: Natacha Metherell
Photographer: Elena Machado

Sea House
(2003)

Commissioned by the Aldeburgh Festival
Aldeburgh beach, Suffolk
June 2003

Simon Daw: 'A performance installation featuring a house designed to float on the sea, which is discovered beached on the shore and filled with water. Surrounding the house, pipes protrude from the shingle through which snippets of a narrative can be heard. Inside the house, a figure struggles with his underwater predicament. Created in collaboration with writer/artist Alistair Gentry and performer Jake Oldershaw, *Sea House* developed out of a visual starting point with the text/soundscape and actions being created in response.'

Director and Designer: Simon Daw
Soundscape and text: Alistair Gentry
Performed by: Jake Oldershaw
Photograpers: Simon Daw and Alistair Gentry

Michelle Reader

Experimental Anatomy
Michelle Reader and Tessa Wills (2005)

The Old Clock Shop, Brighton
May 2005

Michelle Reader: '*Experimental Anatomy* is an exploration of people's relationships with their bodies, and the capabilities and limitations of the human form. Using information gathered from people, I am designing objects that modify the human form. This series arose out of my collaboration with performance artist Tessa Wills, and a pair of mechanical wings. Together we explored their possibilities, both physically and thematically. This led to two different performances, which draw on similar elements. The first was a three-hour piece in a shop window in Brighton as part of *Clockworks*; the second was a half-hour performance at the *Fresh* festival at South Hill Park. Both pieces follow Tessa's attempts to learn how to fly. This ritualistic process includes elements such as covering the body with feathers, drawing diagrams, redistributing weight by counterbalancing, using bags of stones, and a sequence of movements designed to prepare the mind and body for take-off.'

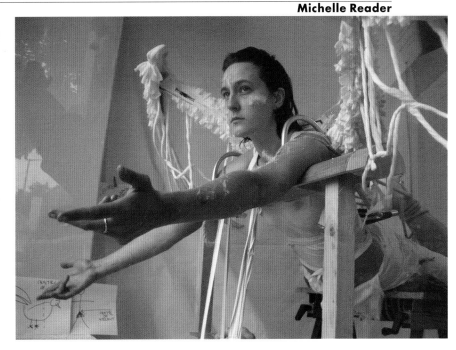

Mechanical Wings

Director: Michelle Reader
and Tessa Wills
Set and Costume Designer:
Michelle Reader

Imogen Cloet / Jacob Polley

Mirror

I'm the mirror, half a moon above the hearth
where your faces surface then disappear:
rearrange the room and you rearrange me.
But I'm tired of looking, from wherever I'm hung
or stood, tired of never closing, tired of never turning off.
I abide by whatever's before me:
whatever's before me, I become.
Drape me in a sheet: under it I'm working.
Turn me to the wall: I pay it the closest attention.
Break me and every piece of me is full.

Trace
Devised (2004)

Derelict Room, White Knights,
Newcastle.
July 2004

Imogen Cloet: 'A series of stills from
part of an ongoing collaboraton with
poet Jacob Polley. We have been
working together for the past couple of
years creating various pieces of work
and also researching and developing
new ways of working and responding to
each other's work. Some have resulted in
public showings, one such project being
Trace. Working with director Ian Fenton,
I styled a derelict room with evocative
furniture and objects, peopling it with
strange, timeless characters - a kind of
"happening", the documentation of
which resulted in my creating a series of
intriguing photographic tableaux. I then
sent these unexplained images to Jacob,
who responded with a series of poems
that evoked lost worlds by giving voice
to the people and objects within the
images. The resulting poems and
corresponding images formed part of
a permanent public exhibition of work
displayed in Secco, Newcastle.'.

Director: Ian Fenton
Set and Costume Designer:
Imogen Cloet
Poet: Jacob Polley

Elizabeth Wright

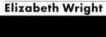

Wallflowering
Peta Murray (1991)

The Studio, Theatre by the Lake, Keswick
May 2003

Elizabeth Wright: 'The director, Stefan
Escreet, was keen to use mirrors as part
of the design to express both the literal
and the metaphorical themes of
reflection in the play. The ballroom
dancing, which occurs throughout the
play, prompted me to look at art deco
dance halls to inspire the mirrored motif.
I worked with lighting designer Jo
Dawson to anticipate the problems of
lighting such a reflective surface and to
build solutions into the design where
possible. Jo's lighting design totally
enhanced the functioning of the

Accordion

*My fingers on the yellow keys
and the black, the parachute strap
across my back. All I do is squeeze.*

*Bellows. A huge book draws breath in my lap.
I'm a strongman, bending air
till it squeals, a charmer struggling*

*to snap the latch on a creel of snakes.
The tattoos on my arms ache.
Behind its folds I hide my face.*

Telephone

*I'm drinking her voice from the telephone.
I ask Are you scrupulously alone?
She's in company, but out on her own.
I tell her I can hear my neighbour's phone
through the wall, the man who lives on his own,
the man I would be if I stayed alone.
If she misdialled, she'd get his phone.
I tell her my house is full of her gone –
the lamps casting their lonely yellow cones,
the tortoiseshell of the telephone.
I ask Are you glad you left me at home?
She's glad, and shuts me back in the phone.*

reflective surface, creating a
kaleidoscope effect and an expanded
sense of space within the small studio.
The shapes made on the floor by gobos
continued the circular line of the motif,
creating a unified sense of space and
light. The outcome of this collaboration
was a particularly poignant visual
effect.'

*Director: Stefan Escreet
Set and Costume Designer:
Elizabeth Wright
Lighting Designer: Jo Dawson
Sound Designer: Paul Bunn
Choreographer: Lorelei Lynn
Cast Members: David Alcock,
Amanda Bellamy
Photographer: Keith Pattison*

Christopher Giles

Ten Belles
Franz von Suppé

The Royal Welsh College of Music and Drama
Sherman Theatre, Cardiff
July 2005

Christopher Giles: '*Ten Belles* is a light-hearted comic romp with a widowed military man trying to marry off his ten exotic daughters. A tenor appears and the prospects look good, but which one will he choose? The design consisted of a bare stage; ten trap doors and items of scenery brought on gradually, like a puzzle. The daughters' "champagne" dresses maximised the sense of celebration. Later, they perform a display of their talents for which the costumes needed to portray their different nationalities.'

Director: John Labouchardiere
Set and Costume Designer: Christopher Giles

Conor Murphy

The Turn of the Screw
Benjamin Britten (1954)

Nationale Reisopera, Holland
Stadsschouwburg Amsterdam
March 2002. Revival in April 2006

Conor Murphy: 'In *The Turn of the Screw*, we decided to focus on the dark and intense atmosphere of the piece. We agreed that the design should facilitate the key spatial relationships between the performers at specific moments and also reflect the strong musical structure. The opera's narrative begins to unravel with the appearance of the ghosts. A space of black-painted wood, with apertures and platforms, allowed the piece to unfold logically at first. In the scene pictured all logic has broken down; choreography and space merge in abstraction.'

Act 2: The Piano

Director: Stephen Langridge
Set and Costume Designer: Conor Murphy
Lighting Designer: Guiseppe di Lorio

Bophelo Mandla
Bawren Tavaziva (2006)

Tavaziva Dance
UK tour
Premiere: Clore Studio, Royal Opera House, July 2006

Abigail Hammond: 'As a costume designer working predominantly with contemporary dance, I see the collaborative relationship as being primarily with the choreographer and also the dancers, music and lighting. A collaboration is working together and requires trust and instinctual understanding brought to a fulfilling conclusion through the utilisation of tools and articulation of ideas in verbal, visual and both 2D and 3D forms. I see my collaborative role as that of an interpreter of the choreographic intent, aiming to conceptualise the meaning of movement and have an effect on the perception of that movement and the space it inhabits through the visual language of costume.'

Choreographer: Bawren Tavaziva
Costume Designer: Abigail Hammond
Lighting Designer: Jonathon Samuels
Music by: Bawren Tavaziva
Photographer: Hilary Shedel

Abigail Hammond

Susannah Henry

C-90
Daniel Kitson (2006)

Higgledy Piggledy Productions
The Traverse Theatre, Edinburgh
July 2006

Susannah Henry: 'C-90 was set in a repository for lost compilation tapes. The creation of these precious objects was the result of collaboration on a vast, yet personal, scale. We were a creative team of two, myself and Daniel, the writer and performer. We made many compilation tape covers ourselves, but families and friends also produced them in their hundreds. The shelves of the set came to contain tapes titled with family names, important addresses, lost loves, favourite bands and private thoughts. Realising C-90 broadened my understanding of who our potential collaborators in theatre might be. They are always the immediate colleagues who share our aspirations and vulnerability as a new work gets off the ground. But they are also the people who inform our work with real histories and their generosity contributed to bringing this production to life.'

Director: Ben Kitson
Set and Costume Designer:
Susannah Henry

Laura McEwen

The Crane
Reiner Zimnik (circa 1950). Adapted for stage by Wendy Rouse

*Red Earth Theatre
Leicester Haymarket Theatre
June 2006*

Laura McEwen: 'This is the magical story of a little man who lives on top of the tallest crane in the world. From this viewpoint he sees the world differently. The play was designed for deaf and hearing audiences, so the story was told physically, with hands as much as with voices. Our creative process involved collaboration with writers, dancers, puppeteers, schools, sign interpreters and ultimately the local deaf community. The visual language was fundamental to

Prema Mehta

Fine Line
Robin Howard Commission (2005)

*The Place, London
March 2005*

Prema Mehta: '*Fine Line* was a contemporary dance performance commissioned in 2005.
The choreography, music and design created a dynamic environment.
The dancers interacted with the set and light with a sense of playful curiosity of discovering an abstract world.
The piece was split into three sections; music, silence, music. Their carefully constructed movements, sharp and accurate, played within a large performance space where areas were highlighted by a selected palette of

Hannah Gravestock

Chimaera
Fran Barbe

*Fran Barbe Dance Theatre
Cecil Sharp House and Hoxton Hall, London
April 2006*

Hannah Gravestock: 'The costume designs for this dance/theatre performance developed through observations and drawings of the performers' early explorations and rehearsals of the show's theme, transformations. While the performers embodied character through movement, I embodied their interpretations through drawing, making instant, intuitive choices about what was drawn, whilst simultaneously interpreting this through how I drew. For example, exaggerating or omitting gestures, body angles or the production. We used puppets, miniature worlds, a model steam train and a red mechanical crane. The design explored scale and perspective, enhancing the way the story was perceived by the audience.'

Director: Amanda Wilde
Set and Costume Designer:
Laura McEwen
Lighting Designer: Ciaran Bagnall
Choreographer: Joanne Moven
Puppetry Director: Sean Myatt
Puppet Maker: Polly Laycock
Photographer: Robert Day

bright, electric, neon gels. Side lighting helped sculpt the dancers, whilst an overhead rig painted the floor and fluorescent tubes mounted on to the set provided linear rays of light, with a soft outer glow.'

Director: Rashpal Singh Bansal
Set Designer: Pamela Rayfield
Costume Designer: Sharon Coleman
Lighting Designer: Prema Mehta
Choreographer: Rashpal Singh Bansal
Music: Nobukazu Takemura,
Icefall: Susumu Yokota, Kawano
Hotorino Kinoshitade

space around the body. These drawings became my "script", analysed by cutting and pasting the images to find new relationships between the characters, developing a language through which to discuss their characterisation.'

Director: Fran Barbe
Costume Designer: Hannah Gravestock
Lighting Designer: Tia Hassan
Sound Designer: Keith Johnson
Choreographer: Fran Barbe

Francis O'Connor

Faust
John Clifford (2006)

Royal Lyceum Theatre, Edinburgh
March 2006

Francis O'Connor: 'Faust was my
second collaboration with writer John
Clifford, again at the Lyceum.
The production and setting were
contemporary although the story and
events remained close to Goethe.
John's work is thrilling and theatrical and
the production used film, masks and a
very open Lyceum stage on which to tell
the story. Two huge semi-circular steel
structures were at once bookshelves,
a climbing frame and cell bars.
Gretchen's home reappears in stages
of decay to represent home to hell.
Simple devices recurring and reforming,
creating a disturbed and disturbing
world.'

Director: Mark Thompson
Set and Costume Designer:
Francis O'Connor
Lighting Designer: Simon Mills

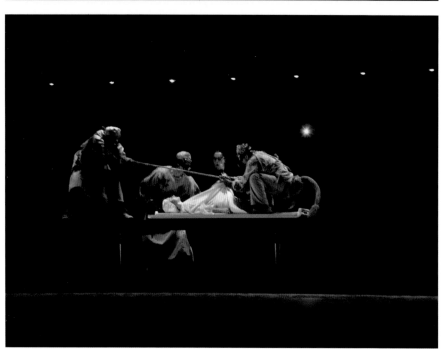

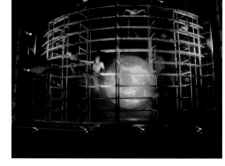

Anna Karenina
John Clifford (April 2005)

*Theatre Company Royal Lyceum
Royal Lyceum Theatre, Edinburgh
April 2005*

Francis O'Connor: 'The first of my collaborations with John Clifford. I created a landscape in which the entire play could unfold. Sometimes the world was confined within the wooden box with its myriad doors, but then it could open out to the forest. The trees always present, reflected and multiplied through the mirrors upstage. Shards of mirror and coloured glass formed the leaf canopy. The bed and other furnishings lived in the forest - the interior and exterior worlds coming together. The train started as a small light from way upstage but grew as it travelled forwards. The entire front of the train was built, but was glimpsed for seconds, the light silhouetting and blinding Anna. The design took real advantage of the fantastic depth available at the Lyceum.'

*Director: Muriel Romanes
Set and Costume Designer: Francis O'Connor
Lighting Designer: Chris Davey
Composer: Max Richte*

Jean-Marc Puissant

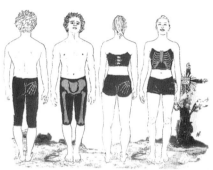

Nopalitos
Music: Lila Downs

Phoenix Dance Theatre
Sadler's Wells, London
March 2006

Jean-marc Puissant: 'The theme for *Nopalitos* is the Mexican Day of the Dead, the music, a collage of songs by Mexican chanteuse Lila Downs. As a result, my palette was the collision of research on Mexico's indigenous heritage, the colonial Christian faith, the Rancheros' Americana, bleeding from the Texan border, the *Lucha Libre* (Mexican wrestling) and Mexico's Pulp cinematic culture of the 50s.
The set is a circular track, hung and stabilised with ropes and sand bags. It supports four cloths, moved by dancers throughout the piece, painted on both sides. This flexible solution constantly reorganises the stage, visually and spatially.
As the choreography evolved, for each sequence we devised the configuration of the set and assembled various elements of clothing taken from each theme. The dancers moved the set and took care of quick costume changes themselves (on and off stage, behind the cloths), so the design decisions were practical as much as dramaturgic or visual.'

Set and Costume Designer:
Jean-Marc Puissant
Lighting Designer: Michael Mannion
Choreographer: Javier De Frutos

collaborators

Oh, WoT a lovely war?
Kevin Fegan and Andy Farrell (2006)

The Lowry Community and Education, Quays Theatre, The Lowry, Salford April 2006

Andrew Wood: 'Taking inspiration from Joan Littlewood and the Theatre Workshop movement, the process here was to devise a piece about the impact that war, including the War on Terror, has on people's lives now.
Primary sources were the experiences and artefacts brought by the project's participants who then became the cast in performance.
The script, scenographic environment, music and direction all developed simultaneously through workshops, discussions and finally rehearsals. The largely empty stage space was surrounded in performance by the cast and the souvenirs required to tell their stories, overlooked by the large, projected, global context for their deeply personal experiences.'

Gillian's story
Cold war

Director: Andy Farrell
Set Designer: Andrew Wood
Lighting Designer: Dave Clare
Music Director: Beth Allen
Video/AV Designer: Porl Cooper
Photographer: Ben Blackall

Andrew Wood

'Installation 496'
The Royal Family of Thebes
Nona Shephard (2004)

RADA-Jerwood Vanbrugh Theatre June 2004

takis: 'In thinking about Sophocles' work, the questions began to emerge about how we value our cultural heritage, what that heritage is and why it is valuable, what it gives us, what we as inheritors of that culture need to do to maintain it, whether we put a price on it and if we do, how much is it? 'Installation 496', based on Sophocles' trilogy, was commissioned in association with RADA's centenary and the Hellenic Foundation of Culture, as part of its *Greece in Britain* series of events organised on the occasion of the 2004 Athens Olympic Games, celebrating the 2,500 years between Sophocles' birth and the RADA's Centenary.'

Director: Nona Sheppard
Set and Costume and Lighting Designer: takis
Composer: Stamatis Kraounakis

Presented by the Hellenic Foundation for Culture as part of *Greece in Britain 2007*, a nationwide series of events illustrating the wealth and diversity of contemporary Greek culture.

takis

Emma Ryott

Der *Sandmann*
*Robert Schumann, Alfred Schnittke,
Martin Donner*

*Stuttgarter Ballet
April 2006*

Emma Ryott: 'A dark fable based on
an ETA Hoffmann story. The main
character, Nathanael, fights for his
sanity after the traumas of his childhood.
He is pushed into madness by the gift of
an Occular, a lense which skews his
shaky view of reality.
In my third collaboration with Christian,
designs were developed by first trying
lots of real clothes on the dancers, an
organic approach to finding a costume
language. In Act 1, the simple dresses
and suits and unusual use of short ankle
boots for the *corps* served to underline
the stability and parochial nature of
small town life. By contrast, in Act 2,
the *pointe* shoes and more severe,
structured costumes give the feeling of
a rigid society from which Nathanael is
even more alienated.'

*Set Designer: Dirk Becker
Costume Designer: Emma Ryott
Lighting Designer: Rienhard Traub
Choreographer: Christian Spuck
Dramaturge: Jens Schroth
Photographers: Stuttgarter Ballet*

Lulu; Eine Monstretragödie
Demitri Shostakovitch/Alban
Berg/Arnold Schönberg

Stuttgarter Ballet
Staatstheater, Stuttgart
December 2003

Emma Ryott: '*Lulu* was my first
collaboration with Christian Spuck.
He was looking for a designer who had
a broad base in all areas of theatre, not
purely ballet. I did not want to be
confined to a particular time period.
The design of the costumes had to
emphasise the character of the
protagonists and make them instantly
recognisable, despite being, at the start,
seated at tables in the empty, crumbling
ballroom, as they wait for their part in
the drama to unfold. The simplicity of
Lulu's costume was intended to
emphasise her initial purity and to steer
clear of the "vamp" image. That side of
her character was to be fully illustrated
through the choreography.'

Set Designer: Dirk Becker
Costume Designer: Emma Ryott
Lighting Designer: Reinhard Traub
Choreographer: Christian Spuck
Film: Fabian Spuck
Photographers: U.Beuttenmüller
and B.Weissbrod

..., la peau blanche ...
John Adams

Stuttgarter Ballet
Staatstheater, Stuttgart
April 2005

Emma Ryott:' A detective story
inspired by *Gabrielle d'Estree and her
Sister*, a 16th-century painting.
Gabrielle, mistress of Henry IV of
France, died in terrible agony on the eve
of their wedding, rumoured poisoned for
political ends. The protagonist Vignac
tries to decipher the painting, which
contains tantalising clues to Gabrielle's
murder. A dark palette for the costumes
suggests a world of intrigue and
shadows. Period detail is used out of
context to unsettle, i.e. the *corps* girls
wear a humorous combination of
Elizabethan bodices teamed with men's
"onion" breeches, while the boys are in
contemporary suits with ruffs. As Vignac
becomes entangled by his theories, the
manic score emphasises his increasing
frustration.'

Set Designer: Christian Spuck
Costume Designer: Emma Ryott
Lighting Designer:
Stephan Seyrick-Hofmeister
Choreographer: Christian Spuck
Dramaturge: Jens Schroth

Emma Ryott

collaborators

TEAMWORK

"Good teamwork!" we say of particular performances
and productions, meaning that it all works together, there is
a coherence and sense of combined purpose. Of course there
is teamwork at each stage of the design process.

Many young designers spend an invaluable period working
as assistants and model makers before - and while - designing
themselves. The relationship between designer and assistant takes
different forms, but becomes essential in the development,
particularly, of very large-scale projects, often operas, which can
take two, three or even four years to be realised. Paul Brown
and Les Brotherston both acknowledge the importance of these
collaborations and the respect needed within them for individual
skills and intuitions which can enable a fruitful and rigorous
shared process.

Teamwork, of course applies when the empathy, critical
understanding and skills that production staff bring to
interpretation and realisation of designs, blends the design
and making processes into one.

Teamwork can also relate to the rare collaboration that is devised
performance work, in which the designer contributes to the whole
process, very often offering visual images as starting points as
well as interpreting and developing images from moments that
arise in the rehearsal room, in site-specific research and in
workshops with community or school groups. Designers mention
different ways of working within the devising process. Some, such
as Penny Saunders of Forkbeard, describe the need for
withdrawal, at some points, into their own mental space and
vocabulary in order to develop ideas and actual production
artefacts. Others, such as Bob Frith of Horse and Bamboo discuss
total collaboration, where the individual skills are part of a
melting pot and each member contributes in all areas of the work.

Interestingly it is the collaborative aspects of working with
performers that designers have mentioned the most, in both
professional theatre contexts and even more so when working
with community and education groups. On these occasions,
the audience too can become collaborators in uncovering the
story, discovering it together. Such opportunities to directly engage
with and contribute to the emerging characters, to advance
design ideas through one-to-one problem solving and to refresh
one's own aesthetic and understanding of various cultures and
stratas of society offer a continuing and stimulating education.

Cordelia Chisholm

The Dubya Trilogy: The Madness of George Dubya, A Weapons' Inspector Calls, and Guantanamo Baywatch
Justin Butcher (2002-2004)

New Players Theatre, London
October 2004

Cordelia Chisholm: 'These satirical, revue-style plays were designed in collaboration with Justin Butcher (writer and director) as the scripts were being written. We had locations and scenarios but no concrete dialogue. Design decisions were shaped by the emerging scripts, but initial design ideas were also able to shape the structure and content of the plays. For *A Weapons' Inspector Calls* (echoing Ian MacNeil's design for *An Inspector Calls*) we designed a miniature White House out of which

Simon Banham

Geneva / Grace
Jane Arnfield (December 2003)
Devised (October 2005)

Newcastle Playhouse
Contact Theatre, Main Stage

Created by Quarantine between December 2003 and May 2006

Simon Banham: 'Quarantine make work through collaboration, from the histories woven by the participants, the multi-layering and texturing of real stories and lives transforming the very ordinary into the extraordinary. Three generations of a Glaswegian family explore their relationships beneath a cloud of mirror balls; a dancer and his mother catalogue their shared house across a dance floor; young men from Manchester are locked in a "dirty ballet" over a pool table. There are invitations to dance, share food, ask questions; all the elements of a real event. A performance-mediated encounter between people, and between people and space.'

Director: Richard Gregory
Set and Costume Designer:
Simon Banham
Lighting Designer: Mike Brookes
Sound Designers:
John Alder and Dan Steele
Choreographers:
Jane Mason and Leo Kaye
Other creative collaborators:
Renny O'shea

George Dubya is taken at the top of the show. This decision inspired the final scene of the play. Following Bush's re-election, White House inhabitants are tucked up safe and sound, and (pastiching *The Waltons*) in turn, they say good night. Outside, the despairing weapons' inspector laments the fate of the world. The design was also shaped by the fact that these three plays were all to be performed on the same day with 15-minute turnarounds.'

Director: Justin Butcher
Set and Costume Designer:
Cordelia Chisholm
Lighting Designer: Mike Gunning
Sound Designer: Jack Arnold
Choreographers: Jane Mason,
Christine Devany, Leo Kaye,
Jane Mason
Music Director: Stephen Daldry

Brighton Rock

*Giles Havergal's dramatisation of
Graham Greene's novel
Composer: John Barry. Lyrics: Don Black*

*Presented at the Almeida in association
with Bill Kenwright
Almeida Theatre, London
October 2004*

Lez Brotherston

Lez Brotherston: 'With *Brighton Rock*, the challenge was to build a convincing Brighton Pier with levels, walkways and corners that could live as pubs, cafes and amusements, as part of the permanent set but that could also transform into hotel interiors and bedsits with minimal additions in the intimate space of the Almeida Theatre, with no flys or wings. This meant that the permanent structure had to relate very closely to the architecture of the theatre. It also demanded a close collaboration between the model maker, the production manager and myself. I gave my assistant designer the rough sketches of the ideas behind the design and he worked with the architect's drawings to enable us to link existing balconies to our built-metal set. The resulting model had to be very accurate as the fit up was over a very short period and had to be exact.'

Photograph of model basic set

Director: Michael Attenborough
Set and Costume Designer:
Lez Brotherston
Lighting Designer: Tim Mitchell
Sound Designer: John Leonard
Choreographer: Karen Bruce
Musical direction: Steven Edis
Assistant Designer: Colin Falconer

Gabriella Csanyi-Wills

The Burglar's Opera
Composer: Jeff Clarke
Author: Stephen Wyatt (2005)

Opera della Luna
Tour
September 2005

Gabriella Csanyi-Wills: '*Burglar's Opera* was an intense, energetic and wonderful collaboration, starting with Jeff Clarke and Stephen Wyatt creating a new G & S from a story by Gilbert and orchestral score by Sullivan. From the moment the decision was taken to stage the opera, ALL ideas were welcomed. With a constantly evolving script, singers, stage manager, wardrobe mistress and ASM, all had an input and a fun, fantastic show ensued. Although fraught, an amazingly happy atmosphere charged the process.'

The image shows the hapless 'burglar' wishing to be caught, but even then having problems, over and above the obvious

Director: Jeff Clarke
Set and Costume Designer:
Gabriella Csanyi-Wills
Lighting Designer: Amy Southeard
Choreographer: Jenny Arnold
Photographer: Brian Slater

Kandis Cook

Beauty and the Beast
Conceived by Lawrence Boswell

RSC
Main stage RSC, Stratford-upon-Avon
December 2004

Kandis Cook: 'The collaboration was an exciting and complex experience. In order to communicate with a young and possibly non-English-speaking audience, we styled the Beast in cartoon fashion, as a remote-controlled monster. We used computerised fibre optics on the body, exaggerating height by using sprung leg extensions which allowed him to spring and leap quickly. Gary Sefton came up with the idea of using leg extensions and Robert Allsopp constructed the costume.'

Director: Lawrence Boswell
Set Designer: Jeremy Herbert
Costume Designer: Kandis Cook
Lighting Designer: Adam Silvermann
Sound Designer: Mic Pool
Choreographers: Heather Habens
and Stuart Hopps
Composer: Mick Sands
Costume props: Robert Alsopp
Movement Director and Performer of
Beast: Gary Sefton
Movement Directors: Gary Sefton
and Darren Tunstall
Photographer: Chris Moyse

BlueBird
John Metcalfe (March 2006)

Liz Lea Dance
Clore Studio, Covent Garden and tour
March 2006

Gabriella Csanyi-Wills: 'In *Bluebird*, set became costume. The costume transformed from three hanging peaks to one vast floating skirt, to pond, 18th-century silhouette, bird of paradise, showgirl, etc. The project grew from Liz's eclectic dance experience: Showgirl, Bharata Natyam, contemporary dance, ballet and creative movement, all are drawn upon to create a world in which both animal and human share emotional expression. It was a great collaborative effort, working out between us not only the form but also the technique of manipulating 40 metres of fabric, enhanced by input from composer and lighting designer alike.'

Director: Liz Lea Dance
Set and Costume Designer:
Gabriella Csanyi-Wills
Lighting Designer: Mike Gunning
Choreographer: Liz Lea
Composer: John Metcalfe
Photographer: Lara Platman

Rosemarie Cockayne

Thread of Gold
Rosemarie Cockayne

Producer: Colin Clark
St Bartholomew-the-Less,
St Bartholomew Hospital, City of London
February 2006

Rosemarie Cockayne:
'We give to one another
a thread of gold
Respect for one another
Compassion for one another
Courage for one another
Commitment to one another
We give to one another a thread of gold

This moment in time is when all the threads as expressed in the artwork are drawn together and offered for peace and healing in the world. Candles symbolising light. We stand together.'

Candles Symbolising Light.

Director, Set and Costume Designer:
Rosemarie Cockayne
Lighting Designer: Mike Gunning
Sound Designer:
The Reverend Peter Cowell
Other creative collaborator:
The Reverend Ben Rhodes
Photographer:
The Reverend Anthony Morley

Anne Curry

Romeo and Juliet
William Shakespeare (1590s)

Shakespeare in Education - Schools Touring, West Midlands
Birmingham Theatre School
February 2003

Anne Curry: 'Girls played boys... in our production, Mercutio and Tybalt were played by girls. This costume design represents Mercutio in action during the fight with Tybalt. I attended rehearsals and made sketches of the actors during the blocking of scenes. I tried to capture the "look" of each actor, skin tone, hair colour, facial characteristics, and movement.
The concept was to set the action in the club world of Ibiza, incorporating contemporary youth culture, with retro-clothing, for the new romantic style "tribes" of the Capulets and Montagues to club mix music.'

Original Costume Drawing for: Act 3 Scene 1 'Mercutio' (played by a girl)

Director: John Paul Cherrington
Set and Costume Designer: Anne Curry
Lighting Designer: John Paul Cherrington
Choreographer: Mandi Ashwood
Music/Sound: Pete Hammond

Atlanta Duffy

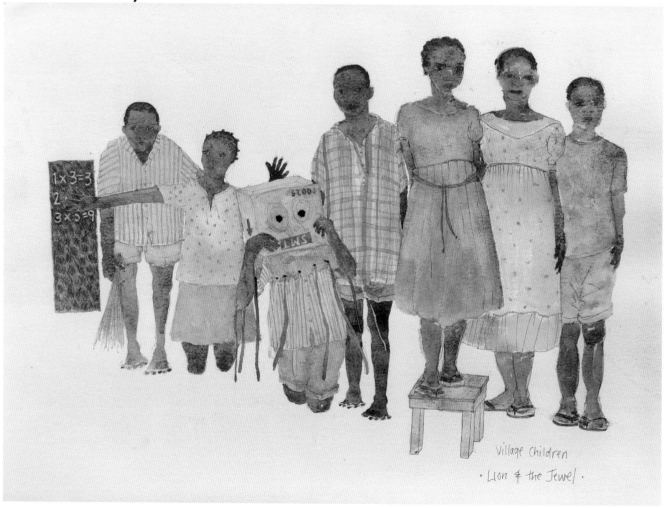

Village Children
- Lion & the Jewel.

Macbeth
William Shakespeare (1590s)

*Shakespeare in Education - Schools
Touring, West Midlands
Birmingham Theatre School
February 2003*

Anne Curry: 'Costume helped the
visual narrative, when I collaborated
with a young cast; actors played
multiple parts, girls played boys, and
there were many quick changes.
My designs were flexible, because
I created them from contemporary and
retro-clothing, stock and hired costume
sources. Collaboration focused on
characterisation. It helped to do costume
fittings in the rehearsal rooms, where
director and designer could view a
costume in a spatial context, and actors
could practise movements and quick
changes. The concept was to set the
action in a cool, minimalist, "corporate
world", using only tones of black, white
and red.'

Macbeth and Lady Macbeth

*Director: John Paul Cherrington
Set and Costume Designer: Anne Curry
Lighting Designer: John Paul Cherrington
Choreographer: Mandi Ashwood
Music/Sound: Pete Hammond*

The Lion and the Jewel
Wole Soyinka (1963)

*Collective Artistes with the Young Vic
and Bite:05, Barbican
Barbican Pit and tour
November 2005*

Atlanta Duffy: "A village clearing
under a huge Odan tree....." At the start
of rehearsals we all agreed that what we
most wanted was for our audience to
have felt that they had been immersed in
the atmosphere, character and heat of a
Nigerian village.
The play includes a series of mimes,
dances and masquerades; stories within
a story. With skilful acting,
choreography and lighting, simple
though evocative elements were utilised
to meld the stories. An oil drum was first
water butt then fiery brazier. Beaten
metal benches became the school, a
railway, market stalls and the Bale's bed.
All under a canopy of rusting oil lamps.'

*Director: Chuck Mike
Set and Costume Designer: Atlanta Duffy
Lighting Designer: Catriona Silver
Choreographer: Koffi Koko
Composer: Juwon Ogungbe
Costume Supervisor: Nicola Fitchett
Photographer: Keith Pattison*

Richard Downing

The Water *Banquet*

Richard Downing (2003)
The Water Banquet was originally
commissioned by Aberystwyth
Arts Centre

U Man Zoo
Tactile Bosch, Cardiff
April 2003

Richard Downing: 'For me the key
collaboration is with the "guest", a term
I prefer to "spectator" and one
particularly apt for the *Water Banquet*.
Here, a group of 18 strangers gathered
each evening at our table of water, and
individually selected several courses of
sound, image, object and story from a
menu of possibilities. I rather like it that
you cannot rehearse such a thing – at
least not beyond a set of strategies and
contingencies. I think it champions
something of the vitality of presence and
the ultimate performance space of
another's imagination. You really had to
be there.'

Director: Richard Downing
Photographers:
Simon Banham (Filed of Forks)
Dan Buxton (Figure/Rain)

Es Devlin

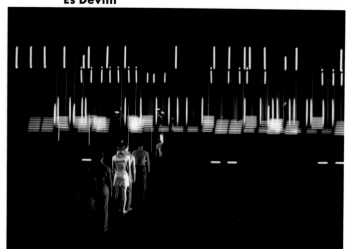

Essence
Fin Walker and Ben Parks (2005)

Walker Dance Park Music
Linbury Studio, Royal Opera House,
London
March 2005

Es Devlin: 'This was a setting of poems by WB Yeats. My brief was to incorporate text kinetically. The set comprised hundreds of vertical and horizontal light tubes which formed phrases of Yeats' poems as they flew slowly past one another. Depending on their position within the raked auditorium, members of the audience saw the phrases coalesce at fractionally different moments. The concept was entirely dependent upon the skilful programming of the Linbury Studio's formidable Nomad automated flying system.'

Choreographer: Fin Walker
Set Designer: Es Devlin
Costume Designer: Jack Galloway
Lighting Designer: Ben Ormerod
Dramaturg: Jonathan Myerson

Paul Farnsworth

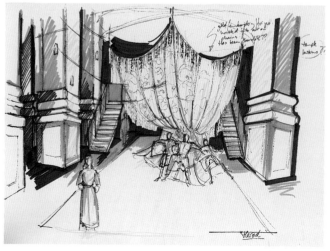

Dog in The Manger/Spanish Golden Age Season
Lope de Vega (1613)

Royal Shakespeare Company
Swan Theatre, Stratford-upon-Avon
April 2004

Es Devlin:'The brief was to create an environment for the four plays that comprised the RSC Spanish Golden Age Season. In collaboration with the RSC lighting team, we created a brass floor inscribed with glowing slots describing the molecular structure of gold.
The costumes were based on 16th-century practice of women being dressed by men's tailors with little accommodation for curves and a taste for heavily embroidered and jewel-encrusted surfaces. The Olivier Award was gratefully received by the designer but should have been divided among the myriad artists from Stratford, London and Pakistan who took part in their creation.'

Rebecca Johnson as Diana

Director: Laurence Boswell
Set and Costume Designer: Es Devlin
Lighting Designer: Ben Ormerod
Sound Designer: Tim Oliver
Choreographer: Heather Habens
Costume Supervisor: Emma Williams
Photographer: Ellie Kurttz

Jesus Christ Superstar
Tim Rice/Andrew Lloyd Webber (1971)

Bill Kenwright Ltd
UK tour
September 2004

Paul Farnsworth: 'Two directors, a company of actors playing multiple roles, a variety of locations to be accomplished swiftly and dramatically within a single, encompassing environment, and the changing spatial and technical demands of major touring venues around the UK. Locations were framed by the large, overhead, brass sculptural element, which could fly, tilt or spin, while simple props - a huge lantern for The Temple, a tablecloth for The Last Supper, gave a changing point of focus. Collaboration was required at every moment of rehearsal and production by all involved.'

Storyboard.

Directors:
Bill Kenwright and Bob Tomson
Set and Costume Designer:
Paul Farnsworth
Lighting Designer: Nick Richings
Sound Designer: Mick Potter
Choreographer: Henry Metcalfe

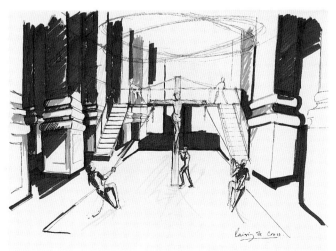

Becky Hawkins

Godspell
Stephen Schwartz (1971)

Northcott Young Company
Northcott Theatre, Exeter
April 2005

Becky Hawkins: 'This youth theatre production, with a cast of 40 and a youth band, was set in a stylised, bombed-out church, inhabited by a raggedy, gothic tribe. We wanted to create a post-apocalyptic world in which the contrasts of light and dark, and all their inherent symbolism, were heightened. The costumes were created by dyeing, ripping and customising old costumes and charity shop finds, making a virtue of our limited budget, and contrasting with the pristine, white, velvet coat worn by Stephen. Probably the cheapest to date, these costumes were voted the "coolest ever" by the youth theatre members.'

Directors: Rachel Vowles
and John Whitehead
Set Designer: Michael Vale
Costume Designer: Becky Hawkins
Lighting Designer: Chris Owen
Choreographer: John Whitehead
Musical Director: Peter Kyrke-Smith
Wardrobe:
Tina Marchant and Beth De Tisi
Photographer: Alan Winn

Ken Harrison

The Tempest
William Shakespeare (1611)

Nottingham Playhouse
November 2004

Ken Harrison: 'Ariel is a spirit put to work by Prospero to torment his adversaries. In this scene he appears to the shipwrecked lords as a vengeful harpy. Actor/dancer Matthew Bugg made use of a flying harness to achieve great flexibility of movement, whilst the flying lines suggested a lack of real freedom under Prospero's control.'

Director: Richard Baron
Set and Costume Designer:
Ken Harrison
Lighting Designer: Matt Pritchard
Sound Designer: Jon Beales
Choreographer: Rita Henderson

Mother Goose
John Crocker (2002)

Northcott Theatre, Exeter
December 2002

Becky Hawkins: 'Designing the Dame's costumes for the pantomime begins with the usual dialogue with the director, but the collaboration of the actor, designer and costume maker is even more important. It is essential to ensure that the costumes will make the necessary visual impact, be durable, comfortable, and give the actor the physical freedom demanded by pantomime. Working together from an early stage means that issues can be resolved without compromising any of these requirements. These are my costume proposals for *Mother Goose*, the first step in that process of problem solving and negotiation.'

Director: John Crocker
Costume Designer: Becky Hawkins
Lighting Designer: Russell Payne
Choreographer: John Whitehead
Costume Maker: Sue Hazemore

Lark Rise to Candleford
Adapted by Keith Dewhurst from the book by Flora Thompson (2005)

The Finborough Theatre, London
Shapeshifter and Berwick House in association with Concordance
September 2005

Alex Marker: 'Close collaboration with the artistic team is essential on a project as complex as this: two promenade plays, myriad locations, performed in rep, with a cast of 13 actor musicians, playing 75 characters. I produced an environment that included a two-storey hayloft, ladders, a hill, folding tables, a counter on castors, flaps, doors and a tin bath. No corner left unfilled; we even had an actor enter from the lighting box window.'

Directors: John Terry and Mike Bartlett
Set Designer: Alex Marker
Costume Designer: Penn O'Gara
Lighting Designer: John Terry
Arrangements and Musical Direction:
Tim Van EyKen
Choreographer: Kitty Winter

Alex Marker

Sophie Jump

Boxed
Devised by the company (2006)

Seven Sisters Group
A wooden box in the shop windows of
John Lewis, Debenhams and House of
Fraser, Oxford Street, London
15 July 2006

Sophie Jump: 'Placing a woman in a box in a shop window on London's Oxford Street raised questions about who was being observed and why, and explored women's roles. Was the box a constraint, a place of privacy, a protection or a vantage point? As a collaborative company we often discuss the most suitable term for our roles. As associate artist, I contribute from conception to choreography. Programmes say that pieces are "devised by the company" and stick to our usual titles. I am sometimes described as designer/collaborator or dramaturg. None of these terms seems satisfactory but we have not found any which are more appropriate.'

Director: Susanne Thomas
Set and Costume Designer: Sophie Jump
Dancer: Kristin McGuire
Photographer: Kevin Davis

Madeleine Millar

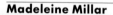

The Good Person of Setzuan
Bertolt Brecht (1941)

Crucible Youth Theatre
Crucible Studio, Sheffield
February 2004

Madeleine Millar: 'It was Nick Nuttgens' vision to use half masks and as there were so many actors/characters (some of the young people taking on two or more roles) this proved a golden opportunity to involve the whole group. Liz Dean and I cast their faces and with our help and encouragement they each designed their own mask, using clay and brown paper tape in layers to build up their character-exaggerated features. The masks were given a final mosaic patterning from ripped up magazines.'

The Forest
Devised by the company (2004)

Newlands Corner near Guildford
Seven Sisters Group
September 2004

Sophie Jump:
"I walk through the wood until all its perspectives converge upon a darkening clearing; as soon as I see them, I know that all its occupants have been waiting for me; with the endless patience of wild things, come alive from the desire of the woods."
Angela Carter.

The Forest tapped into the primeval emotions stirred by being in a forest, as well as touching on modern associations. The audience were given headphones to listen to a soundtrack as they followed a trail through the forest, coming upon installations and performers along the way, whilst dusk fell around them.'

Director: Susanne Thomas
Set and Costume Designer: Sophie Jump
Sound Designer: Quentin Thomas
Photographer: Mattias Ek

" The Whole Town is at your service, Illustrious Ones"

Director: Nick Nuttgens
Set and Costume Designer:
Madeleine Millar
Lighting Designer: Gary Longfield
Sound Designer: Nick Greenhill
Composer: Luke Carver Goss
Student Design Assistant:
Elizabeth Dean
The young people themselves
Photographer: Chris Saunders

Ralph Koltai

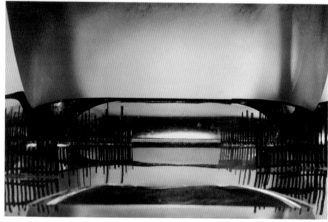

Fred Meller

giving

Timon Of Athens
William Shakespeare (1605-1608)

*Cardboard Citizens Theatre Company
and The Royal Shakespeare Company
Queen Elizabeth Hall, Stratford-upon-
Avon and Waterside, Belfast.
October 2006*

Fred Meller: 'In *Timon of Athens* the
language used to tell the story comes
from the artificial corporate world of
conferences and integrates stories from
both companies' actors. The performer
numbers are expanded using video
conference calling, blogging and
texting, enabling a larger number of
collaborators. Selected audience
members are "trained up" at the interval
to play an integral part as teams
engaged in team-building exercises.

The Romans in Britain
Howard Brenton (1980)

Sheffield Theatres
Crucible Theatre, Sheffield
February 2006

Ralph Koltai: 'The theme of *The Romans in Britain* is Britain's involvement in "The Troubles" in Ireland, drawing a parallel with the Roman invasion of Britain during the reign of Julius Caesar. The press at the time focused on a male rape scene by actors in the nude. The moral crusader, Mary Whitehouse instigated a private proscecution of the director Michael Bogdanov for obscenity, but the case came to nothing when it emerged that Mary Whitehouse had not actually seen the show. It was first produced by the National Theatre in 1980. The play had not been staged again in the interim 25 years. The rape scene in the Crucible production was cleverly staged by Sam West in a pool of water which I had conceived for the purpose. It caused no offence or derogatory comment.
My set represents Britain symbolically as a grassy circular terrain, i.e. our island Britain, an alien milieu for the invading Romans. The sculptural set structure is based on a tree root, linking it to dead bone. The central aperture may be seen as a tenuous reference to the rape.'

Director: Samuel West
Set Designer: Ralph Koltai
Costume Designer: Peter McKintosh
Lighting Designer: Peter Mumford
Sound Designer: Gareth Fry
Movement Director: Michael Ashcroft
Composer: Jason Carr
Set Builder: Stephen Pyle

Stephen Pyle: 'My first meeting with Ralph was as a very junior prop-maker at Scottish Opera in 1967 where he was designing *The Rake's Progress*. Almost every project of his that I have been invited to work on, over the years, has involved an element of risk, as they required original approaches to the method of scenic construction. Ralph's daring and adventurous spirit has enabled my workshop to develop materials and techniques that have totally transformed the physical palette available to the modern set designer. From the "lead" walls of *Richard III* at the NT, to the three-metre-ball bearing for *The Planets* ballet at the ROH, via the gigantic torso sections for the Ken Russell-directed production of *Die Soldaten* in Lyon, the challenges have been intriguing. I was approached by Ralph in late 2005 to collaborate on his sculpted root piece for *The Romans*. Together, we spent some time struggling to adapt the concept to the available funds. In construction, I was able to create the sculpture in transportable sections and assemble it on stage, where it was a permanent fixture for the duration of the show. The bleached, bone-like quality of the sculpture was achieved with a combination of carving, applied texture and painting. I eagerly await the next challenge.'

Katya Kabanova
Leos Janácek (1921)

Teatro La Fenice, Venice
January 2003

Ralph Koltai: '*Katya Kabanova*, an opera in three acts by Janacek with text by Cervinka is based on Ostrovsky's *The Storm*. Janacek and his librettist adhered very closely to the original story. At the age of 63 Janacek fell deeply in love with Kamila, a married woman of 25. Two thirds of his greatest music was written in his last dozen years, much inspired by his love for Kamila. The first of the operas thus influenced was *Katya*. It is a very powerful piece, musically and dramatically. The setting is on the banks of the Volga, in Russia. Katarina (Katya) is trapped in that remote environment both physically and emotionally. In a loveless marriage to Kabanov, and much maligned by her mother-in-law, Kabanova, there is no escape. The opera has many scenes, including the exterior and interior of their house. My photograph conveys the vastness of the land, with the typically Russian fences implying Katya's imprisonment. These fences are a permanent feature of the set, irrespective of the other scenic, architectural structures.'

Director: David Pountney
Set Designer: Ralph Koltai
Costume Designer: Sue Willmington
Lighting Designer: Mimi Jordan Sherin
Conductor: Lothar Koenigs

Motivational team leader Timon gives away absolutely everything and is reduced to eating the flower displays, spilling earth and cups of tea on the pristine carpets and into laptops and projectors then, curiously, under the dirt, he finds more money.'

First Drawings.

Director: Adrian Jackson
Set and Costume Designer: Fred Meller
Lighting Designer: Ian Saunders
Sound Designer: David Baird

timons banquets

Dana Pinto

What Does it Take?
Second Wave Artists (2006)

*Second Wave/the Albany Theatre
Albany Theatre, London
August 2006*

Dana Pinto: '*What Does it Take?* tells the story of two families in conflict. Based on Shakespeare's *Romeo and Juliet*, this contemporary urban play was a collaborative project between Second Wave and the Albany Theatre and the local community. We involved 30 local young people, aged 16-25, in a programme of training with theatre professionals in set, costume, prop-making, sound, DJ and VJing, lighting and multimedia. The result was an exciting colourful production.'

Act1 Scene 8, Uncle Steadman preparing sunday morning breakfast with Rommell

*Directors: Ann Considine, Judith Dove, Angela Michaels and Talmud Bah
Set and Costume Designer: Dana Pinto
Lighting Designer: James Rovira
Sound Designers: Dimples Vadher, Tope Omowale and Mikko Gordon
Choreographer: Tori Taiwo
Projection Design: Carrie Harvey, Ade Ogundare-Ali and Allan Okello*

Kimie Nakano

Festival for Fish
Yu Miri

*Yellow Earth Theatre Company
New Wimbledon Studio Theatre
Spring 2004*

Kimie Nakano: 'The youngest son commits suicide, a ritual to try to bring his separated family back together. The play starts with chairs in silhouette, then a video projection of a koi fish (the boy's spirit) swimming in the darkness. The koi fish is used as a symbol of *Boys Day* in Japan. The set includes a fish tank with a real koi. Here it represents the dead son's body in a coffin. The final image is of the family taking a souvenir photo. This combines with a video projection of several koi, flying in a changing blue sky. The complete design is minimal, with a clever use of simple Japanese screens for scene changes.'

*Chairs in silhouette (top)
Koi fish and blue figure shadows (bottom)*

*Director, Set and Costume Designer:
Kimie Nakano
Lighting Designer: Adam Crosthwaite
Sound Designer: Fung Lam
Video Art: Kimie Nakano
and Matthew Deely*

collaborators

Nerissa Cargill Thompson

Risk it? : A Story of Love, Life & STIs
Devised by Aqueous Humour with Boarshaw YIP for Rochdale MBC (2005)

*Aqueous Humour
Touchstones, Rochdale
August 2005*

Nerissa Cargill Thompson: 'Aqueous Humour collaborated with Rochdale Youth Service to explore issues surrounding sexual health and relationships with a group of young men at Boarshaw Youth Inclusion Project. We focussed on their ideas around sexually tranismited infections - the myths and the reality. As designer, I created a set of ten masks to visualise the symptoms. The director gave them personalities. The performance dealt with how a couple (played by professional actors) could leave themselves open to extra guests in their bed and their lives by not using protection. A successful premiere at Rochdale Touchstones led to invitations to perform at various youth centres.'

*Director: Tom Hogan
Set, Costumes and Mask Designer:
Nerissa Cargill Thompson*

Our Lady of the Drowned
Nelson Rodrigues (1947)

*StoneCrabs
Southwark Playhouse, London
June 2006*

Kimie Nakano: 'A Brazilian bourgeois house is juxtaposed against the world of dockyard brothels to real truths hidden for 19 years. The set is clear glass frames and chairs within a dark, brick-walled space. The play has themes of murder and revenge. The frames create transparent, psychological barriers which move and slice through this tense play. Projections of rain, running like blood and a photo sinking in the water add to the atmosphere. The neighbours/gossips, like a Greek chorus, are a constant presence throughout. They witness all murders through the frames. The costume key colour is black, with some red and white.'

*Director: Kwong Loke
Set and Costume Designer:
Kimie Nakano
Lighting Designer: Adam Crosthwaite
Sound Designer: Dinah Mullen
Video Art: Kimie Nakano
and Matthew Deely
Photographer: Marian Alonso*

Stuart Nunn

Close to Home
Daniel Jamieson (2005)

*Theatre Alibi
Small-scale touring
February 2005*

Stuart Nunn: 'A bridge to nowhere or anywhere, incongruously reaching out across the moor of South West England. Theatre Alibi offered three stories of exile and alienation, hope and homecoming. Three lifelong-journeys to define home conjoin in an indefinable time and space. Delivered on the first day of rehearsals, the basic set was developed in collaboration with the part-devised nature of the rehearsal process. Pathway and vantage point, the space transfigured through movement and lighting to house the storytelling and from which to survey the journey ahead. A shelter in which to share a sense of longing and belonging.'

Pathway, vantage point and shelter

*Director: Dorinda Hulton
Set and Costume Designer: Stuart Nunn
Lighting Designer: Marcus Bartlett
Sound Designer: Duncan Chave
Composer: Helen Chadwick
Scenic Artist: Meg Surrey
Photographer: Tim Sheader*

Tom Piper

Henry VI   Parts I, II, III
William Shakespeare (1590)

*RSC
Courtyard Theatre, Stratford-upon-Avon
August 2006*

Tom Piper: 'This design opened the RSC's new theatre. I worked on the set and the theatre in parallel. We went through 27 versions of the auditorium, which were tested in debate between the RSC's artistic team and theatre consultants Anne Minors and Charcoalblue. The use of steel in the design is a response to the rusted box created by architect Ian Ritchie as the outer shell of the building. It is a versatile playing space which will be the basic environment for a cycle of eight history plays to be staged by Michael Boyd and an ensemble of actors over the next two years. A true collaborative event.'

*Battle of Towton (left), Set for Henry VI
- Part I, II, III in Courtyard Theatre (right)*

*Directors: Michael Boyd
Set and Costume Designer: Tom Piper
Lighting Designer: Heather Carson
Sound Designer: Andrea Cox
Choreographer: Liz Rankin
Costume Supervisor: Emma Williams
Photographer: Ellie Kurttz*

Oz
Patrick Shanahan (2006 rewrite of 1994 original)

The Unicorn Theatre
The Weston Stage at the Unicorn Theatre, London
August 2006

Stuart Nunn: 'In colourless, Victorian Chicago, streetwise Dot breaks into the home of Mr L Frank Baum and stumbles into the biggest adventure of her life. With the reluctant help of housekeeper Bridget they tear through the study like a cyclone and bring Baum's fledging manuscript of *The Wonderful Wizard of Oz* to life, discovering along the way that it's not just the scarecrow, Tin Man and Lion who feel they're missing something crucial. A rehearsal room stacked by stage management with period furniture and props allowed the director, actors and designer to collaborate in inventing Victorian inspirations for 1940s icons.'

'Come on Mr Oz, deliver!'

Director: Greg Banks
Set and Costume Designer: Stuart Nunn
Lighting Designer: Olivier Fenwick
Photographer: Ben King

Katherina Radeva

5.Christian trying to get it on with Letisia

Daffodils
Maria Neikova

Robin Howard Dance Theatre,
The Place, London
March 2005

Katherina Radeva: '*Daffodils* tells the
story of four people - travellers - two
males and two females, going from one
place to the next, in between places and
experiences. The piece was inspired by
the music of Maria Neikova, a Bulgarian
singer famous for *Walking Together*,
a song that formed the soundtrack of
The Goat's Horn, a Bulgarian movie
made in the 1960s. I tried to limit the set
and costumes to the most necessary and
basic; flowers, a long pole on the end of
which rests a tap, a commode and two
types of toilet paper. Both the set

Nettie Scriven

Dragon Breath
Peter Rumney (2004)

Collaboration between Dragon Breath
Theatre; Creative Partnerships,
Nottingham; Theatre Design,
Nottingham Trent University

Waverley Theatre, Nottingham Trent
University
February 2004

Nettie Scriven:
'*A child's sculpture of a dragon*
(fiery tongue licking red across the
space)
shifts the writer's mind...
And so the George and Dragon myth
echoes
in a modern parable of grief and anger.
This moving image depicts
Great Dragon's rage against the twin
towers of a medieval city,
its previously fragmentary limbs
synchronised to create the whole,
its theatrical potency a consummation of
artists
speaking together in collaboration.'

Directors: Rosamunde Hutt
Set and Costume Designer:
Nettie Scriven
Horse Design: Kathy Barnes
Baby Dragon Puppet Design:
Claire Harwood
Lighting Designer: Arnim Friess
Sound Designer: Duncan Chave
Choreographer: Liz Clark
Puppetry Consultant : Sean Myatt
Dramaturg: Esther Richardson
Photographer: Robert Day

and costumes were made to inspire a sense of Home (in the sense of returning to something following an absence) and in particular, its ethos of working with the land. The objects used in the set were a reminder of my childhood in Bulgaria and a symbol of reverence for both my grandparents, whom I lost whilst working on the project.'

Choreographer: Philip Amann
Set and Costume Designer:
Katherina Radeva
Photographer: Benjamin Jenner

Reaching for the Moon
Peter Rumney (2005)

Dragon Breath Theatre at NTU SPACES
Waverley Theatre, Nottingham Trent
University
March 2005

Nettie Scriven: *'Responding to the 2004 Tsunami, 23 theatre design undergraduates join five professional artists to devise a puppet show for children aged between four and seven. An open-ended, improvisatory process generates a modern myth, exploring relationships, creativity and resourcefulness, and how the power of imagination and creativity can enable a child to project beyond her perilous circumstances to a place of safety – "reaching for the moon".*
The writer/director, puppeteer, lighting designer, choreographer and scenographer collaborate to express their own visions and concerns, enabling the student designers, makers, puppeteers and performance facilitators to generate the imagery, themes, characters, conflicts, and theatrical gestures that drive and stimulate the devising process.
Can we create a giant, interactive wave with nothing but light and a plastic sheet? Should we be showing it to tiny children at all? What are the responsibilities of the artist? What do we learn from the playfulness of the children we work with?'

Director: Peter Rumney
Scenographers: Sean Myatt, Nettie Scriven, in collaboration with NTU students
Designed, made, facilitated, performed and workshopped by NTU Theatre Design undergraduates

Ashley Shairp / Sam Heath

Front Window
Devised by the company (2005)

Planning A Trifle
Unity Theatre 2, Liverpool
October 2005

Ashley Shairp: 'This was a puppet-based performance devised, made and performed by three theatre practitioners, a designer, a set builder, a costume maker, and a scientist. The original idea was inspired by Hitchcock and growing up on terraced streets. The show developed by all four of us talking, making and experimenting in a fairly playful way. We ended up with an empty black space into which little worlds in boxes floated past the audience at a variety of scales.

Ian Teague

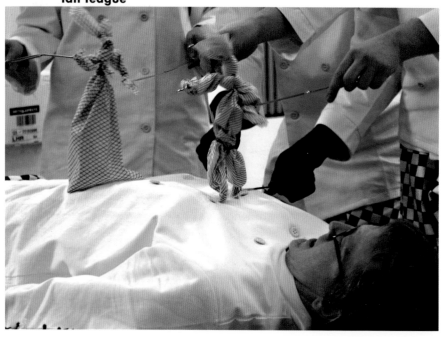

Gulliver's Travels
Devised (2006)

MakeBelieve Arts
Schools tour
May 2006

Gulliver meets Emperor and Empress of Lilliput (as played by puppets made from dish cloths)

Ian Teague: 'This devised production grew out of development work collaborating with a maths expert, numerous teachers and several hundred children, exploring the use of story in primary school maths. We were determined to tell Gulliver's story from the Lilliputian viewpoint, to engage children in the mathematical, logistical and moral questions involved in looking after a giant. Our actors became four

Johanna Town

Macbeth
William Shakespeare (1606)

Out of Joint
Warehouse, Batley
September 2004

Johanna Town: 'Out of Joint's production of *Macbeth* was a collaboration of set, lighting, and venue design. The brief was to be able to tour a show around the world into often forgotten buildings, ranging from a warehouse in Yorkshire, to a castle in Wales, to the British Embassy in Nigeria. All the lighting had to be non-theatrical and look as if it either belonged to the production (a modern, war-torn African state) or to every venue visited. Here we see the company, up lit with floodlights, disguised inside ammunition boxes at the front of the

The finale formed a tableau of a domestic galaxy, complete with twinkling stars.'

Director: The company
Set Designer: Ashley Shairp
and the company
Costume Designer: Ann Preston
and the company
Lighting Designer: Sam Heath
and the company
Sound Designer: John Preston
and the company

chefs from the Lilliputian royal kitchens preparing giant quantities of food.
To tell the story, the chefs used whatever they had to hand. In this case, dish cloths made into Emperor and Empress puppets.'

Director: Trisha Lee
Set and Costume Designer: Ian Teague
Sound Designer and Composer:
David Baird
Movement: Rose Ryan

Pericles
William Shakespeare (1607/08)

National Theatre Education Department
Schools tour
January 2006

Ian Teague: 'This cut-down version of *Pericles* was set on a beach, where a group of fisherfolk told the story of the King who was washed up on their shore. Here Pericles puts on his armour made of objects found on the beach. Often, doing a small show in a large organisation can be problematic but the enthusiasm, skill and commitment of the production staff at the National Theatre made it a pleasure to collaborate with them. A designer working in educational theatre rarely has such resources to call upon.'

Pericles puts on his armour made of objects found on the beach

Director: Karl Heap
Set and Costume Designer: Ian Teague
Music: Joe Townsend
Movement: Rose Ryan

acting area.'
Image 2: This corresponding image shows the actors (here playing the witches as voodoo witch doctors) again up lit in another location, this time using an industrial sodium flood, up-ended to look as if part of the rubble, left strewn around the venue.'

Orchestrated Finale
The Witches

Director: Max Stafford Clark
Set and Costume Designer: Es Devlin
Lighting Designer: Johanna Town
Sound Designer: Gareth Fry
Music: Felix Cross
Photographer: John Haynes

David I. Taylor

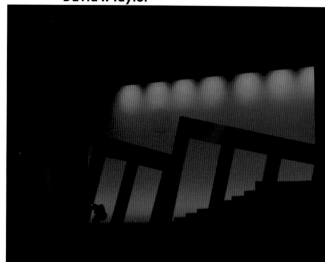

Lucia Di Lammermoor
Gaetano Donizetti (1835)

*Lyric Opera Company of Kansas City
Lyric Opera House, Kansas City,
Missouri USA
March 2006*

David I. Taylor: 'Within one of the
most "old school" opera companies in
North America, the design team for
Lucia di Lammermoor explored the
complex mix of staging, acoustic
arrangement, lighting, colour, singer
relationships, scenic movement,
transparency, projection and texture
through a digital pre-visualisation tool.
All the key team members, whether
originating their work in pencil or data,
utilised Cast Lighting's WYSIWYG
software and uploaded to a workspace
area on the internet where ideas were
shared, explored and refined. Shared,
3D-rendered working images of the
whole production were the main tools of
the team's collaboration leading to an
enlightening production process and a
wildly successful new show.'

*Director: Ward Holmquist
Set and Costume Designer:
R. Keith Brumley
Lighting Designer: David I. Taylor
Stage Director: Marc Verzatt*

Janet Vaughan

25/7
*Devised by Talking Birds, written by
Nick Walker (2006)*

*Talking Birds
Empty unit in new Priory Place
development, Coventry.
May 2006*

Janet Vaughan: 'Talking Birds is a
collaborative company comprising three
core members (a writer/performer,
composer/film-maker and an
artist/designer). It is our belief that
collaboration makes us better artists and
leads to more interesting work.
The company regularly expands to
incorporate other collaborators with
additional skills to devise and realise
ambitious projects. The company's
creative process productively see-saws
between time spent together devising
and time spent developing words, music
and visuals individually. It aims to
produce work where all the performance
elements, including the space or site
(which is as much a collaborator as the
artists involved), are seamlessly woven
together.'

Dudley Holt (Graeme Rose) of the 25/7 News Corporation reporting on "the unfolding situation" puts words into the Sniper's mouth (Janice McKenzie)

Sandra the waitress (Doreene Blackstock) and the Restauranteur (Tyrone Huggins) prepare to serve their themed Olympic meal to 50 captive diners in the revolving restaurant at the highest point in the Olympic City

*Director: Nick Walker
Set, Costume and Lighting Designer: Janet Vaughan
Sound Designer and Composer: Derek Nisbet*

Jessica Worrall

People Show no.117
The Birthday Show
Devised by The People Show (2006)

The People Show
People Show Studios, London
July 2006

Jessica Worrall: 'In 2006 The People Show produced a devised, site-specific performance in its studios in London that both reflected on and celebrated its 40th birthday. The audience were taken on a journey through the building and each room was designed to represent a different part of People Show's story and artistic process. This moment is from the black and white room, which was designed to represent two-dimensional memory. A false wall was built and I covered it with blown-up photocopies of parts of some of the many photographs

Martina Von Holn

Martina Von Holn
Devised (2005)

Site-specific/private home
September 2005 and April 2006

Martina Von Holn:
'*The Tasseographer*, a one-to-one performance piece, revives the ancient ritual of tea leaf reading. Using various objects in the space (e.g. a painting, a travel photograph) as well as a distinct soundscape, it sets out to take the audience on a journey along the lines of the Tasseographer's biography, interweaving sequences of her own life with themes arising from three pertinent questions.
The piece has been created in close collaboration with writer David Lane, through research into fortune telling, popular belief and story telling.

Rebecca Vincent

Lilita
Tracy Keeling and Mary Cimino (1999)

The ALlieS
Underbelly, Edinburgh Fringe Festival
and at the Piccolo Spoleto Festival,
Charleston, USA
June and August 2005

Rebecca Vincent: '*Lilita* unravels why our culture encourages young girls to engage their seductive nature prematurely only to react in horror when they fall victim to a sexual predator. It fuses elements of reality and fantasy and heavily references modern culture/media and fairy tales/folklore. The set consists of a versatile mobile box that transforms into a Wendy house, playpen/cage, cot, shopping trolley, picnic table and finally an electric chair. The box is choreographed and worked which are in the company's extensive archive. I changed the scale of many of the images to try and create a sense of the performers being lost within the images, overwhelmed by them even, which is something that happened to all of us as we tried to deal with and find our way through the company's rich and varied past and make something new from it, that we could feel part of.'

**The Black and White Room
The Main Hall**

*Director: The People Show
Set and Costume Designer: Jessica Worrall
The People Show (the company is a non-hierarchical group of performers, musicians, artists etc. who together, devise and perform the work)
Photographer: Zadoc Nava*

The collaboration took the form of initial brainstorming sessions, moved on to improvisation with performers Hakan Silahsizoglu and Imogen Smith and with the aid of director Caroline Steinbeis started to take on a distinct dramaturgic form which is still being explored.'

*Created and devised by: Martina Von Holn in collaboration with
Caroline Steinbeis
Designer: Martina Von Holn
Writer: David Lane
Performers: Imogen Smith and Hakan Silahsizoglu*

into the action and becomes another member of the cast, ever present and changing/evolving with the unfolding of the story.'

The set, fully worked into the rehearsal process

*Director: Mary Cimino
Set Designer: Rebecca Vincent
Costume Designer: Julie Ziff
Sound Designer/Composer: Oliver Dinsmore and Philip Brown*

Steph Warden

Closer
Patrick Marber (1997)

*The Studio, Theatre by the Lake,
Keswick
February 2005*

Steph Warden: 'Spatial limitations and
the inability to fly scenery contributed to
the overall production design. *Closer* is
a multi-locational play. The design was
minimal, abstract and clinical, a white
box with metal walls making the set
extremely versatile and claustrophobic.
Many scenes were concerned with
capturing and displaying memories.
This concept was utilised putting
objects, actions and characters on
display. Functional storage units formed
a movable set, defining locations and
facilitating the action in each scene.
The actors were responsible for scene
changes and this became integral to the
play. Storing mementoes from each
scene on shelving provided an ongoing
reminder of past actions. '

*Act 1 Scene 5 The Gallery, Alice and Dan
at the opening night of Anna's
photography exhibition*

*Director: Simon H. West
Set and Costume Designer:
Steph Warden
Lighting Designer: Andrew Lindsay
Photographer: Keith Pattison*

collaborators

RESPONSE TO SPACE + PLACE

How does one collaborate with a place?
The importance of 'the place' or of space in which to work,
to which to respond is arguably equal with the material and
team we work with.

This section includes the ever increasing area of 'found space'
work, in which projects such as *Mulgrave* by Louise Ann Wilson
and *Home* by Pip Nash are devised in specific response to the
chosen land or cityscape and to the stories that have originated
from them. In such places the people who live or work there
become vital collaborators. Through them, places are unlocked
and perceived differently.

Finding a non-theatre space for the playing, or re-working,
of a known piece such as *Rusalka* in the cloisters at Iford
(Elroy Ashmore), or *Tom Sawyer* in the park in Lancaster
(Terry Brown) offers moments of conjunction – in which
the re-reading of the piece and the re-reading of the space
can impact on each other at yet another level of signification,
as again with Fred Meller's *Pericles* designs for the Cardboard
Citizens company.

The re-imagining of spaces is absolutely part of designing for
theatres with specific identities and dimensions such as the
narrow shoebox of The Gate, Notting Hill or the 25,000-seat
Arena di Verona or the Donmar Warehouse.

Sometimes the space needs a great deal of work and the teams
assembled to transform or articulate it become key to the project.
This is as true of a performance project, as it is of the design and
construction of a new space, or the redevelopment
of an existing space. Performance spaces currently being
designed and built have a different brief from the past.
They are required to be capable of reinterpretation by their
prospective users. To have adaptable, technically versatile,
designated performance spaces is essential, but the whole
building including its enviroment is made up of spaces
in which a performed something could, might, happen.
A reading, a music performance, part of a promenade,
a moment of dance... with which to re-experience the place
and the people in it.

Rusalka

Rusalka
Antonin Dvorak (1901)

Iford Arts
The Cloister at Iford
July 2005

Elroy Ashmore: 'The design had to be a collaboration with a sleeping partner, in this case the venue. *Rusalka* was staged in the old cloister at Iford, which couldn't be touched in any way. A valuable old well sits permanently centre stage. *Rusalka*, a tale of a water nymph who seeks mortality, finds herself in a place of experimentation but a world shifted from our own. In the centre, a sculpture of pipes, representing the tree of life, carries liquids to and from old rusty machinery and ancient computers. Bare light bulbs hang like fruit from the tree. We are in a world not

Martyn Bainbridge

The Crucible
Arthur Miller (1953)

Clwyd Theatr Cymru
October 2003

Martyn Bainbridge:'An epic play warrants a big set. We decided to remove several rows of seats and build out into the auditorium as far as possible (20 metres front to back). The upstage trees and branches define the space and the forest: a place of excitement for the impressionable girls or a place of terror, with an unknown world beyond.
The stage has a minimum of furniture.
All concentration is on the protagonists.'

Director: Terry Hands
Set and Costume Designer:
Martyn Bainbridge
Lighting Designer: Terry Hands

Terry Brown

The Adventures of Tom Sawyer by Mark Twain
Adapted by Gareth Machin (July 2006)

The Dukes Theatre, Lancaster
Various locations within Williamson Park, Lancaster
July 2006

Terry Brown: 'The open air productions by The Dukes Theatre Company in Williamson Park require a particular form of collaboration (with the exclusion of the weather, that is, which often seems to be deliberately uncooperative!). Productions are promenade in form and the design of each scene is informed by its location in the park – there are no formal stages. So lighting, sound, costume-change areas, as well as the storage of props etc., has to be built in at an early stage

far from 1920s German cinema.
The cloister's stone work played an
important role in the design.'

Director: Jeff Clarke
Set and Costume Designer:
Elroy Ashmore
Lighting Designer: Jeremy Rowe
Conductor: Oliver Gooch

An Inspector Calls
J.B. Priestley (1946)

Clwyd Theatr Cymru
September 2006

Martyn Bainbridge: ' We wanted to
move from naturalism and expressionism
into an abstract world. The well-to-do
Northern family have to face the
consequences of their actions aided by
the mysterious Inspector. The revolving
and pivoting platform is perhaps a
metaphor for the end of an age?
Upstage, an idealised vision of England
is revealed but the satanic mills are
covering the green and pleasant land'

Director: Barry Kyle
Set and Costume Designer:
Martyn Bainbridge
Lighting Designer: Arnim Friess

of the design process, along with the
fact that the park remains a public space
throughout the whole period of the
production.'

*Scene 1 The Mississippi River – Set
sketch/ actual set prior to technical
rehearsal*

Director: Ian Hastings
Set and costume Designer: Terry Brown
Sound and Lighting Designer: Brent Lees
Choreographer: Verity Bray
Composer: Matt Baker

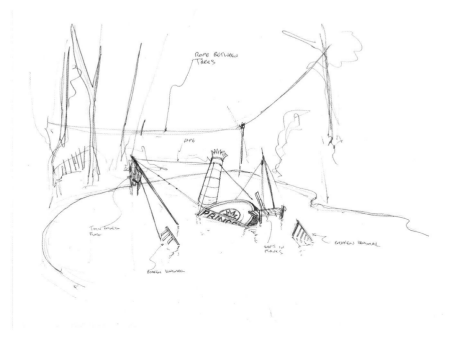

Janet Bird

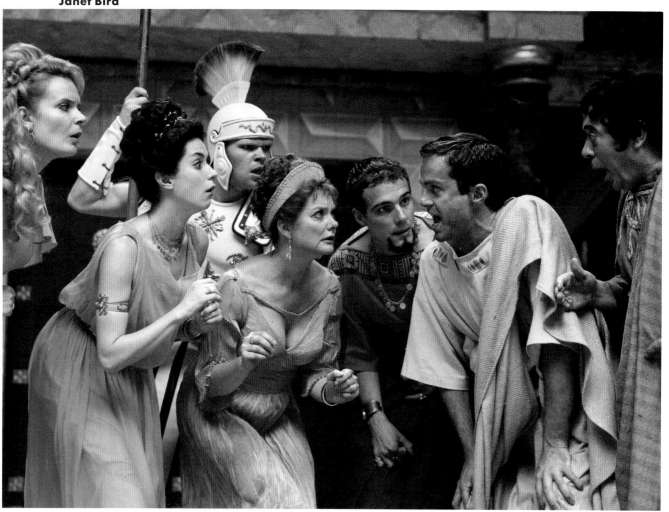

Bunny Christie

The Comedy of Errors
William Shakespeare (1623)

Shakespeare's Globe Trust
Shakespeare's Globe
July 2006

Janet Bird: 'The collaboration of the project was with the extraordinary space itself. The concept was born directly from the Globe. Our *faux* classical theme linked the Tudors' mock classical architecture to the comic 1960s Rome that caricatured that period's own Roman epics. The set design repeated design motifs and colour schemes from the building's pillars and planked *trompe l'oeil*. The design continues into the upstage tiring house, creating a receding Roman Ephesus in false perspective for our characters to race around; our identical twins sometimes appearing simultaneously in different parts of town.'

Director: Christopher Luscombe
Set and Costume Designer: Janet Bird
Lighting Designer: Oliver Fenwick
Choreographer: Jenny Arnold
Composer: Julian Phillips
Photographer: John Tramper

After Miss Julie

Donmar Warehouse
November 2003

Bunny Christie: 'Michael Grandage created a pre-show scene where a meal of liver and onions was cooked onstage, the dishes washed up and the kitchen tidied. The audience had a sense of spying on real lives in a basement kitchen of a large house with a stone floor and over-sized working Aga used to catering for many guests. The kitchen needed to feel full of history and the restrictions of class. It is July 1945. There is a sense of change in the air, the possibility of freedom behind those high-shuttered windows.'

Full Stage
Miss Julie sees John and Christine kiss

Director: Michael Grandage
Set and Costume Designer:
Bunny Christie
Lighting Designer: Neil Austin
Photographer: Ivan Kyncl

Charcoalblue

Courtyard Theatre

Client: Royal Shakespeare Company
Courtyard Theatre, Stratford-upon-Avon
11 June 2006

Charcoalblue: 'In November 2004, the RSC invited us to collaborate on an intensive six-month design period to develop the auditorium concept for the RSC temporary theatre. Charcoalblue worked in close association with Ian Ritchie Architects and design team, the RSC's Michael Boyd, Vikki Heywood, Tom Piper, Simon Harper and Flip Tanner, developing the thrust stage auditorium together. The one room thrust stage is an essential aspect of the RSC's ensemble theatre philosophy. It is the key to bringing a sense of intimacy to the 1000-seat venue. The auditorium and technical galleries surrounding the stage are built as a freestanding structure lightly braced to the walls of the plywood-lined, Cor-ten® steel auditorium building. This "theatre-in-a-box" approach further emphasises the temporary nature of the building which was built in 11 months and within cost.'

Auditorium interior during Builders Night.

Architects: Ian Ritchie Architects
Theatre Consultants: Charcoalblue
Structural: WSP
Mechanical and Electrical:
King/Shaw Associates
Acoustic: Paul Gillerion Acoustic Design

John Brooking

Siobhan Davies Studios

*Client: Siobhan Davies Dance
Siobhan Davies Studios
April 2006*

Charcoalbue: 'The Siobhan Davies Studios is a refurbishment of a Victorian Board School in Lambeth. The building houses offices, therapy rooms and two dance rehearsal spaces, one of which - the Roof Studio - can also be used for performances. The concept driving the design for the main studio was of "dancing on the roof" and was created through the physical, tactile and sensual architecture. Charcoalblue designed the technical facilities for the Studios in close collaboration with both the architects and the dance company. The result in the Roof Studio was a number of custom-manufactured, stainless steel bars, internally wired to provide the necessary technical facilities, which exactly follow the complex curvature of the Studio's ribbon ceiling, thereby allowing the dance company to use the space for technical experimentation and performance without compromising the unique roof design.'

*Architects:
Sarah Wigglesworth Architects
Theatre Consultants: Charcoalblue
Structural: Price and Myers
Mechanical and Electrical:
Fulcrum Consulting
Acoustic: Paul Gillerion Acoustic Design*

A Midsummer Night's Dream
William Shakespeare (1600)

*Stafford Shakespeare Festival
Stafford Castle
June 2006*

John Brooking: 'The auditorium for the Stafford Shakespeare Festival is set on a hill below Stafford Castle. The director, Bill Buckhurst, was very keen to keep the castle in view and to keep the set as open as possible, reflecting the use of the moon in the text. The circular main stage was a reflection of the moon, which rose during the first appearance of Oberon and Titania. Theseus' court, in red, was imposed upon a green set. It was very much the fairy world with a variety of traps and gaps for magical appearances and disappearances.'

*Director: Bill Buckhurst
Set and Costume Designer:
John Brooking
Lighting Designer: Vicky Weymouth
Sound Designer: Matthew Glass
Choreographer: Verity Bray
Composer: David Harper
Photographer: Robert Day*

Paul Brown

La Traviata
Giuseppi Verdi (1853)

Arena di Verona
June 2004

Paul Brown: 'We started with the premise that Violetta was, for a short time, the most famous woman in Paris. Her death was the death of an icon, so we built a huge shrine reminiscent of the one created after Princess Diana's death. After the mournful prelude, the opening party starts with a large doll rotating into view, followed by a saccharine, quilted heart, hanging out of the flowers; the mood has changed dramatically to the superficial and hedonistic. The Utopian retreat that Violetta's lifestyle has paid for is divorced from the reality that Germont brings. The space is furnished with dolls' furniture and the lawn printed with money. A large, glitzy and vulgar fan introduces Flora's "Spanish" party but then inevitably returns to a bleak and morbid landscape with a small space cleared for a simple bed and cabinet.'

Director: Graham Vick
Set and Costume Designer: Paul Brown
Assistant Designer: Adrian Linford
Lighting Designer: Peter Kaczorowski
Photographer: Philip Larter

Steve Denton

Richard Hudson

The Emperor Jones
Eugene O'Neill (1920)

Gate Theatre, London
November 2005

Richard Hudson: 'It was a great
pleasure to design this 50-minute play
for the tiny Gate Theatre, on a very small
budget, and with a wonderfully
enthusiastic and dedicated team.'

Director: Thea Sharrock
Set Designer: Richard Hudson
Costume Designer: Adam Silverman
Lighting Designer: Phil Haldane
Sound Designer: Gregory Clarke
Photographer: Stephen Cummiskey

The Harmony Suite: Elegance, Deprivation and Regeneration in North Liverpool, 2005
Collective Encounters
Site Specific Performance in Anfield, Liverpool
September 2005

Steve Denton: 'Based on months of research with local residents and investigations into policy and provision in North Liverpool, *The Harmony Suite* set out to tell the story of people living through change. Performed in the shadow of Anfield stadium, the show attempted to re-animate a derelict street of houses through the collaboration of lighting, multimedia, music and live performance.'

Opposite: The Researcher enters the Kafkaesque world of Bureaucracy

Director: Sarah Thornton
Set and Costume Designer: Steve Denton
Lighting Designer: Mike Wight
Sound Designer: Kal Ross
Choreographer: Sarah Black
Video: RWP

Tim Foster Architects

The Trafalgar Studios at the Whitehall Theatre, London
2004/5

Client: The Ambassador Theatre Group

Tim Foster Architects: 'Listed building consent was granted for a period of four years only, which meant that the changes had to be easily reversible and have minimum impact on the Art Deco interior. In Studio 1 the original circle front was removed and the rake of the circle extended forward by four rows to meet a new raised stage projecting into the auditorium. The original stalls level, below the circle, has been converted to form Studio 2, a small 100-seat space, with new dressing rooms to serve it provided below the main stage.
Studio 1 opened to critical acclaim with the Royal Shakespeare Company's production of *Othello*, which transferred from the Swan Theatre in Stratford.'

Main Contractor: Mansell Construction
Sub-Contractors:
Steeldeck
Kirwin & Simpson
Fagan Electrical
Mackie Engineering
Theatre Structures
Lighting Consultant:
Howard Eaton Lighting
Acoustic Consultant:
Paul Gillieron Acoustic Design
Structural Engineer: Campbell Reith Hil

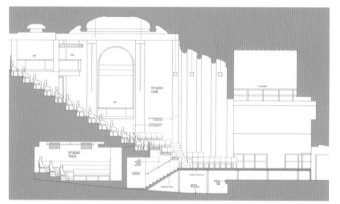

collaborators

The Broadway, Barking
2004

*Client: London Borough of Barking &
Dagenham in association with Barking
College
Civic Trust Partnership Award 2006*

Tim Foster Architects: 'An innovative
partnership between the London
Borough of Barking & Dagenham and
Barking College has led to the creation
of a new community arts centre, within a
converted civic hall, combined with
accommodation for the Performing Arts
Department of Barking College,
including rehearsal and dance studios,
a recording studio and workshops.
The new scheme incorporates a flexible,
328-seat performance space, formed by
the insertion of new hanging balconies
and a retractable bleacher seating
system within the old auditorium.
An extension, at the front of the building,
creates a new profile for the centre and
provides a large, double-height foyer
space with a box office, lift, toilets and
offices and a terrace overlooking the
Barking Abbey grounds.
Accommodation for Barking College is
provided on the lower ground floor.
The new arts and education complex
represents the first stage of the
regeneration strategy for Barking Town
Centre and has featured in two recent
exhibits at the New London Architecture
Gallery.'

*Quantity Surveyors: Trinick Turner
Structural Engineers:
Alan Conisbee & Associates
Services: Waterman Gore
Theatre Consultants: Theatreplan
Acoustic : Paul Gillieron Acoustic Design
Lighting: Light & Design Associates*

Ada Gadomski

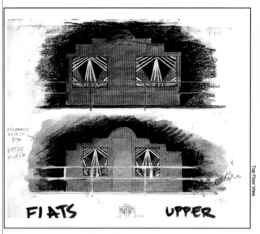

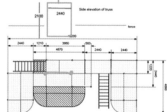

Design for upper floor of set, flats for "Fat Sam's Gran Slam"

Bugsy Malone
*Author; Alan Parker, Music;
Paul Williams (1983)*

*The Young Person's Theatre Company
Lilian Baylis Theatre, Sadlers Wells,
London
February 2004*

Ada Gadomski: 'A challenging brief -
creating 1920s New York streets and
interiors on three levels for a cast of 25
dancing and singing teenagers, in a
dance studio without a backstage area.
The set was the same throughout.
We achieved scene changes by lighting
only sections of the set at a time, with
spots and lanterns hidden inside the
structure. The set needed to be
assembled in four hours so I used Lite
Structures lightweight aluminium trussing
to build a skeleton, which we then
dressed in a minimal 1920s style.'

*Director: Robbi Stevens
Set Designer: Ada Gadomski
Costume Designer: Malin Persson
Lighting Designer: Chris Van Goethem
Musical Director: Steve Higgins*

Richard Foxton

The Country Wife
*William Wycherley,
adapted by Tamka Gupta (2004)*

*Palace Theatre, Watford
October 2004*

Richard Foxton: 'This contemporary
adaptation was commissioned for the
re-opening of the Palace Theatre after
a major refurbishment and total rebuild
of the stage and backstage areas.
The set design aimed to extend the new
colour scheme and architectural feel of
the auditorium on to the stage and
combine it with a modern art gallery
aesthetic, incorporating use of
projection and backlit, Perspex walls.
The rear wall of the set was a flown
piece in the approximate position of the
old rear wall of the stage. This piece
was flown out during the final scene to
reveal a curved mirror, the size of the
proscenium arch, reflecting the
performance and the auditorium
beyond.'

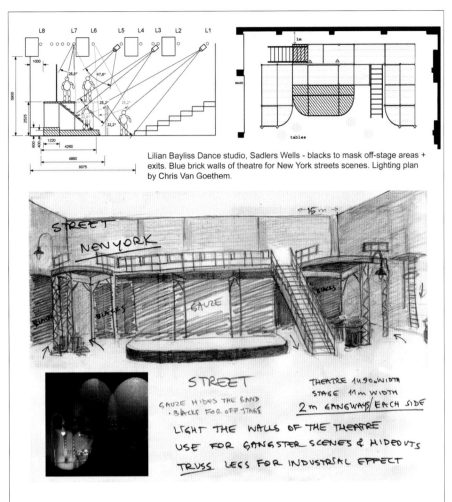

Lilian Bayliss Dance studio, Sadlers Wells - blacks to mask off-stage areas + exits. Blue brick walls of theatre for New York streets scenes. Lighting plan by Chris Van Goethem.

Director: Lawrence Till
Set and Costume Designer:
Richard Foxton
Lighting Designer and Projection
Designer: Jon Driscoll
Choreographer: John Thompson
and Geeta Pendaer
Composer: Dominic Muldowney
Photographer: Jon Driscoll

Peter Higton

Pericles
William Shakespeare (1609)

*Cardboard Citizens Theatre Company
And The Royal Shakespeare Company
Distribution Warehouse, Old Kent Road,
London
July 2003*

Peter Higton: 'This production of
Pericles took place in a complex of
disused supermarket distribution
warehouses. The audience undertook a
journey through the spaces, entering as
asylum seekers to be "processed" under
harsh fluorescent lighting, becoming
shipwrecked alongside Pericles, and
ending in a state of greater well-being
as he is reunited with his family.
The lighting journey reflected that of the
audience: the pitiless, utilitarian nature
of the spaces became less austere as
mercury lamps gave way to sodium,
daylight gave way to darkness, and to
the discovery of largely static, emotive
compositions, which reflected the nature
of event, location and tone. '

*Thaissa Comes Back to Life
The Container With Blood Soaked
Clothes Washed into the Corner
It is the Coffin for Thaissa Believed to
Have Died in the Storm*

*Director: Adrian Jackson
Set and Costume Designer: Fred Meller
Lighting Designer: Peter Higton
Sound Designer: David Baird*

collaborators

Pericles
William Shakespeare (1609)

*Cardboard Citizens Theatre Company
and The Royal Shakespeare Company
Distribution Warehouse, Old Kent Road,
London
July 2003*

Fred Meller: 'Cardboard Citizens
Theatre Company began as a vehicle
for helping homeless people, through
its connection to Augusto Boal's Forum
Theatre in Brazil. It is now a professional
company taking the experiences of
actors from all over the world who take
refuge in the UK.
The designer-director relationship has
been established over ten years.
The Royal Shakespeare Company actors
shared their experience of performing
Shakespeare's text and Cardboard
Citizens shared their first-hand
experiences of the kind of life-changing
events that Shakespeare writes about:
vivid, immediate and relevant.
Pericles' journey as a refugee is
interspersed with real life stories.
The audience initially cast as asylum
seekers experience each of the different
storms in a washing area, a sea of beds
and a shipping container.'

*Dele Adagunodo Tells a Real-Life Asylum
Seeker's Story
The Audience Seated with the Home
Office Asylum Seeker's Form to Fill in
Washing*

*Director: Adrian Jackson
Set and Costume Designer: Fred Meller
Lighting Designer: Peter Higton
Sound Designer: David Baird
Photographer: Louise Stickland*

Becky Hurst

The Sunflower Plot
Devised by Cartoon de Salvo
(July 2005)

Cartoon de Salvo
A site specific piece of outdoor theatre
on two allotments in Farnham and
Newark
July and August 2005

Becky Hurst: 'The Sunflower Plot was
a site-specific piece of outdoor theatre
devised by Cartoon de Salvo, set on an
allotment. The company cultivated the
plot from scratch and the set was
"grown". We adopted the "make-do-
and-mend" aesthetic of the allotment
world in everything we created.
Alllotment community members also lent
us their own plots to feature in show,
where we set up intriguing sets and
installations. They constantly helped us
with gardening tips and donated
numerous plants.'

Director: Alex Murdoch
Set and Costume Designer: Becky Hurst
Lighting Designer: John Mackenzie
Composer and Musician: Jim Marcovitch
Technical Designer: Phil Eddolls
Devisers and Performers: Dennis
Herdman, Clive Holland, Brian Logan,
Paschale Straiton
Photographer: Edmund Collier

Keith Williams Architects

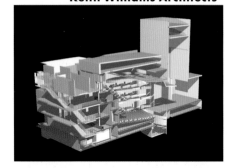

**OPW Architectural Services In
Association With Keith Williams
Architects**

Wexford's New Opera House
*Construction started in July 2006 and
the new building will open for Festival
2008*

Keith Williams: 'The home of the
world famous Wexford Opera is being
redeveloped in a far reaching 30m Euro
rebuilding programme.
The previous Theatre Royal which dated
from 1832, had been much altered, and
was in such poor condition that it had no
viable future, and without major
intervention the existence of the entire
festival was under threat.
The redeveloped Theatre Royal will offer
a larger capacity main auditorium
(750 seats) with excellent acoustics, a
second theatre and other greatly
enhanced facilities. It will be constructed
on the current site, thereby remaining in
the heart of the community, and through
careful design the new theatre will retain
the historic street-scene setting. Though
focussed on the autumn festival, the new
building will also be able to operate as
a year-round arts venue for both
additional Wexford Festival productions
and visiting companies. The new
building has been conceived as a secret

opera house, nestling in the backlands
of Wexford's medieval street pattern.'

*Facilities in the new 7,000 sqm theatre
will include:*
*750 seat state of the art auditorium
specifically designed for opera*
*150 seat second space for drama,
music, rehearsal and cinema*
*Foyer/box office/cloaks/bars and café
/wcs*
Hospitality Areas
Dressing Rooms
Prop Making
Chorus Rehearsal Rooms
*Enhanced backstage facilities for
directors, conductors, designers and
singers*

Main Credits
Client: Wexford Festival Opera
*Project Manager: Office of Public Works
on behalf of the Department of Arts,
Sports and Tourism*
*Architects: OPW Architectural Services
in association with Keith Williams
Architects*
Acoustician: Arup Acoustics
Theatre Consultants: Carr & Angier
*Structural Engineering: ARUP Consulting
Engineers*
*M & E Engineering: OPW M + E
Engineering Services*
Cost Consultant: Nolan Ryan

collaborators

Janis Hart

Consider Rather The River
Robert Rae (2003)

Theatre workshop Edinburgh
The water of Leith, Edinburgh
July 2003

Janis Hart: 'A collaborative project, inspired by stories and myths of water, from the Egyptian river god Hapi, Lorelei, and the Rusalki to the mill workers of the 19th-century. The action took place alongside a historic river in the heart of Edinburgh. The challenge was to collaborate not just with the creative team, but with the many and varied spaces we were using, and with the participants, many of whom had no previous theatre experience. Drawings provided a catalyst for discussion and creativity, and later a map/storyboard of action. Collaborations with Mother Nature ranged from huge tunnels and bridges to tiny, mirrored tears hung from trees. The design team spent many hours in and beside the water, installing artwork, and operating puppets. It was a unique opportunity to observe the life of the river, and to interact with it.'

Director: Morvern Gregor
Set and Costume Designer: Janis Hart
Lighting Designer: Phil Haldane

As Mr. and Mrs Snip Snip argue on the jetty the Egyptians cross the river

Location – Pathway between Bank Gardens & ...

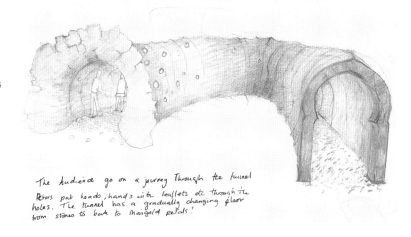

The audience go on a journey through the tunnel. Actors put heads, hands with leaflets etc through the holes. The tunnel has a gradually changing floor from stones to bark to marigold petals!

Unicorn Theatre, Tooley Street, London

'The Unicorn Theatre employs professional actors performing to an audience of children, families and schools. Founded in 1947 by Caryl Jenner, the Unicorn began theatrical life touring in two ex-MOD trucks. From 1967 it shared space at the Arts Theatre in Covent Garden before vacating in 1999. In late 2000 the Unicorn launched a European architectural competition which was won by Keith Williams. The completed building is the result of a five-year collaboration between the architect and the theatre. It must be "rough yet beautiful", to recall artistic director Tony Graham's opening remarks when first briefing his architect, and whilst rich in child-scale detail, what has been created is a unique, "grown up" building for young people. The 300–340 seat Weston Theatre, has its stage level some seven metres above the foyer with the six metre-high Clore Theatre inserted beneath. The Weston's stalls are in amphitheatre form with two arced balconies above, one for audience and one as first technical level. The room can be deployed in either end stage or flat thrust form by inserting or removing seating in the shallow forestage pit.

This multi-award winning building has proved a great success with its young audience, actors, staff and critics alike.'

The main facilities include:
300-340 seat main theatre
(The Weston Theatre)
100/120 seat studio theatre
(The Clore Theatre)
Rehearsal Studio
Foyer/box office/café/shop/wcs
an Education Studio
Meeting Room/2nd Education Studio
Staff Offices and associated facilities
Green Room
Theatre Scene Dock

Programme
Design: Nov 2000 - Sept 2003
Construction: Oct 2003 - Nov 2005
Opening to Public: -1 Dec2005

Main Credits
Client: Unicorn Children's Centre
Architect: Keith Williams Architects
Theatre Consultants: Theatre Projects Consultants with CharcoalBlue
Acoustician: Arup Acoustics
Engineering: ARUP
Main Contractor: Mansell Construction Services
Photography: Helene Binet

Julian Middleton

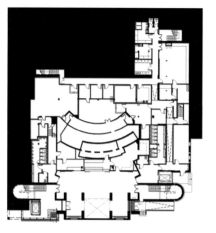

Northern Stage, Newcastle
*Project Duration: Design
Commencement: Autumn 2002
Work Start on Site: Autumn 2004
Formal opening: 27th August 2006*

Julian Middleton: 'The Epic and
Intricate Space. Over the last four
years, working in collaboration with
directors, designers and technical staff
from the Northern Stage company,
we have radically deconstructed and
reformed the former Newcastle
Playhouse to create the new Northern
Stage. The vision has been to create
a European centre for the performing
arts – a home for international theatre in
Newcastle. The project can be distilled
in its simplest terms as three stages, two
bars and one theatre. In real terms this
means a 500-seat main house (known
as Stage 1), a 200-seat studio (known
as Stage 2), and Stage 3, an informal
venue that is part foyer, part
performance space. The engine that
drives this theatre machine, however, is
the ability to interlink Stage 1 and
Stage 2 to create a cavernous empty
space - a factory-like industrial theatre
space. This opens up epic scenic and
directorial opportunities and possibilities
for varying audience/performer
relationships.'

Alexander Lowde

Tobias and the Angel
Jonathan Dove and David Lan

*Young Vic and English Touring Opera
St John's Church Waterloo
October 2004*

Alexander Lowde: 'With a cast of
permanent principals and local
community choruses, this production
toured to a range of churches and
cathedrals. Common to all the spaces
was a central aisle along which the
traverse was placed. Dwellings were
placed at either end of the traverse, with
images of trees, air and water projected
onto the buildings during the journey.'

*Director: John Fulljames
Set Designer: Alexander Lowde
Choreographer: Ben Wright*

View of studio (stage two)
View of main auditorium (stage one)
View of new public frontage
View of internal performance space
(stage three)

Theatre Company: Northern Stage
Erica Whyman
Caroline Routh
Edmund Nickols
Peter Green
Neil Murray

Architects: Arts Team
Julian Middleton
Jason Wilson
Oliver James
Barry Pritchard

Visual art installation "Escapology"
by Cath Campbell.
Photographer: Anthony Coleman

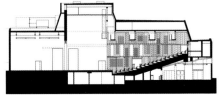

The Egg Children's and Young Persons' Theatre, Bath UK November 2001

*Bath Theatre Royal
2001-2005*

Anne Minors Performance Consultants: Image 1 'This model was made within a month of the start of the design process. The architect had made a model setting the elliptical balcony form into the existing building volume and establishing the relationship between stage and windows. A steep rake of stalls seats gave 90 seats, when the client required 130 to be financially viable. To increase the seat count and also to provide an economic method of changing from raked stalls to a flat floor for workshops, AMPC proposed a seating pit sunk into the floor. This model was made to demonstrate the seating pit, the disposition of the seats and the different configurations possible. A kit of parts of different seating configurations allowed the design team and client to choose a way forward – curved or straight rows, extended stage, flat floor, in the round and thrust configurations. At the top of the room, four options for the lighting bridges and catwalks were made to study the termination of the space and the way that the window wall elevation was framed by the catwalks.'

Anne Minors Performance Consultants: Image 2 'AMPC wanted to involve the children in the design of the seats for the Egg. We had searched the market for fun seats but none combined all facets of the design brief – to be plush, individual, fun and comfortable and to be easy to move and store. One dark November day, we brought ten samples of seats plus boxes of fabrics, paper, braids and glue to Bath and invited the children to first consider all the elements that could be varied on a seat – the back shape, the arms, the upholstery. They coloured in perspective views of the theatre and then embarked on improving the chair samples with padding fabric and designs. From the workshop we learnt the importance of making every seat different from its neighbour, well cushioned and with the comfort of a sofa. With architects Haworth Tompkins, we evolved a new seat for the stalls. Up in the gallery, a bench with divided, tipped up seats allows the audience to sit nearer to the balcony rail.'

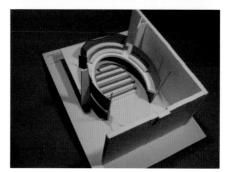

Anne Minors Performance Consultants: Image 3 'Response to the Collaborator's theme, to this moment in the process: To hand over the seats and staging to the theatre, the manufacturers of the staging and the seats explained their products to the theatre staff and proceeded to turn around the space from end stage, raked seating to flat floor and then to in-the-round. At the start of the project, AMPC had made time predictions for the changeovers using different types of mechanism and the theatre measured the time on site. Fortunately we completed the work within the predicted time.'

*Anne Minors Performance Consultants
Other creative collaborators:
Haworth Tompkins, architects
Buro Happold, structural and M&E engineers and quantity surveyors
Fleming & Barron, acousticians*

**Anne Minors Performance Consultants
Menuhin Hall**

*Yehudi Menuhin School,
Stoke d'Abernon, UK
2001-2005*

Anne Minors Performance Consultants: Image 1 'The sight of the steel structure was the first indication on site of the hall's height and scale and how the bulk of it would sit into the landscape. Much of the steel structure, clad in timber, is revealed to the audience within the hall and close collaboration was needed between theatre consultant, architect, acoustician and structural engineer to ensure that the structural mass was great enough to keep the sound of the nearby motorway out of the hall, yet the details within the hall were elegant enough to support the rigging to production and house lighting chandeliers. '

Anne Minors Performance Consultants: Image 2 'Prior to the public opening of any performance space there is normally some kind of acoustic concert when measurements are taken to confirm the space's acoustic performance. In the case of Menuhin Hall, Sound Space Design and AMPC decided to hold our own choral concert called Raising the Roof, during which some electronic sweeps of the sound spectrum would be run through the hall and the hall's properties recorded.'

collaborators

The acoustic tests confirmed what the performers could tell with their ears – that there was sufficient reverberation for the music to float in the air, giving the performers confidence to create sound effortlessly. The hall also allowed each performer to hear all the others, enabling the sound to blend and balance easily.'

Anne Minors Performance Consultants: Image 3 'Historically, music was often composed with particular performing spaces in mind, for example Montiverdi's *Vespers* for St Mark's in Venice, where the placement of the antiphonal choirs was inspired by the architecture.
Malcolm Singer, the director of music at the Menuhin School, composed and choreographed *Opening Rites*, welcoming the musical spirits into the new concert hall. The performers entered the hall and gradually built a field of sound immersing the audience on two levels, crescendoing to a climax before graduating downwards and leaving the space one by one.
Every child in the school was involved, led by the youngest. Stephen Goss composed a work for guitar quartet called *Frozen Music* inspired by five buildings which were important to him. The Menuhin Hall was the first movement where the music was as much about the silence of the space as the sound of the instruments.
All the students at the school compose and new works will be performed regularly in the future.'

Anne Minors Performance Consultants
Other creative collaborators:
Burrell Foley Fischer, architects
Michael Barclay, structural engineers
Michael Popper, M&E engineers
DL quantity, surveyors
Sound Space Design, acousticians

(Left)
Concert Hall choral
concert and acoustic test
1:50 model of Egg theatre showing seat
and balcony disposition
Seating design workshop
Egg Seat and stage turnaround

(Right)
Composition for new Concert Hall
Concert Hall Steel Structure

Pip Nash

My Home

The London Bubble Theatre Company
A verbatim theatre piece presented in
promenade in domestic settings
March 2006

Pip Nash: 'My Home, was performed
in houses across London, using texts
gathered from interviews with people
who were not born in Britain, talking
about their concept of "home".
We adapted each empty property to
create a promenade performance
space, designing some rooms to be the
same from venue to venue, whilst
allowing the ambience unique to each
house, to create a subtext to the
narrative. A recorded soundscape was
used to suggest another story; of unseen
inhabitants of the house or of fractured
memories. Each room, inhabited by a
different actor, was designed to invite
the audience into an environment that
showed aspects of the character within.
Here, the real stories were told, taking
the audiences into worlds suggested by
images evoked by the texts.'

Director: Karen Tomlin
Set and Costume Designer: Pip Nash
Dramaturg; Sara Clifford
Photographer: Steve Hickey

nissenadams

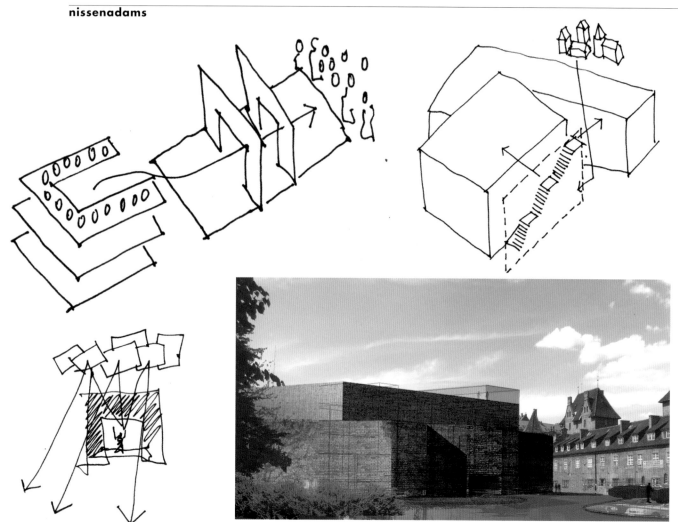

Gdansk Theatre, Poland

nissenadams: 'The theatre embraces the traditional building methods of the old town, whilst providing new and exciting interior and public areas. We have used theatrical techniques throughout the spaces, including a play of materials through light and photographic images. The foyer, for example, casts shadows of people using the spaces, both literally and through artificial means.
Our main strategic move involved redirecting the traffic to form a new public space outside the wall of the theatre area. Part of the theatre wall is removable, providing a theatre in the round close to the Elisabethan theatre. The theatre space is also totally flexible to allow different configurations, including an artificial sky for fencing, to mimic the conditions of traditional jousting at dawn.'

For this project we collaborated with Lighting Designer: Zerlina Hughes Acoustic Consultants: Arup Acoustics Quantity Surveyors: Measur

Dody Nash

'Berio Lounge', part of the festival 'Omaggio: A Celebration of Luciano Berio'
Luciano Berio, 'Coro' (1976)
Curated by South Bank Centre and Dody Nash

SBC and London Sinfonietta
Ballroom Foyer, Royal Festival Hall
April 2004

Dody Nash: 'I approached Maresa Von Stockert to create a dance work in a series of collaborations inspired by the ethos of the composer's work and culture. I felt she could provide a moment of sharp red, to counterpoint the futuristic white and cyan calm of the space, and suggested she explore the architectural openness of the Lounge Circle. Her imagination was also captured by another, more unusual object, the

Ben Pacey

I Am Waiting For The Opportunity To Save Someone's Life

The Other Way Works (2006)
Site specific - an empty shop unit in Birmingham's Mailbox Centre
March 2006

Ben Pacey: 'Ten people collaborated on this site-specific performance. Working together in a vacant unit within a shopping centre, we transformed it from an empty space into a rich, performative environment. Lighting, sound, video and scenography were as crucial as the performers in creating both the atmosphere and the narrative of the production. Upon arrival, the audience were welcomed into a designed waiting area, which established the tone of the experience. Lit with green fluorescent tubes, the space was calming, yet clinical. Light seeped out from this waiting room, through frosted glass, helping to draw curious passers-by into the performance.'

Initial welcoming waiting space, with performer as receptionist

Directors: Katie Day and Jane Packman
Scenographers: Alexandra Boussoulega and Rania Yfantidou
Lighting Designer: Ben Pacey
Sound Designer: Mark Day
Dramaturg: Elyssa Livergant
Video Artist: Chris Keenan
Performers: Sarah Coyle and Louise Platt
Photographer: Chris Keenan

Erik Rehl

Jarman Garden
Devised by the Company (2004)

Flaming Theatre Company
Riverside Studios, Studio 3
February 2004

Erik Rehl: 'The trip we took down to Prospect Cottage in Dungeness stirred our imaginations to better understand Derek Jarman's life and work. Smelling the sea and hearing the shingle beneath our feet were powerful impressions that stuck with us through the four-month, collaborative research period and five weeks of intensive devising rehearsals. The emptiness of the landscape, juxtaposed with the life in the garden became our metaphor of transformation. We wanted the space to be in the round and to incorporate elements of his garden, so we decided on a boardwalk

Listening Shell. Maresa created powerful, intelligent movement which amplified existing relationships between space, music and listening. It also pushed the dancer's physical technique against unusual parameters, extending upwards, backwards, rolling against the padded leather of the circle, rotating, enveloped, absorbed in the spherical intimacy of the Corian shell.'

Listening Shell and Lounge Circle

Director: Maresa von Stockert
for Tilted Productions
Installation Design: Dody Nash
Co-designer of the Listening Shell:
Julian Brown
Lighting Designer: Charles Balfour
Choreography: Maresa von Stockert
Dancer: Roberta Pitre
Photographer: Dee Conway

Slender
Mapping4D (2006)

Mapping4D
BAC, London
January 2006

Ben Pacey: 'Mapping4D created *Slender* through a year-long process of devising and collaboration, between the directors, performers and designers. Exploring the relationships between food, body and soul, *Slender* opens in a "real" suburban kitchen, complete with hot stove, busy mother, and flat, unflattering lighting. This domestic reality quickly distorts as a much-loved son seeks transcendence through starvation. The lighting design heightens this disintegration, becoming increasingly sculptural and unreal as the performance spills through the "fourth wall". Unexpectedly the audience find themselves involved and implicated in the unfolding events'

An ambiguous moment, just before the feast is served.

Directors: Wendy Hubbard
and Sarah Levinsky
Set Designer: Mamoru Iriguchi
Lighting Designer: Ben Pacey
Sound Designer: Lewis Gibson
Performers: Rachel Donovan, Hilda Eusébio, Claire Little, Tom Lyle
Photographer: Melanie Alfonso

style stage with panels that could be removed to reveal the shingle underneath.'

Collage of moments from Jarman Garden

Directors: Ben Gove with Associate Director Cass Fleming
Scenographer: Erik Rehl
Lighting Designer: Mark Jonathan
Sound Designer: Adrienne Quartly
Projection: Josh Appignanesi with Scenografika

Roma Patel

The Tempest
William Shakespeare adapted by Jocelyn Clarke (2006)

*Corcadorca Theatre Company, Cork
On the Pond at Fitzgerald's Park, Cork, Ireland
June 2006*

Roma Patel: 'Pat, Jocelyn and I met on a rainy November morning in 2005 in Cork City to find a place to set *The Tempest*. By the end of that day, wet and exhausted we, decided on the pond in beautiful Fitzgerald's Park.
The adaptation was set in late Victorian times, to blend with the aesthetics of the site. The visual component of each act was influenced by one of the five elements: earth, wind, water, fire and air. The set consisted of tall, vertical structures, platforms (islands) and walkways. Installing these was no easy feat; we had to negotiate with families of ducks, eels, plant life and the tides of the River Lee.'

*Director: Pat Kiernan
Set Designer: Roma Patel
Costume Designer: Joan Hickson
Lighting Designer: Paul Denby
Sound Design: Secret Garden Studio
Composer: Linda Buckley,
Production Manger: Joe Stockdale
Photographer: Eoin O'Riordan*

Roma Patel

The Merchant of Venice
William Shakespeare adapted by
Jocelyn Clarke (2005)

Corcadorca Theatre Company, Cork
Old Irish Distillery, City Courthouse and
Liberty Street, Cork City, Ireland
June 2005

Roma Patel: 'This site-specific
promenade performance took the
audience on a journey through disused
buildings and city spaces. Most of the
creative team meetings took place at
these sites. We spent hours, text in hand,
working out the journeys of the actors
and audience. The set design responded
to various histories of the sites and the
architecture of Cork City. Some spaces
were left as we found them, in others we
intervened with set pieces and video
projections. At points in time it seemed
as if the city and the production
merged.'

Director: Pat Kiernan
Set Designer: Roma Patel
Costume Designer: Joan Hickson
Lighting Designer: Paul Denby
Sound Design: Secret Garden Studio
Composers: Mel Mercier
and Linda Buckley
Video Production: Mick Hurley
Scenic Artist: John Adams

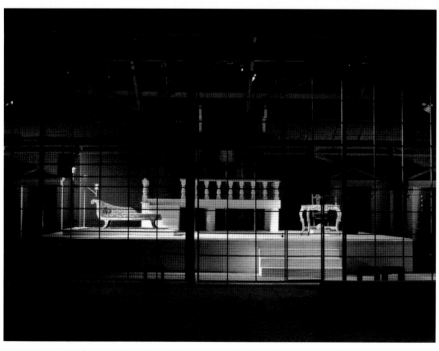

collaborators

Operaen

*Client: AP Møller and Chastine
Mc-Kinney Møller Foundation
Copenhagen, Denmark
2005*

Theatreplan: 'The complexity of a
modern opera house requires serious
collaboration between all of those
involved in its design.
Theatreplan consultants are team players
and contributed fully on all aspects of the
project. We worked in close liaison with
the architects on the space planning and
auditorium design and with the users
and building engineers on all details of
the theatre technical installations.
The success of this collaboration is
reflected by the completion, on time and
on budget, of the Copenhagen Opera
House, a project of the highest quality
and of which the users are justifiably
proud. This realised the expectations of
the funder that the building and its
installations should be second to none.'

*The Auditorium
The Stage*

*Theatre Consultants: Theatreplan LLP
Project Director: Bo Wildfang
Architects: Henning Larsens Tegnestue
Acoustician: Arup Acoustics
Engineers: Rambøll
Main Contractor: E Pihl & Søn
Photographers:
Adam Moerk (The auditorium)
Lars Schmidt (The stage)*

Peter Ruthven Hall

Der Stein der Weisen oder Die Zauberinsel
The Philosophers' Stone or The Enchanted Island
Music: Wolfgang Amadeus Mozart,
Johann Baptist Henneberg,
Benedikt Schack, Franz Xavier Gerl and
Emanuel Schikaneder
Libretto: Emanuel Schikaneder (1790)
Performance Edition edited
by David Buch
With adaptations for this production
by Steuart Bedford and John Cox

Garsington Opera
Garsington Manor, Oxford
27 June 2006

Peter Ruthven Hall: 'Working out of doors means collaborating with Nature. The weather may be unpredictable but often provides welcome surprises: gentle breezes on balmy evenings, glorious sunsets or wild storms. Indoors we might allude to these with lighting effects; outside we must accept the conditions of each performance.
This fantasy opera would have utilised every device in an 18th-century theatre to create its magic: a Genius descends in a cloud chariot; the demon sorcerer appears from the underworld; the chorus drowns in rough seas; and a magic sword is forged.
Out of doors, with little ability even to focus the action with stage lighting, Nature added warmth, wind, rain and sun to our otherwise best endeavours.'

Director: John Cox
Set and Costume Designer:
Peter Ruthven Hall
Lighting Designer: Malcolm Rippeth
Conductor: Steuart Bedford
Choreographer: Scott Ambler
Photographer: Johan Persson

John Risebero

Richard III
William Shakespeare (1592)

Antic Disposition
St Stephen's, Hampstead, London
May 2006

John Risebero: 'The spectacular interior of St Stephen's, built in 1869 but abandoned and left to decay for the past 30 years, provided the perfect setting for Shakespeare's macabre history. Performed in traverse, our darkly comic production used the entire length of the building as a stage – the scarred architecture becoming ravaged England at the end of the Wars of the Roses. As the play begins, a 'red carpet' of light highlights the flag-draped coffin of the defeated King Henry VI, the opulent

collaborators

royal thrones and, in the shadows
beyond, a tableau of characters waiting
to enter the story'

*Directors: Ben Horslen
and John Risebero
Set and Costume Designer:
John Risebero
Lighting Designer: Howard Hudson
Music: James Burrows*

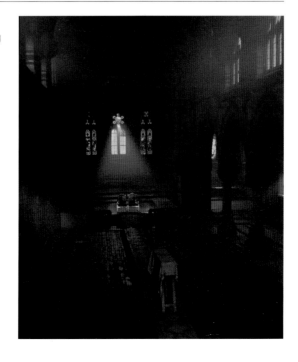

Rachel Scanlon

Little Big World

The Herbert Gallery, Coventry
July 2005

Rachel Scanlon: 'A world of giant story books. A world of familiar places to play in and strange new ones to explore. A world where young minds can create stories, invent new games and revel in their creativity. *Little Big World* was designed with children as the focus. My aim was to stimulate young people's minds and encourage both imagination and play for young and old alike. I created three giant books based on a fairy tale, allowing the children to interact with the installation.'

Set Designer: Rachel Scanlon

Theatre Projects Consultants

The Sage Gateshead

1997
A design competition for a concert hall for Northern Sinfonia, a base for Folkworks, Britain's brightest force in folk music and much more, a music school for the region with 30 plus studios…

2004
The Sage Gateshead opens with a single management, directing the building and the performers, resident and visiting, presenting performances across the spectrum of music for all the citizens of the Newcastle/Gateshead region.

In between
'A deeply collaborative experience involving all aspects of the client, both Council and artists, and a design team headed by Foster and Partners, Arup Acoustics, who led on the 1,700 seat Hall One, and Theatre Projects Consultants, who led on the smaller Hall Two with its 5/10 sided geometry. Ever present were the limitations of money, despite this being the last of the major National Lottery projects: all parties distilling their ideas to capture the essence of the brief – no space wasted, no ostentatious finishes.'

collaborators

Vivienne Schadinsky

Invalid
Theresa Shiban (November 2002)

Angelus Arts
St Bartholomew's Hospital, London
November 2002

Vivienne Schadinsky: '*Invalid* is about the perception of a terminal illness and its treatment from the points of view of the patient, the family and the staff. The venue was unusual - a disused ward at Barts Hospital. We relied on the staff to tell us how the hospital, the ward and the equipment worked. Our props were real hospital furniture and medical equipment. It was shocking to find that one patient during a hypothetical stay of a week, in a general ward, might comes across 58 different staff and take 28 different types of medicine every 12 hours.'

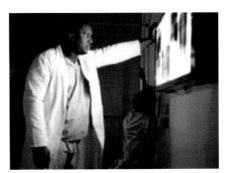

Director: Theresa Shiban
Set and Costume Designer:
Vivienne Schadinsky
Lighting Designer: Stephan Hammes
and Vivienne Schadinsky
Sound Designer and Composer :
Amy Finegan
Choreographer: Theresa Shiban
Other creative collaborators:
Stephan Hammes and Susanne Dietz
Photographer: Jayne West

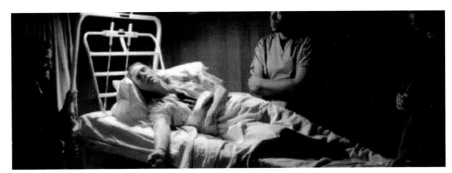

The Result
'A building envelope of soaring beauty under which artists and audiences flourish. The *Guardian* wrote of violinists in Hall Two: "Tonight they were in the centre. There's a visceral intensity to being so close to the performer that you can almost feel their breath. You start to feel bound up in the drama."

Project Team
Architect: Foster and Partners
Acoustics: Arup Acoustics
Theatre Consultant:
Theatre Projects Consultants
Structure/services: Mott Macdonald
Specialist engineer: Buro Happold
Quantity surveyor: Davis Langdon
Lighting: Equation Lighting Design

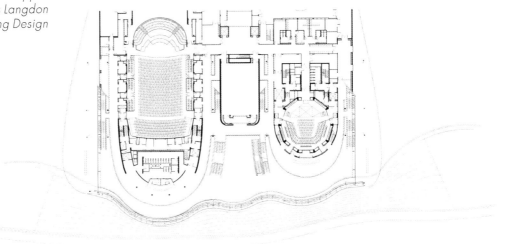

Naomi Wilkinson

Don't Look Back
Dreamthinkspeak (2003)

*Dreamthinkspeak
Stanmer House, Brighton
2003*

Naomi Wilkinson: 'Based on the myth of *Orpheus and Eurydice*, *Don't Look Back* was set in Stanmer House, a derelict Georgian manor, itself left in a decaying limbo, which became a visual metaphor for Orpheus' psyche unable to exist in the present and yearning for his lost Eurydice.
The audience were left to wander these desolate spaces as though in the footsteps of Orpheus, haunted by images of the dead Eurydice, catching glimpses of a life that might have been, in a relentless collision of past, present and future, as if running after something that repeatedly evades, or slips through our fingers as we seem to have it in our grasp.'

*Director: Tristan Sharps
Set Designer: Naomi Wilkinson
Sound Composer: Max Richter*

Happy yet?
Linda McLean (2004)

*Gate Theatre London
2006*

Naomi Wilkinson: '*Happy yet?*, written by Linda McLean, merged and updated four Feydeau farces, all of which thrive on sexual politics and embarrassment. The set is purposefully a cool white space to contrast the heat of domestic fury. The blinds replace the traditional doors required for farce which a character could hide behind, thereby leaving the scene. The ladder was used as a cooling off point, again creating a place for a character to be "absent".'

*Director: Edward Woodall
Set and Costume Designer:
Naomi Wilkinson
Lighting Designer: Charles Balfour*

collaborators

BIOGRAPHIES

INDEXES

Designers /Collaborators
Theatre Architects
Photographers

Productions

Companies

Venues

Keith Allen
Keith Allen stumbled into theatre, post industry and a literature degree at the university of Sussex. He then worked for a number of years touring, in the UK and internationally, as stage, company, and production manager. Following this he worked in administration and project management and organised the odd, small festival. Keith helped to establish an arts centre in Lewisburg, West Virginia, (Carnegie Hall), worked for several years in puppetry, mask, mime and related arts, and for the last 15 years has worked as a consultant, researcher in the fields of arts and culture for local authorities, universities, regional, national and international organisations. He has edited a number of publications, for a similarly wide group, this includes (with Phyllida Shaw) the last three SBTD catalogues.

Becs Andrews
Becs Andrews has a BA in Theatre Design from Wimbledon School of Art and a BFA in Fine Art from the Ruskin School of Drawing and Fine Art.
She was the overall winner of the Linbury Prize for Stage Design in 2003. She has designed costumes and sets for opera, dance, theatre and musical theatre and has also initiated devised work. Her credits include: *La Serva Padrona* (Royal Opera House, Linbury Studio); *The Magic Flute* (New Theatre, Oxford); *Nabucco* (Riverside Opera); *Jeff Koons* (Actors Touring Company, Linbury Prize Commission); *Hamlet* (Al Bustan International Music Festival, Beirut); *Orestes 2.0* (Guildhall School of Music and Drama); *Twelfth Night* (English Touring Theatre); *Perpetua* (Latchmere Theatre); *Our Kind of Fun* (Live Theatre, Newcastle); *Set and Reset* (EDge Dance Company tour); *West Side Story* (Oxford Playhouse); and *What Became of the Witch?* (Theatre and Beyond tour). She designed and lit *Twos* (St Pancras Church Crypt); co-devised *Lounge* (London Contemporary Dance School); and designed and directed *Aperture* (Battersea Arts Centre). Becs has exhibited her installations,films, and photographs in galleries and site-specific spaces. She teaches performance design at Edge Hill University and devised drama in schools.

Richard Andrzejewski
Richard Andrzejewski graduated in Theatre Design for Performance from Central St Martins College of Art and Design in 2001. His design credits include: set and costume for *Ubu Roi*, *Rusalka*, *Baby withThe Bathwater* and, with the Stonecrabs theatre company, with whom he has collaborated on devised projects, *Josephine The Singer* and *Drama Waltz #6*, through which the design elements explored, and grew out of, the rehearsal process with the performers and director.
As co-designer he has worked on: *Auction of Promises*, *The Promise* and *Roccoco-A-Gogo* with the band *The Irrepressibles*. He has also collaborated with a photographer, making realistic masks for a photo shoot and exhibition installation for the Polish Photographic Collective, Galeria Bezdomna, in London.

Liz Ascroft
Liz Ascroft trained at Wimbledon School of Art, where she was awarded the Arts Council Trainee Design Bursary and graduated with a BA Hons. She was also awarded a Unesco prize for the promotion of the visual arts Prague Quadrennial and the TMA Best Designer Award. Liz has worked extensively in the UK. Her credits include: *After You* and *Unwrapping the Ghost Train* (Theatre of Fact, Milton Keynes); *Holding the Reins* (Women's Theatre Group); *The Grapes of Wrath* (RADA); *Hard Times* (Wolsey Theatre, Ipswich); *Zola's Earth* (Cheltenham Everyman and Edinburgh fringe); *Waiting for Godot*, *Metamorphosis* and *Blood Wedding* (Solent People's Theatre); *On Golden Pond*, *Golden Leaf Strutt*, *Sad Arthur's Trip*, *Agnes of God* (Belgrade Theatre Coventry); *Macbeth*, *The Woman in Black*, *The Fosdyke Saga* and *Lie of the Land* (Plymouth Theatre Royal and Orchard Theatre Company); *Trojan Women*, *'Tis Pity She's a Whore*, *Love at a Loss*, *Wild Wild Women*, *As You Like It*, *The Nativity* and *Gargling with Jelly* (Liverpool Everyman); *Alice's Adventures in Wonderland*, *A Midsummer Night's Dream*, *The Importance of Being Earnest*, *The Three Musketeers*, *The Snow Queen*, *Kipling's Jungle Book Stories*, *The Comedy of Errors*, *Death and the Maiden*, *The Winter's Tale* (costumes), *Robin Hood*, *Beauty and the Beast* and *Neville's Island* (Dukes Theatre, Lancaster); *Gargling with Jelly*, *Teechers*, *Bouncers*, *Happy Jack*, *Oliver!* and *Playing Away* (Hull Truck); *Hedda Gabler*, *As You Like It*, *Fast Food*, *Snapshots*, *Ghost Train Tattoo*, *So Special*, *Cold Meat Party*, *The Seagull*, *Little Voice*, *On the Shore of the Wide World*, which transferred to the Cottesloe Theatre at the National Theatre and *Mary Barton* (Royal Exchange, Manchester); *Katherine Howard* (Chichester Festival Theatre); *Cavalcaders* (Tricycle Theatre); *The Bear*, *Dublin Carol*, *A Kind of Alaska*, *and Pygmalion* (Gate Theatre, Dublin); *One for the Road* (St Martin's Theatre, London and Lincoln Centre, New York), *Afterplay* (Charleston, South Carolina and the Gielgud Theatre, London); *See You Next Tuesday* (Albery Theatre); *Vincent River*, *Apocalyptica*, *Give Me Your Answer Do*, *Yellowman*, *Anna and the Tropics*, *Losing Louis* and *Rubenstein's Kiss* (Hampstead Theatre); *Peggy for You* (Comedy Theatre, London and tour); *The Two Gentlemen of Verona* (Swan Theatre and tour); *Honour* (Wyndham's Theatre, London); and *Lucia di Lammermoor* (Scottish Opera).

Elroy Ashmore
Elroy Ashmore trained on the Motley Design Course. After assisting various eminent designers in opera, ballet and drama he became Head of Design at the Belgrade Theatre, the Byre Theatre, St Andrews, the Haymarket Theatre, Basingstoke and the Pitlochry Festival Theatre. He now works as a freelance designer, working in the UK and abroad and has over 250 productions to his credit. Elroy enjoys designing for theatre with music and has worked on many ballets including: *Namouna* (Asami Maki Ballet, Tokyo); *The Natives of Dreamland* (Louisville Ballet, Kentucky); *Little Red Riding Hood* (Sadler's Wells); and *Melodrame* (Royal New Zealand Ballet and NAPAC, South Africa). Musicals have included: *Little Shop of Horrors*, *Aspects of Love*, *Cabaret*, *The Boyfriend*, *Little Tramp*, *Rockin' Mikado*, *They're Playing our Song*, *Gypsy* and *Rock's Progress*. Operas include: *Stiffelio*, *The Bear*, *Cosi fan Tutte*, *The Marriage of Figaro*, *The Barber of Seville*, *La Bohème*, and *I Pagliacci*.
Over the past four years his designs have included: *Tartuffe*, *The Three Musketeers*, *Hay Fever*, *The Canterville Ghost* and *The Beauty Queen of Leenane* (Haymarket Theatre, Basingstoke); *The Elixir of love*, *Eugene Onegin*, *Die Fledermaus* and *Wiener Blut* (Clonter Opera) and *Rusalka* (Iford Arts). Recent credits include: *The Wind in the Willows*, *and the premieres of 3 - 1 - 6* and *Blue on Blue* (Haymarket Theatre, Basingstoke); *Clockwork Orange* (Solent Peoples Theatre); *Private Lives* (Theatre Royal Windsor); *Il Mondo della Luna* (Opera della Luna); *Lucia di Lammermoor* (Iford Arts); and *La Traviata* (Clonter Opera).

Mark Bailey
Mark Bailey has designed over 100 productions of theatre, opera and ballet in Britain, mainland Europe and North America. His work includes designs for the National Theatre, English National Ballet, Opera North and the Gate Theatre, Dublin as well as for many British regional theatres, including Plymouth Theatre Royal, Bristol Old Vic, West Yorkshire Playhouse, Birmingham Rep, Nottingham Playhouse and Clwyd Theatr Cymru, where he is an associate artist. Design credits at Clwyd include: *Equus*, *King Lear*, *Private Lives*, *Present Laughter*, *Hay Fever*, *Blithe Spirit*, *Waiting for Godot*, *One Flew Over the Cuckoo's Nest* and *The Alexander Cordell Trilogy*. His many West End credits include: *The Importance of Being Earnest* (also Toronto); *The Winslow Boy*, *Present Laughter*, *Iolanthe*, *The Gondoliers*, *Rat Pack Confidential*, *Which Witch* (costumes) and *Mack and Mabel*. Other work in music and dance includes: *Melody on the Move* (English National Ballet); *Fiddler on the Roof*, which won the TMA/Barclays award for Best Musical Production 2002; *The Gondoliers*, which won the same award in 2001; *Cabaret* and *Irma La Douce*, both also nominated for TMA awards (all Watermill, Newbury); and operas for Opera de Lausanne and Maggio Musicale Florence, Buxton Festival, ROH Linbury Studio and Almeida Opera.
Mark's designs on tour include: *Hadrian VII*, *Peace In Our Time*, *Entertaining Mr Sloane*, *A Judgement in Stone* and *The Rivals*. For television, Mark designed *Broken Lives* (BBC).

Martyn Bainbridge
Martyn Bainbridge is an associate designer for Clwyd Theatr Cymru.
His most recent theatre designs include: *Brief Encounter* (West End); *The Crucible*, *Under Milk Wood*, *The Norman Conquests*, *Table Manners*, *Living Together*, *Round and Round the Garden*, *Gaslight*, *Night Must Fall*, *The Birthday Party* (Clwyd Theatr Cymru). Other theatre designs include: *A Little Night Music*, *The Birthday Party*, *Kes*, *My Cousin Rachel*, *Outside Edge*, *Pump Boys and Dinettes*, *Absurd Person Singular*, *Charley's Aunt*, *The Shadow of a Gunman*, *I Have Been Here Before* and the national tour of *Master Forger* (all for Theatre Royal Plymouth); *Measure for Measure* (Nye Teater, Oslo); *Deathtrap* (Northcott Theatre, Exeter); *Outside Edge* (Churchill Theatre, Bromley); *The Soldier's Tale* (Oxford Playhouse); *On The Razzle* (Leeds Playhouse); *Intimate Exchanges* (Northcott Theatre, Exeter); *Brief Encounter* (Bill Kenwright tour); *An Inspector Calls* and *Memory* (Theatr Clwyd). Opera designs include: *Béatrice et Bénédict* (Indianapolis Opera); *Ariadne auf Naxos* (Garsington Opera); *The Trial* (Bloomsbury Theatre); *Die Zauberflöte* (Kent Opera); *Madama Butterfly* (Phoenix Opera); *Norma* and *La Traviata* (Opera Northern Ireland); *La Rondine* (Royal Academy of Music) *Le nozze di Figaro* (Guildhall). Ballet designs include: *Daphnis and Chlée* (The Royal Ballet, Covent Garden). Exhibition designs include: *The Astronomers* (London Planetarium); *Armada 1588-1988* (National Maritime Museum, Greenwich); *Lawrence of Arabia* (National Portrait Gallery London); and *Daendels* (Rijksmuseum Amersterdam). He also designed a major permanent exhibition, *Madame Tussaud's Scenerama*, in Amsterdam and a new *Chamber of Horrors* for Madame Tussaud's in London; *Peter the Great* (Queen's House Greenwich); *EMI Centenary Exhibition* in London and *The Explorers Gallery* (National Maritime Museum, Greenwich).

Keith Baker
Keith Baker read drama at Royal Holloway, University of London and theatre design at Nottingham Trent University. From 1999 to 2001 he was Resident Designer at Oldham Coliseum, where he received two *Manchester Evening News Award* Nominations. Designs for Oldham include: *Abigail's Party*, *The Mysterious Mr. Love*, *Misery*, *The Canterbury Tales*, *The Houses in Between* and One for the Road. Other work includes: *James and the Giant Peach*, *Sweetpeter*, *Kadouma's Island*, *Little Angels*, *Just So…*, *Boy*, *Stargazer*, *The Silver Sword* and *The Snow Lion* (Polka Theatre, London); *Into the Woods* (RADA); *River's Up*, *A Christmas Carol*, *To Be a Farmer's Boy*, *More Talking Heads*, *Who's Afraid of Virginia Woolf!*, *Macbeth*, *Night Must Fall*, *Educating Rita*, (Swan Theatre, Worcester); *Postcards from Maupassant* (Old Red Lion, London); *Entertaining Mr. Sloane*, *Cinderella*, *Educating Rita* and *The Rise and Fall of Little Voice* (Courtyard Theatre, Hereford); *Fantastic Mr. Fox* (Belgrade, Coventry); *September in the Rain*, *Intimate Exchanges* and *Hansel and Gretel* (Theatre Royal, Bury St. Edmunds and tour); *Under Milk Wood* (OTTC); *Born to Run* and *In the Bleak Midwinter* (Farnham Maltings and tour); *Cremenville* (Sharpwire); *Peter Pan* (Proteus); *The Owl who was Afraid of the Dark* (Pied Piper); and *Two Sisters* (Two Friends Productions). Film credits: *Heart Thief*, commissioned by Channel 4 as part of the *4 Dance season*.

Simon Banham
Simon Banham has been a freelance designer for 25 years. He has also been Head of Design at the Contact Theatre, Manchester and has had a 25-year relationship with the contemporary chamber opera company, Music Theatre Wales. He is a founder member of Quarantine performance research company (www.qtine.com) and has been responsible for developing the scenography for all the productions in its current portfolio. Quarantine was recently awarded the *Art 05* award for outstanding achievements in the arts.
Recent projects include: *Ion* (Opéra National du Rhin, Strasbourg); *Don Giovanni* (Opera Vest, Bergen); *Rantsoen* (Victoria Theatre Company and Quarantine, Gent); the premiere of Nigel Osborne's new opera *The Piano Tuner* for Music Theatre Wales, (Linbury Studio, Royal Opera House). *Ion* and *Rantsoen* were chosen for presentation at the inaugural *World Stage Design 2005* exhibition in Toronto.
Other designs for Quarantine include: *White Trash* (Manchester); *Butterfly* (Tramway, Glasgow) *Grace* and, most recently, *Susan and Darren* (both at Contact Theatre, Manchester). He is currently designing *Rebekka* for Den Norske Opera - which will receive its world premiere in Oslo in 2007. Since September 1998, Simon has taught in the Department of Theatre, Film and Television at the University of Wales, Aberystwyth. Here he has been instrumental in establishing a new joint honours programme in Scenographic Studies, his contribution to which is fed and informed by his continuing freelance design work.

collaborators

Donatella Barbieri

Donatella Barbieri trained at Central Saint Martin's School of Art and Design. Costume designs for the National Theatre of Ireland include: *Making History* by Brian Friel and *The Hunt* by Ken Burke. Set and costume designs include: *Cuttin' a Rug* (Lyric Theatre, Hammersmith); *Glengarry Glen Ross* (Redgrave Theatre, Farnham); *Going On* and *Sleeping Beauty* (Latchmere Theatre, London - nominated for the *Evening Standard Award* for best set design); *The Voice of the Sea* (Lilian Bayliss Theatre); *The Task* (The Gate Theatre); *Blithe Spirit* (The Embassy Studio); *La Ronde* (Simmons Theatre); and *Silver Thread Anansi* (MAC, Birmingham). Costume designs for opera include: *Rigoletto, Queen of Spades, Luisa Miller* and *Le nozze di Figaro* (Opera Holland Park); *Don Giovanni, Tales of Hoffman, Così fan tutte, Rigoletto* (Stowe Opera); and *Haydn's La Vera Costanza* for the Royal College of Music. She currently teaches costume design at London College of Fashion, where she has established the new MA in Costume Design for Performance. She is an active academic researcher, has curated two exhibitions, co-organised an international symposium on theatre design and co-produced collaborative international projects, including one at DAMU in Prague. She is organising all costume-related events for *Scenofest* at the Prague Quadrennial 2007.

Paul Barrett

Paul Barrett graduated from UCE Birmingham, in 1997 with a BA (Hons) Theatre Design and in 1999 with an MA Scenography. He was awarded a design bursary by the Royal Exchange Theatre in Manchester, where his design experience included: *As You Like It, The English American* and *Bring Me Sunshine*. His freelance credits as a theatre designer include: *Pigtales for Inamorata* and *The Wild Party for The Mousepeople*. Designs the outdoor touring theatre company, Heartbreak Productions, include: *A Midsummer Night's Dream, Macbeth, Hamlet, Much Ado About Nothing* and *Romeo and Juliet*. He is the Course Director of the BA Hons Theatre, Performance and Event Design course at Birmingham Institute of Art and Design.

Dick Bird

Dick Bird began designing in 1998 with Primitive Science. Theatre credits include: *Harvest* and *Flesh Wound* (Royal Court); *Little Match Girl* (The Tiger Lillies tour); *Chimps* (Liverpool Everyman and Playhouse) *Dirty Wonderland* (Brighton Festival, for Frantic Assembly); *Lear* (Sheffield Crucible); *Tejas Verdes, Marathon* and *Une Tempete* (Gate Theatre); *The Night Season, A Prayer for Owen Meany* and *The Walls* (National Theatre); *Defence of the Realm* (Peacock Theatre, Dublin); *The Wind in the Willows* and *The Lady in the Van* (West Yorkshire Playhouse); *True West* and *Great Expectations* (Bristol Old Vic); *Rabbit, Peepshow* and *Heavenly* (all Frantic Assembly tours); *Those Eyes That Mouth* (Grid Iron, site-specific performance, Edinburgh Festival); *Monkey!, The Three Musketeers* and *Poseidon* (Young Vic); *The Invisible College* (Salzberg Festival); *Light* (Theatre de Complicité tour and Almeida Theatre); *Closer* (Teatro Broadway, Buenos Aires); *Icarus Falling, Poseidon, The Invisible College, Half Machine*, and *Vagabondage* (Primitive Science) and *The Banquet* (Protein Dance, UK tour). Opera credits include: *Un Segreto d'Importanza* (Teatro Communale di Bologna); *The Gondoliers* (Oper Am Rhein); *The Gambler* (Opera Zuid, Maastricht); *La Bohème* (English Touring Opera); *Die Kunst des Hungerns* (Schauspielhaus, Graz); *La Cenerentola* (Opera Theatre Company, Dublin); *Thwaite* (Almeida Opera); *Messalina* (Battignano Opera Festival); *Il Tabarro* and *Vollo di Notte* (Long Beach Opera Company); *Little Green Swallow* and *The Rape of Lucretia* (Guildhall School of Music and Drama); and *La Bohème* (LVSO, Vilnius). He recently designed *The Canterville Ghost* for English National Ballet.

Janet Bird

Janet Bird has a BA Hons Theatre Design from Nottingham Trent University (1996). She designed for Nottinghamshire companies until moving to London to study for her MA Scenography at Wimbledon School of Art (2000). She is now based in London where she works from her studio in Elephant and Castle. Most recently she has designed *The Comedy of Errors* (Shakespeare's Globe); *The Rocky Horror Show* for Ambassadors Theatre Group (West End and tour); and *Arms and the Man* (Salisbury Playhouse and tour). More examples of her work can be found at www.janetbird.com.

Madeleine Boyd

Madeleine Boyd trained at Central St Martins College of Art and Design and graduated in 2001. Madeleine's design work includes: *Rhymes, Reasons and Bombass Beatz* at the Oval theatre, London; *The Business of Murder*, Theatre Royal, Bury St Edmunds; Dvorak's opera *Vanda* for UCOpera at Bloomsbury Theatre, London and *True Stories* (Drill Hall Theatre, London). She was Co-designer for the *Philip Lawrence Awards* 2000 and Associate Set Designer for *La Cenerentola* (Opera Ireland, Dublin).

John Brooking

John Brooking trained at Wimbledon School of Art (1977), and has worked throughout the UK as a set and costume designer. As costume prop maker he worked on *Les Miserables* and *The Wizard of Oz*, for the RSC and for three years was Head of Design at the Central School of Speech and Drama. As a costume maker he has produced hats for Dame Edna Everage and Cilla Black. He also worked at Alton Towers for nine years as a costume and set designer, creating a parade, magic shows and various ice shows including *Peter Rabbit on Ice*. He has a studio in Staffordshire, where he continues to design for various clients as well as making costumes, props, hats and 'anything weird for anyone who asks!' John has designed and made extensively for pantomime. *A Midsummer Night's Dream* was his fourth production for Stafford Festival Shakespeare (Stafford Castle). He previously worked on the set for *Macbeth*, and set and costumes for *The Comedy of Errors* and *Romeo and Juliet*. He recently worked on the *Lichfield Mysteries*, a cycle of 24 medieval plays performed by 500 people on three stages in the centre of Lichfield.

Lez Brotherston

Lez Brotherston trained at the Central School of Art and Design and is an artistic associate of Matthew Bourne's company, New Adventures. Productions together include: *Swan Lake* (Tony Award for Best Costumes, Drama Desk Awards for Best Set and Best Costumes, Critics' Circle Award for Best Costumes); *Cinderella* (for which his designs won the *Olivier Award* for Outstanding Achievement in Dance); *Edward Scissorhands, Highland Fling, The Car Man* and *Play Without Words*. He had a ten-year partnership with Christopher Gable, at Northern Ballet Theatre, for which his designs included: *Dracula, Romeo and Juliet, Christmas Carol, Carmen, Hunchback of Notre Dame, Giselle* and *Swan Lake*. In 1999 he won the *TMA Award* for Outstanding Achievement in Dance.
He has designed ballet, opera, musicals and plays for many companies including: the RSC, the Royal Exchange Theatre Manchester, Royal National Theatre, Royal Ballet, ROH 2, Glyndebourne, Opera North, Almeida Theatre, Donmar Warehouse, the Royal Court and various theatres in London's West End, earning him six *Olivier* nominations. Has also designed live shows for French and Saunders and Victoria Wood. In 2005 he began collaborating as a writer/director/designer with Adam Cooper and his company.
In 2003, he was awarded the *Critics' Circle* award for outstanding achievement in design.

Julian Brown RDI

Julian Brown studied postgraduate design at the Royal College of Art, London, worked with the Porsche Design Studio, where he was responsible for the renowned 'Studio' spectacle frame and later co-formed the Lovegrove and Brown design partnership in London, undertaking projects for Knoll, British Airways, Parker Pens and other clients. Since 1990 he has been Director of the independent design company, StudioBrown. He has collaborated with Rexite Spa of Milan and Alfi Zitzmann, Germany for more than ten years, designing numerous acclaimed and commercially successful products. Hannibal, the tape dispenser from Rexite, was awarded Best of Category by *ID USA* in the 1998 *Design Review*. Other clients of StudioBrown include: Haworth and Acco, both in the USA; Curver in Holland; NEC and Sony, in Japan; WMF, Boeker and Henckels, all in Germany. More recently he has been a consultant to IBM, working on future strategies in communication design, and responsible for the 3D wayfinding system at Selfridges' flagship store, London. He was Guest Professor at the Hochschule der Künste in Berlin and at the University of Essen; External Examiner for Industrial Design at the Royal College of Art in London and for the MEDes course at the Glasgow School of Art. His work has won many international design awards and is regularly featured in prominent design exhibitions, publications and books. In 1998 he was elected RDI (Royal Designer for Industry) by the *Royal Society of Arts* in London for 'having attained eminence in creative design for industry'.

Paul Brown

Born in Glamorgan, Paul trained with Margaret Harris at the Riverside Studios. His opera designs include: *The Magic Flute* (Bolshoi Theatre Moscow); *Mitridate Re Di Ponto, Falstaff, The Midsummer Marriage, I Masnadieri, Tosca* (Royal Opera House); *King Arthur* (ROH/Chatelet Paris); *Lady Macbeth Of Mtensk, Moses Und Aron* (Metropolitan Opera New York); *Pelleas And Melisande, Lulu, Turn Of The Screw* (Glyndebourne); *The Magic Flute* (Salzburg Festival); *Peter Grimes* and *Parsifal* (Opera de Paris-Bastille). *Don Carlos* (Sydney Opera House); *Rigoletto* (Madrid); *Thais* (Lyric Opera, Chicago); *Katya Kabanova, Lucio Silla, The Tempest* (Santa Fe); *Fidelio, He Had It Coming* (Birmingham Opera); *L'incoronazione De Poppea* (Bologna); *La Traviata* (Verona); *Mefistofele* (Amsterdam). For the Almeida Theatre designs include: *The Tempest, The Showman* and *Naked*. For the Almeida at the Gainsborough: *Richard Ii, Coriolanus*, For the Almedia at Kings Cross: *Platonov, King Lear, Hamlet* (Tokyo Japan/Sadlers Wells). Paul designed *Giselle* (La Scala Milan) for Sylvie Guillem. Also, *Man Of La Mancha* (Broadway). Film designs include: *Angels And Insects* and *Up At The Villa*.

Terry Brown

Terry Brown trained in theatre design at Wimbledon School of Art and spent the first part of his career designing plays at theatres all over the UK (Manchester, Sheffield, Bristol, Lancaster, Liverpool and Derby). While he has now diversified, he still designs for theatre, most recently a series of outdoor theatre pieces in Williamson Park, Lancaster for the Dukes Theatre, and stage-based productions of plays by Alan Bennett, Dennis Potter, Dylan Thomas and David Mamet. He has been a production designer and art director on animated films for children's television, notably *The Wind in the Willows* and *The Fool of the World and His Flying Ship*. He designs exhibitions both for the art world and for commercial sector. These have included a hands-on, themed exhibition of the work of the company that produced the children's television programmes above and exhibitions on the work of William Morris. Design for live events has ranged from conferences, presentations and product launches (Christian Dior), to Elton John's 50th birthday party and large-scale parties/celebrations (Bloomberg and McLaren), to film premieres. In 2005, for the premiere of *The War of the Worlds* in London's Leicester Square, he used 40 tons of rubble, wrecked cars and 20-feet high flames to convey the impression that Leicester Square had been destroyed by the aliens in the film.

Paul Burgess

Paul Burgess read English at Oxford before training on the Motley Theatre Design Course. Recent set and costume designs include: *Other Hands, Shoreditch Madonna* and *Flush* (all Soho Theatre); *Babel Junction* (Hackney Empire); *Switch ECHO* (WUK, Vienna); *For One Night Only* (touring); *The Most Humane Way to Kill a Lobster* and *Cancer Time* (both Theatre 503); *Party Time/One for the Road* (BAC); *Peer Gynt* (Arcola Theatre); *Have I None* (Southwark Playhouse); *Sherlock Holmes* (La Tea, NYC); *Women and Criminals* (Here, NYC); and *Fred and Madge* (Oxford Playhouse). He designed sets for *Much Ado About Nothing* (Shakespeare's Globe); *The People's Opera* (touring); and sets and video for *Choked* (touring); *The Three Vs* (touring). Assistant design work includes: *The Ramayana* (National Theatre); *Twelfth Night* (Shakespeare's Globe, US tour); and work for Tara Arts. Film includes co-designing/advising on five short films for Ghanaian TV. As a director/designer/video-maker he has collaborated with performers to create two devised, visually led, new works: *Out of Nothing* (The Junction, Cambridge) and *Selfish* (The Arches, Glasgow). With Simon Daw he co-founded Scale Project, which has created work in a variety of locations and media in Siberia and the UK. Other projects range from an installation in Kennington Park to a large-scale, private painting commission. He also works with young people, mainly for the creative and performing arts charity Youth CREATE.

Kate Burnett
Kate Burnett is a theatre designer and educator, Honorary Secretary to the Society of British Theatre Designers and Reader in Theatre Design at Nottingham Trent University.
Previous design work includes *Schweyk in the Second World War, The Ghosts of Scrooge, Merlin* and *Beauty and the Beast* at the Library Theatre, Manchester; Oklahoma! with the National Youth Music Theatre, *The Little Mermaid* at Sheffield Crucible Studio, *Brighton Rock* at West Yorkshire Playhouse, *Mother Courage* and *The Day After Tomorrow* for the National Theatre Education Department and productions at Birmingham Rep, Liverpool Everyman, Leicester Haymarket, the Lyric, Hammersmith. While Head of Design at Contact Theatre she won the Manchester Evening News Award for *The Power of Darkness, To Kill a Mockingbird* and *The Little Prince*, also the Time Out Award for *Doctor Faustus* at the Young Vic, London. Kate has also designed large scale schools and community performance projects for the Halle, Opera North, Huddersfield Contemporary Music Festival, BBC Philharmonic and Glyndebourne Education Departments. She recently gained an MA in Art and Design in Education from The Institute of Education, University of London.
She was designer in residence for the Manchester Arts Education Festival for 5 years, also for the Cornerhouse, Manchester and Whitechapel Gallery, London. Kate is project director for the Collaborators exhibition and catalogue. She has co-organised three previous exhibitions for the SBTD with Peter Ruthven Hall. 2D13D which won the Golden Triga, and 2 Gold medals at the June 2003 Prague Quadrennial and toured to 4 UK galleries, MakeSpace!, which won the Gold Medal at the 1995 Prague Quadrennial and toured to 6 UK galleries, also Time+Space in 1999 at the Royal College of Art and the Theatre Museum in London.

David Burrows
David Burrows has principally collaborated with three directors: Phil Young, David Graham-Young and Alkis Kritikos. Productions for Phil Young include: *Crystal Clear* (Wyndham's); *Knickers* (Lyric Hammersmith); *Blood Brothers* (Heilbronn, Germany); and, in 2005, *Feelgood*, by Alistair Beaton, for Vienna and Frankfurt's English Theatres. Since March 2000 he has designed five productions for Contemporary Stage Company with David Graham-Young. The most recent are *The Tunnel of Obsession* by Ernesto Sabato (Warehouse Theatre, Croydon) then *The Tunnel* (Edinburgh Festival).
Recent work with Alkis Kritikos includes: the music *All Cloned Up* by Mike Bennett (touring), and *The Dinner* by Leah Vitali (Larnaka, Cyprus). For the premiere of Vitali's *Roast Beef* (Riverside Studios, London), he worked as design consultant and coordinator with students from Wimbledon School of Art taking on the set, costume and lighting design. He is Head of the Theatre School at Wimbledon College of Art where he was Course Leader of the Technical Arts Interpretation and Design courses until 2002. He was also Course Leader of the country's first MA in Theatre Design/Scenography from 1989 to 1994. More information at www.davidburrows.com. David's research into the life and work of Richard Negri is at: www.richardnegri.co.uk

Charcoalblue
Charcoalblue is a dedicated team of theatre consultants who have joined together in order to focus on the projects that interest and excite them.
The company uses a holistic and partnering approach in all of its work, and gives special emphasis to collaboration and user consultation.
Our work is rooted in a dual commitment to theatricality and innovation, with a strong desire to focus on exciting user-led projects.
We believe that every part of an arts building should be informed by the lessons of the past, but must also, by taking advantage of new techniques and materials, be capable of meeting the demands of the future.
Our current projects include;RSC Redevelopment, Stratford-upon-Avon; working in close collaboration with architect Bennetts Associates on the redevelopment of the 1930s RST building. RSC Courtyard Theatre, Stratford-upon-Avon; a temporary building constructed in fewer than 12 months, which will host the RSC's performances during its main theatre redevelopment. CBL have worked closely with Ian Richie Architect and the RSC. Siobhan Davies Studios, London; a collaboration with Sarah Wigglesworth Architects for a performance and rehearsal dance space. Young Vic Theatre, London; the refurbishment of the existing 1970 temporary theatre with Haworth Tompkins Architects. National Theatre Studio, London; working again with Haworth Tompkins Architects on the refurbishment of the NT's rehearsal and workshop areas. Camden Roundhouse, London; a unique collaboration with John McAslan and Partners on the refurbishment of the historic engine shed.

Cordelia Chisholm
Cordelia studied English Literature at Cambridge University before training on the Motley Theatre Design Course (2002). Theatre designs include: *The Dubya Trilogy: The Madness of George Dubya, A Weapon's Inspector Calls*, and *Guantanamo Baywatch* (New Players Theatre); *100 Degrees Fahrenheit* (Southwark Playhouse); *Hamelyn Heights* (Young Vic Studio); *Incarcerator* (Old Red Lion); *The Winter's Tale* (Creation Theatre Company, performed in a turn of the century cabaret tent); *An Axe for the Frozen Sea* (touring production for Bedlam Theatre Company); *Masks and Faces* (Finborough); *Multiplex* (Northampton Theatres); *Crimes of the Heart* (Poor School). Opera designs include: *Herodiade* and *Nabucco* (Dorset Opera); *Peter Grimes* (Surrey Opera Company); *Tales of Hoffmann* (Guilford Opera Company). Costume designs include: *Orlando* and *La Scala di Seta* (Independent Opera, Lilian Baylis Studio); *Talk About the Passion* (New End Theatre); *Twelfth Night* (Creation Theatre Company); *The Wedding* (Southwark Playhouse and tour) and an episode of *America's Next Top Model*.

Bunny Christie
Bunny Christie trained at Central School of Art. She has worked extensively at the National Theatre, most recently designing *The Life of Galileo*. She won an *Olivier Award* for *A Streetcar Named Desire* and an *Evening Standard Award* for *Baby Doll* both for the National Theatre. Other work there includes: *President of an Empty Room, Dealer's Choice, Elmina's Kitchen, Fix up* and *War and Peace*, a collaboration with Shared Experience. Other work with Shared Experience includes the much acclaimed British and international tour of *Mill on the Floss*, which won a *TMA Award* for Best Overall Production. Her most recent West End shows have been *Fool for Love* and *The Postman Always Rings Twice*. She has designed for the RSC, The Old Vic, Bristol Old Vic, The Globe, Edinburgh Lyceum, several shows at the Tricycle Theatre and for theatres of all shapes and sizes throughout Britain. She designed *The Vagina Monologues* from when it began at The Kings Head through various West End venues, including its massive charity performances at the Royal Albert Hall and The Old Vic, raising money for woman's charities. This year she is working at the Dramaten Theatre in Stockholm designing *Dance of Death* by Strindberg. For Renaissance Films she designed *Swansong*, starring Sir John Gielgud, nominated for an Oscar as Best Short Film.

Imogen Cloet
Imogen Cloet studied Drama at Hull University graduating with a BA Hons Degree in 1994. In 1995 she received the Arts Council Theatre Design Bursary at Northern Stage where she has continued to work on a regular basis. Productions include: *You'll have had your Hole, V, The Happy Prince, The Elves and the Shoemakers* and *Noir* a co-production with Live Theatre, for which she was nominated Best Designer in the 2002 *Barclays Stage Awards*. Other productions for Live Theatre, where she is an associate artist, include: *Cooking with Elvis, Smack Family Robinson, The Last Post, Charlie's Trousers, Toast, The Lover*, and *Keepers of the Flame*, a co-production with the RSC. In 2001, Imogen was short-listed for *The Arts Foundation Scenography Award*. While a large proportion of her work has been for new writing, she is particularly interested in creating work in found spaces with artists from non-theatre backgrounds. She is currently working on a series of collaborations with poet Jacob Polley, including a site-specific commission for English Heritage at Belsay Hall, Northumberland in May 2007. Other design work for theatre and film includes: *Kaz* (Pinball Films); *The Unexpected Man* (Bath Theatre Royal); *Death and the Ploughman* - Jerwood Young Designer (The Gate); *Mine* and *The Selfish Giant* (Leicester Haymarket Theatre); *Bait* and *In between* (both Channel 4 films).

David Cockayne
Most of David Cockayne's recent work has involved designing for drama, opera, and ballet. His approach to design centres on the flow of the production from scene to scene, determined by the needs of the production as a collaboration between the performers,the creative team and the design. This may involve using a single set on which to stage the many different scenes of a text or a fluid set, often moved by people rather than machinery. In staging period work the period of the production may be determined by the music, the text, the needs of contemporary interpretation, or a combination of these factors.
He trained as a theatre designer at Birmingham College of Art and was subsequently resident designer at Birmingham Repertory Theatre. He has worked at the Liverpool Playhouse; Greenwich Theatre, Theatre Clywd; and Manchester Library Theatre (1973-79), with one production transferring to the National Theatre. Other freelance work has included Greenwich and Traverse theatres; the Leicester Haymarket Studio; Sheffield Crucible; Great Eastern Stage; Leeds Playhouse; MAC, Birmingham; Duchy Ballet; Novaya Opera, Moscow; the Royal Northern College of Music; and Boston Early Music Festival. He has also worked in education and is currently Equity's Theatre Designers' Councillor. David also now works as an artist on projects such as evolving a new opera from an existing play, working as dramaturg.

Rosemarie Cockayne
Rosemarie Cockayne was born in Montreal and returned to Britain with her family as a young child. Coming first to the theatre via ballet, she trained with Stanislas Idzikowski, and the Royal Ballet Senior School, becoming Prima Ballerina with the Basle Ballet Company (Director, Waslav Orlikowsky) and then dancing freelance. It was during this time that she had the first of several one-woman art exhibitions at the Clarges Gallery London, having attended St Martins School of Art and Morley College. Designs for the theatre followed. She is currently working in the community on *Thread of Gold* (St Bartholomew-the-Less and touring). Contributors to the first showing within the Presentation of Christ in the Temple/Candlemas Service (St Bartholomew-the-Less) were mainly artists from the Pembroke Centre, a drop-in centre for people with long-term mental ill health, run by Kensington & Chelsea Council, but also included girls from the Arbour Youth Centre, East London, school pupils and professional artists. *Thread of Gold* currently involves young artists from Kosovo and Lithuania.Rosemarie has worked on many long-term projects in the community across a range of services. These have included *Ancient Traditions and Celebrations* at St Philip & St Barnabas play centre, culminating in a performance with professionals. At the Pembroke Centre, where she has been art tutor for the past 12 years, projects have included model theatre set and costume design, *Sacred Wishes, Space and Light and Environment in the City*. Other projects include: *Doors to the World* (YMCA Youth Hostel) and *Dawn mural design with bird box environment* (Broadway Youth Hostel).
She has worked extensively for Providence Row Charity, in East London, first as artist-in-residence with their Rough Sleepers Shelter, then with other centres (men and women street drinkers, drop-in centres, hostels for young adults and asylum seekers and people with mental health issues).
This collaboration has produced several installation/performance designs including *Circles, Streams of Light* (touring exhibition), *Journey of the Soul, St George*, as well as *Portraits* for the Drapers City Foyer. She was artist-in-residence for the Field Lane Foundation, drawing the relationship between carer and the cared for. Centres included homeless families and single parents, elderly people, people with dementia and those with severe disabilities.
Rosemarie is very interested in international exchange, education and environment. She was art tutor and consultant in the development of the Look Out Education Environmental Centre in Hyde Park.

David Collis
Having studied with Percy Harris on the Motley Theatre Design Course, David Collis was awarded an *Arts Council Traineeship* and sent to work for a year at the Royal Lyceum Theatre, Edinburgh. He became Assistant Designer and worked on several productions with Associate Director, Richard Eyre. When Richard Eyre became Director of Nottingham Playhouse, David joined him as Head of Design, for seven years. During that time he also designed for English National Opera and when he left Nottingham, it was to join ENO as Head of Design, at the London Coliseum. Since leaving ENO, he has worked freelance.

Patrick Connellan
Patrick was the first winner of the Linbury Prize for Theatre Design in 1987. Since then he has designed for regional, touring and West End theatre. He has worked for the New Vic Theatre, Newcastle-under-Lyme, Bolton Octagon Theatre, Leicester Haymarket, Belgrade Theatre, Coventry, Plymouth Theatre Royal, New Wolsey Theatre, Ipswich, the Mercury Theatre, Colchester, Birmingham Rep, West Yorkshire Playhouse, Harrogate Theatre, Hampstead Theatre, Royal Shakespeare Company, Royal National Theatre and various West End and commercial theatres. Notable productions have included: *Julius Caesar, St Joan, Pygmalion, Edward III, Osama the Hero* and *Nathan the Wise*, all with the director Tony Clark at Birmingham Rep, the Royal Shakespeare Company and Hampstead Theatre. In 1995 Patrick was one of the Gold Medal-winning team of British Theatre Designers at the Prague Quadrennial.
Whilst maintaining a keen interest in designing for theatre, Patrick has increasingly been directing plays. He directed *This Lime Tree Bower* (Belgrade Theatre and Edinburgh Festival); *Popcorn* (Bolton Octagon Theatre) and *Abigail's Party* (New Vic Theatre, Newcastle-under-Lyme).

Kandis Cook
Kandis Cook trained with Percy Harris on the Motley Theatre Design Course(1976/77). She has since designed sets and costumes for theatre, ballet, opera and film, in the UK, Australia, Canada, the US, Denmark and Ireland. She was born and raised in Canada and after completing a fine art degree she eventually moved to London, where she has lived since 1974. On arriving in London she had thought of herself as a visual artist, keenly interested in experimental film and video, but more than likely a lost painter. Her influences came from film, performance, sound, and conceptual artists such as Lawrence Weiner, Stan Brakage, Maya Deren, Jonas Mekas, John Cage, Steve Reich, Karl Andre, David Askevald, On Kawara, Simone Forte, Daniel Buren, Charlemagne Palestine, Kaspar Koenig, Sol LeWitt, Vito Acconci, Michael Snow, Susan Sontag, and others. Her knowledge and interest in live, traditional stage performance was limited until she discovered the space it had to offer and the reckless abandonment of a work once it was completed. The selling and storing of work was not an issue. Since this epiphany, living in hope of becoming a collaborator of ideas, regardless of how they came about or what form they took, in order to ask questions and pose possibilities with an audience, she has continued to engage in the ephemeral.

Sean Crowley
Since graduating from Wimbledon School of Art in 1985, Sean Crowley has worked across the design spectrum in theatre, dance, opera, and television. In 1993, he left London and returned to his birthplace, Wales. He has designed over 100 productions for companies including The Tron Theatre, Glasgow, the Grand Theatre, Swansea, the Torch Theatre, Milford, Theatr Nanog, North Wales Stage, Hampstead Theatre, London, Soho Theatre, London, Wales Theatre Company, The Hamburger Kammerspiele and the Danish Royal Opera. For over seven years, he has worked with the Sherman Theatre, Cardiff on its Christmas shows, as a part of the creative team that produced the original *Danny Champion of the World*. Sean became a full time lecturer in Theatre Design in 1998 and in 1999 he became Head of Design at the Royal Welsh College of Music and Drama. He is currently Chair of the Association of Theatre Design Courses in the UK, and is a member of the Linbury Prize committee. He has been the UK Commissioner for the OISTAT Education Commission since December 2003, and is currently Vice Chair of the Education Commission and Project Leader for the Prague Quadrennial Scenofest 2007.

Gabriella Csanyi-Wills
Gabriella Csanyi-Wills, Hungarian by parentage, British by birth, and French by education, has a degree in Humanities from the Open University and a degree in Theatre Studies from Central School of Speech and Drama. Since graduating in 1996, she has worked consistently in theatre, opera and dance, and on the occasional film. Recent work has included: Haydn's *Il Mondo della Luna*, Offenbach's *The Tales of Hoffmann* and *La Belle Hélène*, as well as collaborating on a new Gilbert and Sullivan, *The Burglar's Opera*, for Opera della Luna with the director Jeff Clark; *Bluebird*, with choreography by Liz Lea (the Clore Studio, Covent Garden and tour); as well as *Intoto, Livid, Refract, Inland, Solo, Duet Interrupted, Bartails* and *Tala Rasa, Hellas and Back* and *Shandra/Luna*, for Mavin Khoo Dance; Puccini's *Madama Butterfly*, for Clonter Opera; *Young Emma* by Laura Wade, with director Tamara Harvey; *Dancing in the Dark*, by Jenny Lee and Tom McNab, directed by Mehrdad Seyf. The future holds many exciting prospects working on new works both in opera and dance.

Anne Curry
Anne has a degree in Theatre Design, and an MA in Theatre Design from the Slade School of Fine Art and an MA in Education and Professional Development. In 1977, she received a *Royal Society of Arts Bursary* for her designs, which funded her to research Renaissance drawing and painting in Italy, her report on which received the Jacobs Memorial Medal. In 1982, she was awarded an Arts Council Theatre Design Bursary. She has worked as a resident and a freelance designer for many companies. She designed the set and costumes for *Dreams of San Francisco* (the Bush Theatre), which received the Thames Television Award for Best Production in 1986. She designed the costumes for *The Boys in the Band* (The King's Head, then the Aldwych). Anne has exhibited costume designs in private galleries and Society of British Theatre Designers exhibitions, at the Prague Quadrennial (1999), the Theatre Museum Covent Garden and the National Theatre in Tokyo (2001). Her work was represented in the World Stage Design Catalogue (2005).

She has been Course Director of the BA (Hons) Design for Performance, the BA (Hons) Theatre Design and the MA Scenography at the University of Central England. She has been Senior Lecturer in Costume Design and Interpretation at the Nottingham Trent University since 2002. Anne is also a freelance designer and visiting lecturer. She lectures extensively in drawing and costume design at various higher education institutions.

Charles Cusick Smith
Charles Cusick Smith studied at Glasgow School of Art and Post Graduate at the Slade School of Art in London. He was Resident Designer with the Library Theatre in Manchester from 1982 -86. Since then he has been freelance, designing dramas, musicals, and pantomime for all major repertory theatres in the UK and designing internationally for opera and ballet. He designed the European premiers of Sondheim's *Follies, Pacific Overtures* and *Sweeney Todd* (TMA Award for Best Production 1990), the European premiere of *Ladies Night* in 1989; *Boyzone Something Else Tour 1997*, and *Rock around the Dock Rock Extravaganza* (Granada TV). Most recently in London: *The Guardsman* starring Greta Scacchi (Albery Theatre) and co-designing *Cliff, the Musical* (Prince of Wales Theatre and national tour). International designs for opera and ballets include: *Giselle* (English National Ballet); *Romeo and Juliet, Nutcracker* and *Cavalleria Rusticana/Pagliacci* (Estonia); *Romeo and Juliet* (Indianapolis Ballet International); *Nabucco, Aida, Don Carlos, The Wall* (Rock Ballet), *Otello, Der Rosenkavalier, Cavalleria Rusticana/Pagliacci* (Germany); *Il Trovatore*, and recently, *Spartacus*, Hong Kong Ballet choreographed by Irek Mukhamedov (Hong Kong). His next projects are *The Three Musketeers* for Northern Ballet Theatre and, in Estonia, *Giselle*. Charles received the *TMA Best Designer Award* 1993 and the *Manchester Evening News Award* Best Designer in 1986. He has also exhibited his paintings in the Dragooni Galeri, Estonia, the Royal Academy in London, and in many other galleries in the UK.

Phil R Daniels
Phil R Daniels is a theatre designer and fine artist. He trained in Theatre Design at the Bristol Old Vic. Since graduating in 1983, he has designed shows for repertory theatres around the country, for national tours and the West End. He has designed shows performed at the National Theatre and for the BBC. Some of his theatre designs have been acquired for the permanent collection of the V&A Theatre Museum. In 1987 he set up the design company Upstage Designs with fellow theatre designer Charles Cusick Smith. In addition to designing individually they also collaborate on theatre projects across the world, including opera, ballet, musicals, pantomimes and rock concerts. Originally Phil trained and worked as an illustrator. His illustration work has been included in the Best of European Illustration and the Association of British Illustrators Annuals. He has exhibited his fine art extensively with work shortlisted for the National Portrait Gallery's BP Portrait Award, and included in the *Sunday Times Watercolour Competition* and he has been commissioned to design and paint artwork for the fire curtains of two Frank Matcham theatres, the Cheltenham Everyman and most recently, Theatre Royal Newcastle.

Simon Daw
Simon Daw studied Fine Art at Glasgow School of Art and on the Motley Theatre Design Course, London. He has exhibited photography, film, video and installation work in both the UK and abroad, most recently in the form of an interactive web/performance piece *Wave Structures*, commissioned by the Aldeburgh Festival and his video work *Sea House*, which was exhibited at the 2005 Venice Biennale. Theatre design credits include: *Aladdin*, based on Philip Pullman's book (Bristol Old Vic); *Jackets* (Young Vic/Theatre 503), *The Bodies* by Peter Flannery (Live Theatre); *Rutherford and Son* (Royal Exchange Theatre, Manchester); *Tall Phoenix* by Chris O'Connell (Belgrade Theatre, Coventry); *Romeo and Juliet* (Royal Shakespeare Company, Stratford and the Albery, London); *Adam and Eve* (TPT, Tokyo); six plays for the Imprint Young Writers Festival (Royal Court Theatre Upstairs); *Astronaut* with Theatre O (Barbican Pit); *Rafts and Dreams* and *Across Oka* (Royal Exchange Studio, Manchester); *Relatively Speaking, The Witches, Everyman* and *Habeas Corpus* (Northampton Theatres); *Under The Curse* and *Tragedy: A Tragedy* (Gate Theatre); *Fragile Land* (Hampstead Theatre); *Kes* (National Youth Theatre, Lyric Hammersmith).
Opera and dance includes the revival design of *Fidelio* for Scottish Opera and *Bloom* for Rambert Dance Company. As co-director of Scale Project, Simon has collaborated with fellow theatre designer Paul Burgess on site-specific performances in Harlow Town Hall, The Arches, Glasgow and in a Siberian nuclear bunker.

Steve Denton
Steve trained and worked in architecture before moving into theatre design. Over the past decade he has worked extensively in theatre and dance, designing for a range of main stage, touring and site-specific productions, as well as large-scale community theatre, TIE, youth theatre and educational projects with companies across the UK. Recent work includes: *Unspoken Agreement, Beginnings* and *Tough Love* for Diversions Dance Company; *The Crucible, The Good Person of Szechuan* and *Little Shop of Horrors* (Ustinov Studio, Theatre Royal, Bath); *Dancing at Lughnasa* and *Gut Girls* (Mountview Theatre School); *Jane Eyre, Nothing Compares 2 U* and *Moll Flanders* for the Royal Welsh College of Music and Drama, where he holds a part-time lecturing post.

Es Devlin
Es Devlin studied music, English literature and fine art before attending the Motley Theatre Design Course. She was awarded the *Linbury Biennial Prize* for Stage Design 1995/96, *TMA Best Designer* 1998, was nominated for *TMA Best Designer* 2000, and for *Manchester Evening News* Best Design 2005 and was the winner of the *Olivier Award for Best Costume Design* 2006. In theatre, Es has designed extensively for the RSC, the National Theatre, the Royal Court, Almeida, Bush and Young Vic theatres. Her most recent theatre designs have included a site-specific African *Macbeth* for Out of Joint, and the *Spanish Golden Age Season* and *Hecuba* for the RSC. Designs for dance include: *Essence* for the Linbury Studio; *I Remember Red* for Cullberg Ballet, Sweden; *God's Plenty* and *Four Scenes* for Rambert Dance Company. Her designs for opera have included: *Gadafi* for English National Opera; *Don Giovanni, Flammen* and *Macbeth* all for Vienna's Theater an der Wien; *Midsummer Nights Dream* for Hamburg

Staatsoper; *Orphée* for ROH2 at the Linbury Studio; and Adès' *Powder Her Face* for Ystad, Sweden.
Film production designs include: *Dreams of Miss X*, starring Kate Moss and directed by Mike Figgis; *Brilliant!* for BBC2; and Harold Pinter's *Victoria Station*. Her designs for live music have included: a collaboration with Wire and Jake and Dinos Chapman at the Barbican; the Pet Shop Boys World Tour; and Kanye West US Tour. She is currently designing *Salome* for the Royal Opera House, *Carmen* for ENO and *Billy Budd* for Hamburg Staatsoper. Her work can be viewed at www.esdevlin.com

Chris de Wilde
Chris de Wilde's recent designs include: *Cyberjam* (Queen's Theatre); *Nixon's Nixon* (Comedy Theatre); *Il Trovatore* (Tbilisi Opera and Ballet Theatre, Georgia); *Nine* (Malmö Musikteater, Sweden); *Sweeney Todd* (Värmlandsoperan, Karlstad, Sweden); *Straker Sings Brel* (King's Head); *Love, Lust and Loss* (BAC); *Queer Counsel* (Croydon Warehouse and tour); *Ceremony of Carols/Winter Words* (Streetwise Opera at New College Chapel, Oxford); *The Very Magic Flute* (Krazy Kat Theatre Company on tour); *Such Sweet Thunder* and *The Late Sleepers* (two new musicals for NYMT at Newcastle Theatre Royal); and five showcase productions for the annual *Musical Voices* season at Greenwich Theatre. Previous designs include: *Crazy For You*, with a cast of 250 in which 60 chorus girls emerged from a limousine, and a full-scale production of *The Cunning Little Vixen* in a barn in Berkshire. Chris worked for many years as a production manager, overseeing a wide variety of productions including eight major shows in the West End, 17 national tours, 34 productions for the RSC and three seasons for Almeida Opera.

Liam Doona
Liam Doona studied Theatre Design at Trent Polytechnic (now Nottingham Trent University.) He graduated in 1986 and has worked variously in design for theatre, conferences, exhibitions and the heritage industry. Since 1992 he has combined design with an increasing commitment to working in education. He has developed and run theatre design programmes at Bretton Hall (University of Leeds), University of Central England and Nottingham Trent University where, until recently, he was Head of Narrative and Interactive Arts. Recent design work includes: national tours of *The Seagull* and *The Rivals* for Compass Theatre Company under the direction of Neil Sissons; *The Beauty Queen of Leenane* directed by Marcus Romer (York Theatre Royal); and *The White Album*, directed by Giles Croft (Nottingham Playhouse). Other notable productions include; *Frankenstein*, a new adaptation by Richard Hurford; *Romeo and Juliet*; *The Glass Menagerie*, all directed by Damian Cruden (York Theatre Royal); *The Merchant of Venice; Endgame*; *A Christmas Carol* for Compass Theatre. Liam now lives and works in Ireland where he is Head of Art and Design at The Institute of Art, Design and Technology, Dublin.

Richard Downing
Richard Downing is the founder and Artistic Director of the Wales-based arts company *U-Man Zoo*, initially formed in 1994 to create *Motorcity*, a wordless performance conducted upon cars suspended from trees. Since then, the company has proceeded to make a series of original and distinctive works at diverse locations (both indoor and outdoor, locally and internationally)

drawing upon (and often blurring) a diverse range of performance practices. Whilst each event is unique in itself, the company typically seeks to offer extraordinary encounters in unorthodox places, with the work often being inspired by location and object, and delivered with characteristic challenge, warmth and wit. As well as his work with *U-Man Zoo*, Richard has also lectured in scenography at the University of Wales, Aberystwyth, since 1996.

Atlanta Duffy
Atlanta Duffy trained on the Motley Theatre Design Course and at the Lyric Hammersmith. In 1995 she was a finalist in the Linbury Prize for Theatre Design. Designs for theatre include: *Cleo, Camping & Emmanuelle* (Bolton Octagon); *Come out Eli* (awarded *Time Out Best Fringe Production*); *Afterbirth* (Arcola Theatre); *The Way of the World* (Wilton's Music Hall); *Inside Out* (Clean Break); *Brokenville* (St George's Church); *Women of Troy, A Month in the Country* (RADA); *Fairy Tales* (Cegrane, Macedonia); *Hansel and Gretel* (Lyric Hammersmith); *As You Like It, The Basset Table* (Bristol Old Vic); *The Farmer's Bride* (Stephen Joseph Theatre). Since 2003, she has collaborated with director Chuck Mike on *Women of Owu* (UK tour); *Sense of Belonging* (Arcola Theatre); *Death and the Maiden* (Muson Centre, Lagos); *It's Just a Name* (The Door, Birmingham Rep); *The Lion and the Jewel* (Young Genius Season, Barbican Pit and tour); and *Tegonni* (University of Richmond, Virginia). Opera designs include: *Burning Mirrors* (ENO Studio); *Die Gärtnerin aus Liebe*, (Royal Academy of Music); *Apollo and Hyacinth* (Classical Opera Company); *Hugh the Drover, Don Giovanni* (ETO). Designs for dance include: *Waingi Yoruba Masquerade Costumes* (Greenwich and Docklands Festival) and collaborations at Chisenhale Dance Space. Atlanta has also curated a number of exhibitions including: *The Brokenville Exhibition* (National Theatre) and has made giant puppets for carnivals, processions and outdoor events.

Paul Edwards
Paul Edwards was born in Australia and graduated with honours from the Royal Academy of Dramatic Art, where he is now an Associate Member. Theatre design credits include: *Little Women* (Sheffield Crucible); *The Last Yankee*, (Leicester Haymarket); *The Importance of Being Earnest, Cat on a Hot Tin Roof, Private Lives, The Odd Couple, On The Piste, Gasping, Romeo and Juliet*, (Harrogate Theatre); *Vita and Virginia*, (Sphinx Theatre Company); *The Young Idea*, (Chester Gateway); *Noises Off, Great Expectations, The Sound of Music, The Turn of The Screw, Dames at Sea*, (Queen's Theatre Hornchurch); *The Servant of Two Masters*, (Wolsey Theatre, Ipswich); *Threesome, Stupid Cupid, F***ing Martin*, (Sweatshop Theatre Company); *Fair Game*, (Theatre Royal Plymouth); *Kiss Me Kate*, (Norwich Playhouse); costumes for *Brighton Beach Memories* (Stephen Joseph Theatre, Scarborough); *Pygmalion, Hamlet, The Seagull, School for Scandal*, (Theatr Clwyd); *The Importance of Being Earnest*, (National Theatre of Israel); *No Flies on Mr. Hunter*, (Chelsea Arts Theatre); *The Pleasure Principle*, (Young Vic); *Viva Espana*, (Arts Theatre); *The Taming of the Shrew*, (Regent's Park Open Air Theatre); costumes for *Is That All There Is?* (Almeida, London and New York); *Trelawny of the Wells*, (West End); *Jyro-Scape and Boutique*, (Sadler's Wells); Designs for opera include: *The Bartered Bride, Orfeo ed Euridice,*

Die Zauberflte, Costumes, (The New Israeli Opera, Tel Aviv); *The Mikado*, (Sherman Theatre Cardiff); *L'égoïste*, (Royal Academy of Music); *Il Mondo della Luna, L'Italiana in Algieri*, (Garsington Opera); *Der Jakobin, Eva*, (Wexford Festival Opera); *Carmen*, (Riverside Opera); *Orfeo ed Euridice* (Opéra National Du Rhin, Strasbourg and Theatro Calderon); *The Marriage of Figaro*, (Opera Ireland); *La Finta Semplice*, (Opéra de Nice and L'Opéra Comique, Paris); *Die Walküre*, (Teatro Teresa Carreno, Caracas); *Il Matrimonio Segreto*, (L'Opera Comique, Paris); *Die Fledermaus, L'Incoronazione di Poppea*, (Royal College of Music); *Chérubin*, (Teatro Lirico di Cagliari); *Lucia di Lammermoor*, (Opernhaus Halle); *Les Pêcheurs des Perles* (Kazan Opera and Den Haag).

Lis Evans
Lis Evans trained at Cardiff Art College and what was then Trent Polytechnic, graduating in 1987. She made props and painted for various productions, exhibitions and tradeshows. As Head of Design at the New Vic Theatre (one of the very few UK theatres retaining such a post), Lis has designed over 60 productions, including *Oliver!, Stags and Hens, Poor Mrs Pepys, Sizwe Bansi is Dead, The Graduate, Amadeus, Kes, Carmen, My Night with Reg, Lonesome West, The Railway Children, Cleo Camping Emanuel and Dick, Top Girls, Moll Flanders, Kiss of The Spider Woman, Translations, The Tempest, A Comedy of Errors, Bright and Bold Designs, The Jolly Potters* and *The Cherry Orchard*.
For Northern Broadsides, Lis designed tours of *Vacuum, The Tempest* and *The Storm*. She also works with the New Vic Education Department, Creative Partnerships, and local schools, colleges and adult education groups, designing, leading workshops, giving talks, and mentoring students.

Mike Elliott
Mike graduated from Nottingham Trent University in 2004, with first class honours in Theatre Design. Since then he has assisted Liam Doona on The *Beauty Queen of Leenane* for York Theatre Royal and *The Seagull* for Compass Theatre Company. Working with the Education Department at the Nuffield Theatre, Southampton, he has also designed sets and costumes for productions of *Red, Red Shoes, The Rover* and *Brave Boys*. Mike also works as a prop-maker, most recently two seasons for Glyndebourne Opera House where he worked on: *La Cenerentola, Giulio Cesare, Cosi Fan Tutte, Betrothal in a Monastery* and *Turn of the Screw*. During this time he has also worked with Kate Burnett on a large NHS project and on hosting the OISTAT Education Commission at NTU.

Colin Falconer
Colin Falconer studied Interior and Environmental Design at Duncan of Jordanstone College, University of Dundee and Theatre Design at Nottingham Trent University. He has designed productions of *Romeo and Juliet* and *Three Sisters* (Chichester Festival Theatre); *The Merchant of Venice* (RSC at the Barbican Pit and the Swan, Stratford-upon-Avon, regional and international tour); *Endgame* and *Dominos* (Theatr Genedlaethol Cymru); *Madam T* (Meridien Theatre Company/Cork European Capital of Culture); *Acis and Galatea* and *Dido and Aeneas* (RSAMD); *The Blue Room* (Minerva Theatre Chichester and Theatre Royal Haymarket); *The Misanthrope, The Secret Rapture, Hysteria* (Minerva Theatre, Chichester); *Twelfth Night* (Liverpool Playhouse);

costumes for *Aladdin* (Scottish Ballet); *Blue Funk* and *Hospitality* (Old Red Lion); *A Family Affair, The Chalk Garden, Summer, Heartbreak House, Arcadia* (Questors Theatre).

Paul Farnsworth
Paul Farnsworth trained in Theatre Design at Wimbledon School of Art. He has designed more than 20 productions for Minerva Studio (where he was resident designer) and Chichester Festival Theatre, including: *The Power and the Glory, Adam was a Gardener, Point Valaine, 70 Girls 70* (also in the West End), *Love's Labours Lost, Summerfold* and most recently, *Entertaining Angels*.
Other designs include: numerous productions for the Open Air Theatre in Regent's Park, among them: *Troilus and Cressida, The Merry Wives of Windsor, The Two Gentlemen of Verona, High Society* (also in the West End), *Kiss Me Kate, A Funny Thing Happened on the Way to the Forum* and *The Boyfriend*.
Other work includes: *A Warwickshire Testimony, Transit of Venus* (RSC); *The Crucible, A Little Night Music, Sweeney Todd, Into The Woods, Hedda Gabler, A Woman of No Importance* (Leicester Haymarket); *Lady In The Van, My Father's House* (Birmingham Rep); *Safe Sex* (Contact, Manchester); *The Merchant of Venice, Volpone* (English Shakespeare Company); *Hayfever, A Flea in her Ear, My Fair Lady*, and *The Producers* (Det Ny Theater, Copenhagen). West End productions include: *The Cherry Orchard* (Aldwych Theatre); *Fallen Angels, Sleuth* (Apollo Theatre); *Ghosts* (Comedy Theatre); *A Man for All Seasons* (Theatre Royal, Haymarket); *Scrooge* (Palladium and UK tour, US tour and Australia); *Passion* (Queen's Theatre); *Moby Dick - A Whale of a Tale* (Piccadilly Theatre).

Jonathan Fensom
Jonathan Fensom trained at Nottingham Polytechnic. Recent theatre productions include: *The Faith Healer* (The Gate Theatre, Dublin and Broadway); *Smaller* (West End and UK tour); *Chatroom, Citizenship* and *Burn* (National Theatre); *God of Hell* (Donmar); *What the Butler Saw* (Hampstead and West End); *National Anthems* (Old Vic); *Twelfth Night* (West End); *Journey's End* (West End and national tour). Jonathan has also worked with many of the major producing theatre companies in the UK including: Shared Experience, Out of Joint, Oxford Stage Company, Bath Theatre Royal, The Royal Court, West Yorkshire Playhouse, The Bush, Sheffield Crucible, and Hampstead Theatre. He was Associate Designer on Disney's The *Lion King*, which premiered at the New Amsterdam Theatre on Broadway and has subsequently opened worldwide.

Rick Fisher
Originally from the US, Rick Fisher has worked in British theatre for over 20 years. He is currently Chairman of the Association of Lighting Designers. He has won the *World Stage Design Bronze Medal for Lighting Design* (2005); an Olivier Award (1998 and 1994); and Tony, Drama Desk and Critics' Circle awards. He participated in PQ 95 with Ian MacNeil showing *An Inspector Calls* and *Machinal*; in PQ 99 with Adventure in Motion Pictures' *Swan Lake*; and in PQ 03 with *Wozzeck* for Santa Fe Opera.

Tim Fosters Architects
Tim Foster Architects are a medium-scale architectural practice established in 1979. Tim Foster trained at the Cambridge University School of Architecture, where he also worked as a stage designer. Before establishing his own practice, he worked for Roderick Ham and Partners and as consultant architect to Theatre Projects Consultants. He is chair of the ABTT Theatre Planning Committee and represents the UK on the OISTAT Architecture Commission. The practice has established a reputation for the design of theatres and performing arts venues. Projects include the Tricycle Theatre and the Gate Theatre (London); the Cliffs Pavilion in Southend-on-Sea; school theatres at Dulwich College and St Paul's Boys School; the refurbishment of the Salisbury Playhouse; the Tricycle Cinema (winner of four major design awards in 1999/2000); and the remodelling of a large 1937 cinema as a multi-purpose entertainment venue at the Broadway in Peterborough. Recent work includes: the redevelopment of the Broadway Theatre in Barking; a low-cost studio theatre for Kingston College and the remodelling of the Whitehall Theatre in London's West End as the Trafalgar Studios. Current projects include: Norwich Theatre Royal; the Annenberg Theatre at the American School in London; an extension to the Salisbury Playhouse; a new performing arts centre for Cheltenham Ladies' College; and proposals for a new home for the Southwark Playhouse.

Helen Fownes-Davies
Helen Fownes-Davies graduated from Nottingham Trent University with a BA (Hons) in Theatre Design in 1995. The following year she was appointed a Resident Designer at the Arts and Education Centre in Nottingham. Since becoming freelance, Helen has produced designs for theatre at many different levels and continues her educational work in theatres and for communities.
Theatre credits include: *Ballet Hoo!* (a collaboration between Birmingham Royal Ballet and Channel 4); *The Retirement of Tom Stevens* and *A Who's Who of Flapland* (Lakeside Theatre, Nottingham); *Misery* and *Our Day Out* (Harrogate Theatre); *Satin 'n' Steel* and *The Man Who* (Nottingham Playhouse); Momentum Festival (Theatre Writing Partnership, Lakeside Theatre, Nottingham); *The Emperor's New Clothes, The Snow Queen, Arabian Nights* and *The Firebird* (MAC, Birmingham); *Safahr* (Birmingham Royal Ballet) *The Selkie Girl* and *The Emerald Cave* (The Playhouse TIE, Birmingham); *Two Minutes Silence* (site-specific show for Focus Productions). Touring shows include: *Booty Call* (Big Creative Ideas); *Natural Breaks and Rhythms* (Northampton Theatre Royal and Theatre Writing Partnership); *21 Tales* for the Fionnbarr Factory (touring); *The Elves and the Shoemaker* (MAC, Birmingham); *Bowled a Googly* (OTTC and New Perspectives); *The Bad One* (Women and Theatre); *Chalk Stories, Zagazoo, Nightmaze, Come With Me* and *Stepping Stones* (Roundabout Theatre, Nottingham Playhouse); *Acts of Love, Brethren* and *3 Tales of Courage* (Eclipse Theatre).

Richard Foxton
Richard trained at Trent Polytechnic, Nottingham. He was Assistant Designer at Contact Theatre, Manchester then Resident Designer at the Octagon Theatre, Bolton before going freelance in 1999. He has designed over 100 productions including national tours of *Brassed Off* (Sheffield Theatres); *Office Suite* (Theatre Royal, Bath); *The Importance of Being Ernest* and *Hector's House* (Lipservice); *Ladies' Day* (Hull Truck); and *A Clockwork Orange* (TAG). He has also designed *Neville's Island* and *All My Sons* (Theatre Royal, York); *Macbeth, The Miser, Equus, Noises Off* and *Dead Funny* (Salisbury Playhouse); *The Price, A Family Affair* and *Double Indemnity* (New Wolsey Theatre, Ipswich); *Good Golly Miss Molly* and *Feels Like the First Time* (Oldham Coliseum); *Blue/Orange, Queen's English, The Country Wife, Big Night Out...* and *Cor, Blimey!* (Palace Theatre, Watford); *Things We Do For Love* and *Death of a Salesman* (Library Theatre, Manchester); *Wuthering Heights, 1984, Under the Whaleback, Up on the Roof* and *Lonesome West* (Hull Truck Theatre); Kvetch (West Yorkshire Playhouse); *Oedipus Tyrannos*, and *Man Equals Man* (Contact Theatre, Manchester); *Midnight Cowboy* (Assembly Theatre Ltd, Edinburgh).
He has designed 50 productions for the Octagon Theatre, Bolton in a variety of formats: thrust, end stage, in the round, and traverse. These include: *Blood Wedding, Saved, Macbeth, A Midsummer Night's Dream, Eight Miles High, Four Knights in Knaresborough* and *Dancing at Lughnasa*. He has won the *Manchester Evening News* Design Award four times (1992, 1994, 1999 and 2000).
His design for *Murderer Hope of Womankind* (Whitworth Art Gallery) was part of the Gold Medal-winning British Exhibit at PQ95. In 1997 he was a judge of the *Linbury Prize*.

Bob Frith
Bob Frith founded Horse + Bamboo Theatre in 1978. He remains Artistic Director of the company and works as the lead artist with a team of creative collaborators – designers, makers, performers, puppeteers, composers, musicians and film-makers. His current main role is writing, designing and directing the company's international touring productions.

Ada Gadomski
Ada Gadomski was a musician before training in Scenography at the Academy of Applied Arts and Design in Belgrade and at Central Saint Martins College of Art and Design. She works as a freelance set and costume designer and assistant in theatre and film.
She has created devised theatre work with her own company, Opala Group and worked with Pamela Howard on Scenofest - Prague Quadrennial 2003. Ada is Visiting Lecturer at the Scenography Department of the Academy of Applied Arts and Design in Belgrade. In 2005-6 she spent five months in Japan researching Japanese Theatre on a scholarship from the Japanese Agency for Cultural Affairs.

Christopher Giles
Born in Brussels, of a French mother and English father, Christopher Giles had a former career as a graphic designer and ballet dancer. He performed with major companies in Europe, but mainly with Northern Ballet Theatre as Principal Dancer. He then retrained as a theatre designer at the Royal Welsh College of Music and Drama. He was a finalist in the 2005 *Linbury Biennial Prize* and had a design featured on the front cover of the Nov/Dec 2005 issue of the *Opera Now* magazine. He has since designed *Umbilica* for Diversions: The Dance Company of Wales, as well as a double-bill opera of *The Medium* by Menotti and *Ten Belles* by Von Suppé, directed by John Labouchardiere and created for the Sherman Theatre main stage.
He has assisted David Nixon, director of Northern Ballet Theatre and designers including Es Devlin, Mark Thompson, Peter McIntosh and Tanya McCallin. He is currently on an internship at the Royal Opera House.

Hannah Gravestock
Hannah Gravestock graduated from the Central School of Speech and Drama in 2001 and has since worked designing set and costumes for theatre and film. She is currently in the final year of a PhD at the Wimbledon School of Art, researching the embodiment and understanding of character through the movement of the performer and the movement of the designer, in order to develop processes of costume design. Her theatre work includes *Annie* and *Oliver!* (Palace Theatre, Manchester); *West Side Story* (the Arts Theatre, Cambridge); a promenade production of *A Midsummer Night's Dream* (Ripley Castle); and costume designs for a dance/theatre performance, *C.'17imeara*. Hannah also runs costume and design workshops for schools and theatre companies, which most recently include A Piece of The Pie Theatre Company.

Abigail Hammond
Abigail Hammond studied Dance Theatre at the Laban Centre, London, specialising in Costume Design. For the past 20 years she has been a freelance designer and lecturer. She has designed and realised costumes for over 100 choreographic works.
She was the Resident Designer for the National Youth Dance Company for 13 years and for Union Dance for three years. Her theatre work includes costumes for *The Hobbit*, produced by VFP Ltd (West End). Abigail has lectured at the Royal Academy of Dance, London College of Fashion, Laban and currently holds a part time post at Wimbledon School of Art.
Her commitment to education is also through community projects, most recently with the National Theatre Education Unit, English Heritage, English National Ballet and the Barbican Centre, London. The designs for *The Hobbit* and an accompanying educational video were part of the Society of British Theatre Designers' 2002 exhibition *2D13D*, and this exhibit was selected to be part of the UK's contribution to the World Stage Design Exhibition in Toronto in 2005. Abigail was nominated for an *Arts Foundation Fellowship Award* for Costume Design in 2004. She is currently designing a second touring production for Zimbabwean choreographer Bawen Tavaziva, whose *Umdlalo Kasisi* was runner up in *The Place Prize for Choreography* in 2004.

Ken Harrison
Ken Harrison trained at the Ruskin School, Oxford and with Motley at the Riverside Studios, London. He won an *Arts Council Design Bursary* for a season at Watford Palace Theatre and has been Head of Design at Colchester Mercury Theatre. Recent designs include: *Tales from Hollywood, Humble Boy* (Perth Theatre); *Vanity Fair* (Northcott Theatre, Exeter); *Travesties, The Tempest* and *The Hound of the Baskervilles*, with projection designer Tim Bird (Nottingham Playhouse).
He has designed national tours of *Time and the Conways, Travels With My Aunt, The LadyKillers, The 39 Steps* and *Mindgame*. He has also designed productions in each season at Pitlochry Festival Theatre since 1990. These include: *Amadeus, Double Indemnity, Man and Superman, Kind Hearts and Coronets, Summer Lightning* and *Man of the Moment*.

Janis Hart
Janis Hart gained a degree in Textile and Fashion Design, and studied Theatre Design at the Slade School of Art in London. Her career as a designer has been varied, including residencies at Theatr Powys, Worcester Swan Theatre, Derby Playhouse and South Hill Park, Bracknell, and freelancing. It has encompassed repertory, touring, TIE and community theatre. A long collaboration with London Bubble Theatre Company produced exciting new work for site-specific and outdoor performance; *A Midsummer Night's Dream, Gilgamesh, Gulliver's Travels* and *Pericles*. An enjoyment of non-theatre spaces that she has developed since moving to Scotland has led to *Consider Rather the River* (theatre workshop at the Water of Leith); *The Lost Forest* (Tramway); *Digging up the Future* (site-specific community theatre at Methil Docks in Fife - National Theatre of Scotland). An enjoyment of traditional theatrical forms, such as pantomime, puppets and mask, and traditional stories from around the world, has led to many Christmas and children's productions including: *Jack and the Beanstalk, Ali Baba, Cinderella, Red Riding Hood, Sleeping Beauty* (London Bubble); *Treasure Island* and *Peter Pan* (South Hill Park); *Saame Sita, Last Little Fish in the Net, Hogmanay Boys* and *Hans Christian Anderson* (Theatre Workshop). She has also worked as an educator for theatre design in both academic and community settings, and has designed many community plays, developing methods of involving community participants in the creative process, and visual workshops for actors.

Becky Hawkins
Becky Hawkins trained in Theatre Design at Bristol Old Vic Theatre School, after graduating from Goldsmiths College with a BA (Hons) English and Drama. She has recently completed several years of part-time study at the University of Plymouth, achieving a Masters in Fine Art.
Becky has designed over 60 productions, many of them youth theatre shows, including: the world premiere of *Korczak* (Plymouth and Poland); *Brother Jacques, The Threepenny Opera, Oh, What A Lovely War!, Sweeney Todd* and *The Hired Man* (The Drum, Plymouth); *Macbeth, Custer's Last Stand, The Rime of the Ancient Mariner, Blood Wedding* and *Into the Woods* (Salisbury Playhouse); *The Polychronicon*, a millennium community play (Chester Gateway Theatre); and touring productions of *The Weir* and *Grimms' Tales* (Nuffield Theatre, Southampton). For the Northcott Theatre, Exeter, Becky has designed *Aladdin, Hamlet, Bouncers, A Passionate Woman, The Curse of the Werewolf* (which also toured to the Minack), *Fiddler on the Roof*. Designs for Northcott Young Company productions include: *The Boyfriend, Godspell, Around the World in Eighty Days, Oh, What A Lovely War!, Tin Pan Ali, Oliver!, The Wizard of Oz* and *The Wind in the Willows*; costumes for *Days of Hope* and *Matthew Miller* (a large-scale community project); and the Dame's costumes for the last five pantomimes.

Simon Head

Simon Head trained as an engineering draughtsman before graduating from the London College of Printing where he studied typography, photography and print management. He has designed the catalogues for 'time+space', '2D13D' and 'collaborators' for the SBTD and has produced many books, journals and magazines in his career. He directed and produced three educational/documentary films for the Tate Gallery. 'Engaging with Pollock', 'Tate international open day/Socrates project' and 'Grace Nichols/Visual Paths'; also 'Architectives' for London Open House. He organised the Park Studios education programme, including the workshop 'Park Studios/Theatre de Complicite'. At the heart of his working practice lays the interface of photography and film making. His subject is landscape and the people found within it. Work is inspired during many journeys and field trips. He recently exhibited his 'film-frame-reference' series; 'autoexposure', 'denial', 'walkin' and 'new york/sky'. 'bridge', which was exhibited in 2005, at the Kingsgate Gallery, London NW6, is a series of site-specific works, that go far beyond conventional documentary.
website: www.simonhead.co.uk

Susannah Henry

Susannah Henry trained at Wimbledon School of Art, later taking an MA Scenography at Central Saint Martins College with the support of an AHRC award. Recent design work includes; C-90 by Daniel Kitson (Riverside Studios, London and the Traverse Theatre, Edinburgh); The Crowning of the Year (Watermill Theatre, Newbury); and Sweet Yam Kisses, for Kushite Theatre (Lyric Hammersmith, London). Susannah works with two young theatre companies based in Leeds and London. For Silver Tongue Theatre, she designed Shiver by Oliver Emanuel (premiered at the Pleasance, Edinburgh in 2006); and for Pleasure Seekers Theatre she co-devised Ariadne and Point & Shoot, under the Tonic scheme for emerging theatre artists (Camden People's Theatre). Design for dance encompasses a fruitful collaboration with choreographer Amy Voris, with whom Susannah has designed two new works of contemporary dance: Hover and Overlap, presented as part of the Springheeled season (Blue Elephant Theatre, London).
Other dance-related work includes The Light Chapters, a short film with performer/choreographer Gary Lambert.
She has a design position with The Wrestling School, which produces the work of playwright and director Howard Barker. She is also active within theatre education as Lecturer in Stage Design on the MA Scenography for Dance at Laban and as an Associate Design Tutor at Mountview Academy of Theatre Arts.

Peter Higton

Formerly Resident Lighting Designer at the Chester Gateway Theatre, Peter Higton now works in an entirely freelance capacity, both as a lighting designer and as a lecturer in theatre lighting design. Recent work includes: Kaos Theatre Company's interpretation of Richard III (national tour); Alice Through the Looking Glass, Mother Goose and Cinderella (London Bubble Theatre); Woyzeck and Pericles, a site-specific co-production for Cardboard Citizens Theatre Company and the RSC, performed in a disused supermarket distribution warehouse off the Old Kent Road; Exit Allen, for the International Festival of Musical Theatre, Cardiff; David Copperfield and East Anglian Psychos for Eastern Angles Theatre Company. During his residency at the Gateway Theatre, Peter lit over 40 productions including the award-winning Macbeth and Torch Song Trilogy, and premieres of Wuthering Heights, Strangers on a Train, Vertigo, Crush, Girls' Night Out, Taking Liberties, Heart and Soul and All at Sea. Peter's freelance credits also include: Steven Berkoff's Coriolanus (Mermaid Theatre, London); Dishonorable Ladies, Honor Blackman's one-woman show (Criterion Theatre); The Wars of the Roses (Henry VI and Richard III), Twelfth Night, Tom Jones, Moll Flanders, Habeas Corpus, Up 'n' Under and Frankenstein (Theatre Royal, York). Peter's work has toured nationally with Confusions, Girls' Night Out, Three Steps to Heaven, for Paul Farrah Productions, and the highly acclaimed Cat on a Hot Tin Roof for Moon River Productions. Peter is an Associate Lecturer on the BA (Hons) Design for Performance course at Central Saint Martins College of Art and Design, London.

Simon Holdsworth

Simon Holdsworth trained at Wimbledon School of Art, London and at the Kunstacademie, Maastricht. Designs for Second Movement include: a double bill of The Medium and The Impresario (Covent Garden Film Studios, London); and Trouble in Tahiti (Hoxton Hall) all directed by Oliver Mears. More recently he designed Rinaldo (RSAMD, Glasgow and Edinburgh Festival Theatre) directed by Annilese Miskimmon. Theatre includes: screwmachine/eyecandy or: How I Learned to Stop Worrying and Love Big Bob (Assembly Rooms, Edinburgh) directed by John Clancy. For Steven Berkoff, Simon designed Richard II (Ludlow Festival); Messiah (Old Vic, London and West End); and The Secret Love Life of Ophelia (London, Edinburgh and Denmark). Work for repertory theatre includes: Ritual in Blood (Nottingham Playhouse) directed by Timothy Walker and Dracula (Derby Playhouse) directed by Stephen Edwards and Uzma Hameed. On London's fringe he designed 'Tis Pity She's a Whore (Southwark Playhouse) directed by Edward Dick. For children's theatre he designed The Invisible Monkey (New End Theatre) directed by Linda Marlowe. For dance, he devised and designed Frigidaire (Place Theatre, London) choreographed by Lea Helmstädter. Working in television, he designed The Waltz King (BBC 1) directed by Rupert Edwards.

Pamela Howard

Pamela Howard has worked as a stage designer in the UK, Europe and USA since 1960, and has realised over 200 productions. She has worked at all the major national and regional theatres, including the creation of several large-scale, site-specific works with the late John McGrath. She is now a director and designer, especially for opera and music-theatre. In 2005 she directed and designed the Greek premiere of The Greek Passion, the opera by Bohuslav Martin and Nikos Kazantzakis for the Opera of Thessaloniki, performed in the old Byzantine citadel/the former town prison. As writer/director/visual artist, she realised The New Jerusalem, a true story of evangelism in Britain in 1811. Productions as part of teaching assignments in 2005 for the National Theatre School in Copenhagen include: Why Do You Always Wear Black? and A Labour of Love (2006). In 2005, for University of the Arts Belgrade and BITEF Festival, Please take a Seat! - a memory play. Director/designer, At the End of the Earth (Julia Pascal). She is currently Artist in Residence at Carnegie Mellon University, Pittsburgh, where she has created an installation and performance piece in The Miller Gallery of Contemporary Art, Three Fragments from The Marriage. For December 2006, she was director of a site-specific event in the old City of London with writer Julia Pascal, The Petition – a Kind of History. In 2008 she will direct and design a new production of The Marriage, a comic chamber opera by Bohuslav Martin for Opera-Theater Pittsburgh, a European tour and the Martin Festival Prague 2009.

David Howe

David Howe's West End lighting design credits include: Pageant (Vaudeville Theatre); Seven Brides for Seven Brothers (Haymarket Theatre); Forbidden Broadway (Albery Theatre); The Vivian Ellis Awards (London Palladium); The Last Five Years (Menier Chocolate Factory); and Rags (Bridewell Theatre). Broadway: Primo (Music Box Theatre); recreation of the original National Theatre design. UK national tours of: Me and My Girl, Disney's Beauty and the Beast, Fiddler on the Roof, Carousel and The Demon Headmaster. Additional credits: Primo (Hampstead Theatre); Big Love (Gate Theatre); Corpse (Salisbury Playhouse); Turn of the Screw (Playhouse, Sevenoaks); My Darlin' Janey (King's Head); The Italian Straw Hat, Orestes 2.0 (Guildhall School of Music and Drama). Ballet includes: Toad for National Youth Ballet (UK tour); Images of Dance Triple Bill (UK tour); and Dame Beryl Grey Gala (Sadler's Wells). Opera work includes: La serva padrona, for the Royal Opera House. International design work: Woyzeck, (New York); Cabaret, for English Speaking Theatre (Frankfurt); Stars of the Musicals (Malaysia); Sunset Boulevard (Cork Opera House); and Who Shot the Sheriff? and Dracula (Tivoli, Copenhagen); Jesus Christ Superstar (tour of Sweden). Many other productions in Europe. As Associate Lighting Designer: Lord of the Rings, (Toronto and London); The Woman In White (West End and Broadway); Hamlet (Old Vic); Humble Boy (West End and UK tour); Into the Woods (Donmar Warehouse); Alarms and Excursions (UK tour and West End); Nine (Donmar Warehouse and Teatro de Blanco, Buenos Aries); Electra (UK tour and Donmar Warehouse); The Royal National Theatre's Carousel (West End, Japanese and US tours).

Richard Hudson

Richard Hudson was born and brought up in Zimbabwe. He trained at Wimbledon School of Art. He has designed plays for the Young Vic, Old Vic, Almeida, Royal Court, National Theatre, Royal Shakespeare Company, and theatres in the West End and on Broadway. For opera he has worked at the Royal Opera House, English National Opera, Glyndebourne, Metropolitan Opera, New York, Opéra National de Paris, Wiener Staatsoper, La Scala Milan, Lyric Opera of Chicago, Bayerische Staatsoper, the Bregenz Festival, and in Venice, Florence, Turin, Pesaro, Munich, Copenhagen, Opera North, and Scottish Opera.
He designed the sets for Disney's The Lion King, for which he won many awards, and which has been seen in New York, London, Tokyo, Nagoya, Osaka, Los Angeles, Chicago, Sydney, Melbourne, Hamburg, Amsterdam, and Shanghai.
He is the British Scenography Commissioner to OISTAT. In 2003 he won the Gold Medal for Set Design at the Prague Quadrennial and in 2005 he received an Honorary Doctorate by the University of Surrey.

Becky Hurst

Becky Hurst trained on the Motley Theatre Design Course. She is Resident Designer for Cartoon de Salvo for whom she has designed six shows: The Ratcatcher of Hamelin, The Sunflower Plot, The Chaingang Gang, Ladies and Gentlemen, Where am I?, Meat and Two Veg and Bernie and Clive. Other designs include: Kes, Knives in Hens, Electra, Pomegranate, Maybe Tomorrow and Pictures of Clay (Manchester Royal Exchange); Metamorphoses, Alice through the Looking Glass and Punchkin/Enchanter for London Bubble (site 2); Memory of Water (Watford Palace Theatre); The Real Thing (Northampton Theatre Royal); The Tempest (New Wolsey, Ipswich); Master Harold and the Boys (Bristol New Vic Studio and Southwark Playhouse); Breaststrokes (BAC); Measure for Measure (Cambridge Arts Theatre); Women of Troy and This Cookie May Contain Nuts (The Orange Tree Theatre); Taniko (The Queen Elizabeth Hall); Monogamy (Riverside Studios); and Logic (The Chelsea Centre Theatre). She has designed productions for LAMDA, Mountview Theatre School, Webber Douglas Academy, Oxford School of Drama, the London Sinfonietta Education Department and Share Music. Currently, she is designing Birds Without Wings for Eastern Angles and Romeo and Juliet for the New Wolsey Ipswich.

Martin Johns

Martin Johns started his career at the Belgrade Theatre, Coventry and then became Head of Design for the Tyneside Theatre Company, York Theatre Royal and Leicester Haymarket Theatre. During the latter period he designed the set for the West End production of Me and My Girl (the Adelphi and subsequently in Berlin, Broadway, Japan, Australia, South Africa, and British and American tours). The design was nominated for a Drama Desk Award and a Tony Award in America. Other West End shows include: Master Class (Old Vic and Wyndham's); Passion Play (Wyndham's); West Side Story (Her Majesty's); The Hired Man (Astoria); The Entertainer (Shaftesbury); Brigadoon (Victoria Palace); A Piece of My Mind (Apollo); The Secret Lives of Cartoons (Aldwych); Rolls Hyphen Royce (Shaftesbury); Let the Good

Stones Roll (Ambassadors); *Mack and Mabel* (Piccadilly); and the set for *The Romans in Britain* (National Theatre), Recent designs include: *A Different Way Home, The True Life Fiction of Mata Hari, Sitting Pretty* and *One Last Card Trick* (Watford Palace Theatre); *Breaking the Code* and *A Passionate Woman* (Chester Gateway Theatre); *The Daughter in Law* and *Thérèse Raquin* (Haymarket Theatre, Basingstoke); the LipService productions of *Very Little Women* and *Horror for Wimps*. He is now Resident Designer at Theatre by the Lake, Keswick and has designed the last eight seasons in the main house.

Mark Jonathan
As a lighting designer, Mark Jonathan's many international opera productions include: *Gianni Schicchi, Bluebeard's Castle* (Washington Opera); *Salome, Das Gehege* (Bavarian State Opera); *Ariadne auf Naxos* (LA Opera/Israeli Opera); and *Samson et Delila* (Israeli Opera) all with director William Friedkin; *Carmen* (Israeli Opera); *Hansel and Gretel*, director/designer Doug Fitch; *Peter Grimes*, director John Schlesinger; *Falstaff* and *Don Pasquale*, director Stephen Lawless, all at Los Angeles Opera. Musicals include *Marlene* playing in the West End, Paris and Broadway. His extensive work in ballet includes: *Cyrano* and *Beauty and the Beast*, for David Bintley, Birmingham Royal Ballet. For the Royal Ballet at the Royal Opera House, he has lit *Cinderella* (also at the New York Met, BBC TV and international tour); *The Sleeping Beauty* and *La Sylphide*. He lit Christopher Newton's recreation of Sir Frederick Ashton's *Sylvia* (a co-production with American Ballet Theatre at the Met), which was nominated for an Olivier Award for outstanding achievement in dance. He lit *Skylight* (Olivier Award for Best New Play) and *Honk!* (Olivier Award for Best New Musical) when he was Head of Lighting at the Royal National Theatre from 1993-2003. He has worked in many of the UK's repertory theatres and studios and became an Associate Artist of the Chichester Festival Theatre in 2006 where he lit the critically acclaimed *Nicholas Nickleby*.
For more information see www.markjonathan.com

Sophie Jump
Sophie Jump works in both theatre and dance and is a founder member and Artistic Associate of the Seven Sisters Group dance company. The company has become well known for its site-specific work and has toured nationally and internationally.
Theatre work includes; *Full Moon* (Theatr Clwyd and Young Vic); *The Tempest* (Shared Experience); *The Tempest* (A and BC Theatre Company); *The Difficult Unicorn* and *Blackbird* (both Southwark Playhouse). She is on the Equity Designers' Committee and is a Director of the Society of British Theatre Designers. She has received awards from the Society for Theatre Research and the John Hodgson Theatre Research Trust for her research into the London Theatre Studio and the Old Vic School.
Her work was chosen to form part of the British exhibit at the Prague Quadrennial in 1999 and 2003.

Simon Kenny
Simon Kenny trained in set and costume design at the Central School of Speech and Drama, graduating in 2001 with first class honours. His work has been seen across the UK and internationally, in Europe, the USA and Central America. His designs for theatre include: *The Comedy of Errors* (Cambridge Arts Theatre); *Are You Now or Have You Ever Been, Twelve Angry Men* (Tricycle); *The Veiled Screen, True or Falsetto?* (Drill Hall, and international tour); *Hansel and Gretel* (Windsor Arts Centre); He has designed for European tours of *A Midsummer Night's Dream* and *Relatively Speaking; Lord of the Flies* (West End); *Romeo and Juliet - The Panto!* (Kino-Teatr Bajka, Warsaw); *Carmen* (Hampstead Garden Opera); *The Ruffian on the Stair, The Erpingham Camp* (Greenwich Playhouse); *F***ing Romeo* (Young Vic Studio); *The Snow Queen* (Edinburgh fringe and tour); *Twelfth Night, King Lear* (Central); *The Very Nearly Love Life of My Friend Paul* (Finborough); *Savage/Love, The Mouse* and *The Woman* (Union); and two seasons of *Shakespeare for Breakfast* (Edinburgh fringe, and tour). Simon has also worked extensively as an assistant designer. His work as an associate designer includes: *The Caretaker* (Sheffield Crucible); *World Cup Final 1966 (UK tour)*; and Lysistrata (Arcola). He has also presented a number of site-specific installations and tours across Europe and designed a series of devised education projects for Creative Partnerships.

David W Kidd
Over 180 of David W Kidd's lighting designs have been seen in theatre, opera, ballet, music events and corporate theatre. His most recent work includes the ballet double bill *Andersen's Fairy Tales* for the Bulgarian National Ballet at Opera Sophia, *Die Walküre* for Den Ny Opera, Denmark, *Unsuspecting Susan* starring Celia Imrie and *Tabloid Caligula*, both in New York, the premiere of Pam Gems' *Nelson* and *Don Quixote* by Richard Curtis at the Nuffield Theatre, Southampton. West End credits include: *The Anniversary, The Female Odd Couple, The Dice House, Mademoiselle Colombe, Paul Merton Live at the Palladium*, plus numerous designs for the National Youth Theatre, most recently *Savages* (Royal Court); and Sextet (Soho and leading producing theatres across the UK). David originally studied graphic design and photography but ended up working as a theatre electrician for some years before becoming a freelance lighting designer. For more information see www.davidwkidd.com

Bridget Kimak
Bridget Kimak's designs for opera include: *Il Viaggio a Reims* and *Semele* (Chicago Opera Theatre); *La Cenerentola* (Royal Opera House, Linbury Studio); *Figaro's Bryllup*, (The Marriage of Figaro) and *Elskovsskolen* (Cosi fan tutte) for De Ny Opera, Denmark; *Cendrillon, Falstaff, The Marriage of Figaro* and *Idomeneo* for the Royal Scottish Academy of Music and Drama; *The Magic Flute* and *A Midsummer Night's Dream* for British Youth Opera; *The Maid of Norway* for Norway's Opera Vest; *Agrippina* for the Handel Society (Royal College of Music); and *The Man who Mistook his Wife for a Hat* (Bridewell Theatre, London). Other theatre credits include: *The Adventures of the Stoneheads* (Lyttelton Theatre, National Theatre); the world premiere of Stephen Sondheim's *Saturday Night, After Magritte, On the Twentieth Century, On a Clear Day You Can See Forever, Antony and Cleopatra, The Jewess of Toledo, Othello* and *The Best of Times* at the Bridewell Theatre; *Othello* at the Cochrane Theatre; *Hamlet, The Tempest, Macbeth, Twelfth Night*, and *A Midsummer Night's Dream* for the Young Shakespeare Company; *Hamlet* at Greenwich Theatre; *The Woman Who Cooked Her Husband, George's Marvellous Medicine, Mr Wonderful, The Thirty-nine Steps* and *Alice's Adventures in Wonderland* at Chester Gateway Theatre; and *A Midsummer Night's Dream* at the New Vic Studio. Bridget also leads workshops for the Royal Opera House.

Kevin Knight
Kevin Knight trained at the Central Saint Martins School of Art in London and has worked extensively as a set and costume designer in the United Kingdom and abroad. He has worked at most of the country's leading repertory theatres and on numerous West End productions. He has designed premieres of plays and musicals that have toured throughout Europe and America where productions have gained international recognition and won numerous awards. As an international opera designer he has worked for many of the world's leading opera companies. Credits include: *Lady Macbeth of Mtsensk* (Canadian Opera Company, Toronto); *Pastorale* (World Premiere, Staatstheater Stuttgart); *Tannhäuser* (La Scala, Milan); *Il Trovatore* (Bologna/Japan); *Il Lombardi* (Florence); *I Capuletti eil Montecchi* (Spoletto Opera Festival, USA). *The Miserly Knight/ The Florentine Tragedy* (Teatro San Carlos, Lisbon); *Les Contes d'Hoffmann. Summer and Smoke* (Central City Opera Festival, Denver USA); *Death in Venice* (Chicago Opera Theatre, USA); *Die Drei Pintos* and *Mirandolina* (Wexford Opera Festival and Lugo Opera Festival, Italy); *La Finta Giardiniera* (Garsington Opera Festival); *Daphne* and *Ariadne auf Naxos* (Teatro La Fenice, Venice and Vlaamse Opera, Antwerp); *Königskinder*, winner of the Premio Abbiati (Teatro San Carlo, Naples); *Sweeney Todd* and *Don Giovanni* (Opera North). Current projects include: *La Bohème* for Santa Fe Opera Festival 2007 and *Die Frau ohne Shatten* for Lyric Opera Chicago.
His theatre work includes directing and designing the world premiere of Naomi Wallace's stage adaptation of *Birdy* for the West End and American productions, which won the Barrymore Award for Outstanding Contribution to Stage Design); and *The Truman Capote Talk Show*, which won an *Edinburgh Fringe First Award* and was also produced in London, Off Broadway and on a European Tour. British premieres of the plays *Oktoberfest* and *Webster* in London. He is currently a Senior Lecturer in Performance Design at Central Saint Martins.

Ralph Koltai
Hungarian by descent, Ralph Koltai served with the British Intelligence Service at the Nuremberg Trial and War Crimes Interrogation at the end of the Second World War.
He subsequently studied Stage Design at the Central School of Art and Design in London. He has designed some 250 productions of drama, opera and dance throughout the world, and is generally regarded as the innovator of British theatre design of the mid-last century. As an Associate Artist of the Royal Shakespeare Company he has designed some 30 productions, including a distinguished *Cyrano de Bergerac* and Hochhuth's *The Representative* on the subject of the Holocaust. For The National Theatre *Brand* - and the ground-breaking all-male *As You Like It*. His most memorable recollection is the Brecht/Weill, *Mahogany* for Sadler's Wells Opera, under the supervision of the legendary Lotte Lenya, the original Jenny in 1928. He has won numerous national and international awards, including several at the Prague Quadrennial where he has exhibited on all occasions since 1975. He has had several exhibitions of his work in Britain, mainland Europe and Asia. In 1983 he was awarded Commander of the Order of the British Empire (CBE). His book *Designer for the Stage* states: 'Ralph Koltai's distinguished career covers half a century and continues to inspire new ways of looking at well known classic works, as a result of his strong personal aesthetic. From the first collaboration with the Ballet Rambert, through his huge variety of drama work with national companies, opera, dance and musicals, Koltai is renowned as a designer internationally. He has created over 200 productions, vividly demonstrating his unique ability to respond to the demands of the individual commission while maintaining a clear and personal voice. His particular way of working with fact and fiction, art and metaphor, investigating different forms of reality, is the essence of the designer's art.
His work demonstrates his instinctive ability to translate a vast emotional subject into a simple abstract image, which lives in the imaginary world of the theatre.'

Wai Yin Kwok
Wai Yin Kwok achieved first class BA Honours in Theatre Design at Rose Bruford College. She was amongst the 12 finalists who contributed to the Linbury Biennial Prize exhibition for Stage Design at the National Theatre in 2005. Her recent set designs include: *The Mona Lisas*, in collaboration with Theatre Mélange and Teatrul Municipal Ariel, Romania (UK tour including The Brewhouse Theatre, Taunton and Riverside Studio 2, London); and *Homesick* (New End Theatre, London and Leeds International Jewish Festival). Set/costume designs include: *Dead Fiddler* (New End Theatre, London); *Easy to Love* (Catford Broadway Theatre); *Inflame* (BAC, London); and *Gascoyne Circus/ Twist Da Hood* (Immediate Theatre Company). Assistant work includes: *What Does It Take* with Dana Pinto and *Antiphony* with Mike Lees. Upcoming designs include *I Sing* at The Union Theatre, London.

Stefanos Lazaridis
Stefanos Lazaridis has worked extensively in Britain and abroad, notably in theatre (Chichester Festival Theatre, the West End, Almeida Theatre, RSC) and opera. He has designed more than 30 productions for ENO including. *Rusalka* (also Frankfurt and Rome); *Lady Macbeth of Mtsensk* (also Amsterdam); *Hansel and Gretel* (also Venice and Amsterdam); *Macbeth, Wozzeck, The Adventures of Mr Broucek* (also Munich); *Doctor Faust, Madam Butterfly, The Mikado* (also Los Angeles, Houston, Venice and New York); *Tosca* (also Florence and Houston); and all seven productions in the 2000 Italian Opera Season. He has also designed *Der Ring des Nibelungen*, Royal Opera House, Covent Garden between 2004-2006 with the first full cycle in 2007; the 1988 arena production of *Carmen* at Earl's Court and international tour; the Athens Olympics in 2004. and many productions in Europe and the USA including for the lake stage at the Bregenz Festival of *Der Fliegende Holländer. Nabucco* and *Fidelio* (all produced by David Pountney); *The Greek Passion* (Bregenz Festspielhaus and Royal Opera); *La Fanciulla del West* (La Scala, Milan, Turin and Tokyo); *Peleas et Mélisande* (Nice); *Werther* (Vancouver); *I Pagliacci* and *Cavalleria Rusticana* (Staatsoper, Berlin); *The Turn of the Screw* (La

Monnaie, Brussels); *Moïse et Pharaon* (1997 Rossini Festival at the Palasport, Pesaro); *Katya Kabanova, Faust* (Bayerische Staatsoper Munich); *Lucia di Lammermoor* (Tel Aviv); *Lohengrin* (Bayreuth Festival); and *Wozzeck* (Royal Opera Covent Garden). He directed and designed: *Oedipus Rex* (Opera North, Leeds); *Oedipus Rex, Bluebeard's Castle*, and *Maria Stuarda* (Scottish Opera); *Orphée et Eurydice* (Australian Opera); *The End of Life* (Athens); and Duran Duran's 1993 Rock Show (North American tour). Awards include *London Evening Standard* and *Olivier Awards* for his work for ENO; *Olivier Award for Best Opera Production* for The Greek Passion; the 1998 Opernwelt German Critics' award for Designer of the Year for Julietta (Opera North) and The Turn of the Screw (La Monnaie); the 2000 Martinu Foundation Medal; a Diploma of Honour at the 1999 Prague Quadrennial; the 2003 Laurence Olivier Award for *Wozzeck* at The Royal Opera House, Covent Garden. He was a member of the Golden Triga winning UK exhibition at PQ2003, and is now Artistic Director Of the Greek National Opera in Athens.

Marie-Jeanne Lecca
Marie-Jeanne Lecca was born in Bucharest where she studied at the Beaux Arts Institute. She now lives in London and works extensively in opera. Her set and costume designs include: *Therese Raquin* (World premiere, Dallas); *Falstaff, The Stone Guest, Pelleas* and *Melisande* (ENO): and *Carmen*. (Houston, Seattle, Minnesota). Among her recent costume designs are: *The Ring Cycle, Wozzeck, Greek Passion* (Royal Opera House, joint winner Oliver award); *Julietta, The Dwarf* and *Seven Deadly Sins* (Opera North, South Bank Show Award); *Moses and Aron, Faust, Katya Kabanova* (Bayerische Staatsoper, Munich); *Die Soldaten* (Ruhr Triennale); *Maskarade, West Side Story* (Bregenzer Festspiele); *Turandot* (Salzburger Festspiele); *Peter Grimes, Macbeth* (Opernhaus, Zurich); *Jenufa, Rienzi* (Wiener Staatsoper); *Salammbo* (Opera National de Paris); *The Turn of the Screw* (La Monnaie, Brussels): *Magic Flute* (Wiener Volksoper); *The Nose* (De Nederlandse Opera, Amsterdam); *Der Freischutz, The Adventure of Mr Broucek* (ENO). She received the Martinu Foundation Medal for *Julietta* and *The Greek Passion* and was nominated by Opernwelt Magazine as costume designer of the year for *Maskarade*. Her theatre work includes sets and costumes for *As You Like It* and *La Bête Humaine* (Nottingham Playhouse); and costumes for *The Taming of the Shrew* (RSC); and *Napoleon* (West End); for film and TV *Amahl and the Night Visitors* (BBC, Wales, BAFTA nomination). She was part of the British team that won the *Golden Triga* at the 2003 Prague Triennale.
Current projects are *L'Etoile* (Zurich), and *Khovanshchina* (WNO).

Adrian Linford
Adrian Linford trained at Wimbledon School of Art in London. Work includes: *Betrayal* (Mercury Theatre, Colchester); *Die Fledermaus* for Scottish Opera-Go-Round 2006/7; *The Turn of the Screw* for Macedonian Opera; and Judith Weir's *The Vanishing Bridegroom* (RSAMD, Glasgow). He has also designed: *Bay at Nice/Family Voices* (Mercury Theatre); Grange Park Opera's *Così fan tutte* (Grange Park and tour); and *Assassins* for Pimlico Opera (Ashwell and Coldingly prisons). Other opera includes: *Albert Herring* (Aldeburgh Festival); *Nabucco* and *Così fan Tutte*, Opera West; *Orlando*, Cambridge Handel Opera; *Il Seraglio* for English Touring Opera; and the co-design for Il Trovatore (Bastille Opera), directed by Francesca Zambello. Other theatre work includes: *Stars in the Morning Sky, Fen, The Promise, The Shoemaker's Wonderful Wife, Inside the Firm, A Cat on a Hot Tin Roof, Blood Wedding, The Glass Menagerie* and *Camino Real* and the UK premiere of *When Five Years Pass*. Adrian has designed in Singapore and the Far East on productions of *Blithe Spirit, They're Playing Our Song, Art* (a musical who-done-it), *A Twist of Fate*, and *A Little Shop of Horrors*. Adrian was Associate Designer to the artist Anish Kapoor on his designs for *Idomeneo* (Glyndebourne Opera, 2003), and worked closely with Maria Bjørnson on a number of her productions including: *Katya Kabanova* and *Don Giovanni* (Covent Garden), realising her sets for *Les Troyens* (Metropolitan Opera, New York); and *The Little Prince* (Houston Opera).

Keith Lodwick
Keith trained at Central School of Speech and Drama. Work includes: *Full Frontal Diva* (Finborough); the UK premieres of *A...My Name is Alice* (Bridewell); and *Ruthless!* (Stratford Circus). Ruthless was awarded Best Musical on the Fringe by *Musical Stages* magazine. Other work includes: *Sweeney Todd* (UK tour); *The Lady of the House of Love* (BAC); *The Little Prince* (Linbury Studio, Royal Opera House); *Take It to the Green Light, Barry* (Latchmere 503); *Bent* (Courtyard); *Great Expectations* (Shaw Theatre); and *Oliver!, Mr Cinders, Is There Life After High School* and *The Laramie Project* for the Arts Educational Schools. Keith's stage adaptation and design of Angela Carter's *The Bloody Chamber* won a Herald Angel Award for Outstanding Achievement at the Edinburgh Festival and was nominated for a Best Design Award. Keith has also worked for the V&A Theatre Museum and recently curated/designed an exhibition on the work of Oliver Messel. *Oliver Messel: Making & Doing* is an interactive exhibition with an emphasis on theatre design and prop-making for children and young adults and is currently touring the UK.

Sophia Lovell Smith
Sophia Lovell Smith has just completed a large creative project, *Mapping the Body*, with Jubilee School, Hackney. She is at present designing *Beneath the waves* for Tell Tale Hearts, a promenade interactive show for 5 - 7 year olds. In 2006 she has been involved in designing *Master Juba* for a GLYPT touring dance production using digital animation as part of the design. Also *In Praise of Fallen Women*, a Fingersmiths production with Jeni Draper, Jean St Clair and Kate OReilly, using BSL and film (Drill Hall, London). Sophia has designed for touring shows, outdoor promenade events, collages, schools shows and exhibitions.
Last year Sophia designed for ENO, installations for the Coliseum's Sky Bar, working with the season's opera themes. She loves the collaborative process required for good theatre, working with long-term working partners, discovering new people and new skills. She is currently exploring the possibilities of digital animation and film in theatre. Previous companies worked with include: Theatre by the Lake in Keswick, Shaker, Lyric Hammersmith, Scarlet Theatre, Young Vic, Graeae, Theatre Rites, Unicorn, Little Angel, Theatre Centre and M6 Theatre. In 2007 Sophia is back working with Tony Graham at the Unicorn with *Jemima Puddle Duck and her Friends* and later with Jenny Sealey, at Graeae, with *The Flower Girls*.

Alex Lowde
Alex Lowde attended the Motley Course having read Drama at the University of Hull. He spent a year on a bursary with the Newcastle Playhouse where his designs included: *Angelic to Alnwick* and *Romeo and Juliet*. He has designed *Triptych, Candide* and *The Threepenny Opera* for the Opera Group; *The Gentle Giant* and *The Nose* for ROH2; and *Tobias and the Angel* for the Young Vic and ETO.

Alex Marker
Alex Marker trained in theatre design at Wimbledon School of Art and has designed over 40 productions. He is Associate Designer at the Finborough Theatre and for Shapeshifter. At the Finborough Theatre, his designs have included: *Eden's Empire, The Representative, Red Night, Lark Rise to Candleford, Albert's Boy, Hortensia and the Museum of Dreams, Trelawny of the Wells, Happy Family, Soldiers, How I Got That Story*, and *The Women's War* - a Centenary Celebration. Other designs include: *Cooking With Elvis, Gym and Tonic, The Opposite Sex* and *Inside Job* (Lyceum Theatre, Crewe): *Oklahoma!* (New Wimbledon Theatre); *Hush* (The Pleasance, Edinburgh and Arcola, London); *Marat/Sade* (University College Northampton); *Twelfth Night* and *Been So Long* (Broadway Theatre, Catford); *Marília Pêra Sings Ary Barroso* (Bloomsbury Theatre); *Oedipus, Agamemnon* and *Androcles and the Lion* (The Scoop, City Hall, London); and *A Doll's House, The Ruffian on the Stair* and *The Erpingham Camp* (Greenwich Playhouse). He recently designed an exhibition to commemorate the 100th anniversary of Brentford Football club held at Gunnersbury Park Museum in London. He is part-time Lecturer in Theatre Design and related subjects at Kingston College and is Director of the Questors Youth Theatre, the largest non-agency run youth theatre in London.

Tanya McCallin
Tanya McCallin trained at Central School of Art and Design. After a period designing for several of the principal repertory companies throughout Britain and many fringe theatres in London, she began a series of productions of new plays for Hampstead Theatre, including the original productions of Mike Leigh's *Abigail's Party*, filmed for the BBC, and *The Elephant Man*. Her work in the theatre continued with many productions in the West End, at the National Theatre and throughout the UK, Australia, the USA and on the continent.
Her opera work includes: Jonathan Miller's production of *The Barber of Seville*, (ENO and Barcelona); and in collaboration with David McVicar, *Manon* (ENO, Houston Grand Opera, New Zealand Opera and Dallas Opera); *Macbeth* (the Mariinsky-Kirov, St Petersburg, Covent Garden, the Met and Kennedy Centre, New York); *The Tales of Hoffmann* (Salzburg Festival 2003 - video and DVD); the set for *Semele* (Theatre des Champs Elysées 2004,video and DVD); the costumes for *Der Rosenkavalier* (Scottish Opera and Opera North); and *Rigoletto* (Royal Opera, Covent Garden, video and DVD, BBC).
Her most recent work includes: the costumes for *Così fan tutte* in Strasbourg; *Le nozze di Figaro* for Covent Garden; and *The Turn of The Screw* in St Petersburg. She is currently designing *Carmen* for the Royal Opera House and is soon to begin a new collaboration with David McVicar on *La Traviata*. Tanya has been closely associated with the Theatre Department at Central St Martins and was External Examiner from 1996 to 2000. She has exhibited in London, Sheffield and Manchester and was part of the winning entry at the Prague Quadrennial 2003 with her designs for the Kirov's Macbeth.

Gary McCann
Gary McCann trained in Theatre Design at Nottingham Trent University. His design credits include: a new opera, *Promised Land* (Marlowe Theatre, Canterbury); *Les Pêcheurs de Perles, La Bohème, The Barber of Seville, La Fille du Regiment* (Swansea City Opera); *The Glass Menagerie, The Man of Mode, Goblin Market, Merry Christmas Betty Ford, The Government Inspector, Twelfth Night, Tearing the Loom, The Visit, Iphigenia in Aulis* (Lyric Theatre, Belfast); *Thieves Carnival, Jungle Book, Broken Glass, Arabian Nights* (Watermill Theatre, Newbury); *The Witch, The Government Inspector* (RADA); *Song of the Western Men, Shang-a-lang, One Snowy Night, The Lost Child* (Chichester Festival Theatre); *Elizabeth, Oriana, Romeo and Juliet* (Kabosh Productions, Belfast); and *Top Girls* (Live Theatre, Newcastle). He has worked as Art Director and Assistant Designer on major TV, theatre and opera productions including: *Les Troyens* (The Met, New York); *The Breath of Life* (Haymarket Theatre, London); *The Woman in White* (Palace Theatre, London); *The Queen of Spades, Sophie's Choice* (Royal Opera House, Covent Garden); and *The Turner Prize* (Channel 4).
Gary is Associate Artist with Belfast-based Ransom Productions. His designs with them include: *Hurricane* (Soho Theatre/Arts Theatre London, 59th St Theatre New York); *Protestants* (Soho Theatre); *The Half* (touring) and their next commission, *The Early Bird* by Leo Butler (2006).

Laura McEwen
Laura McEwen has a first class degree in Theatre Design from Nottingham Trent University. Since graduating, she has designed for numerous companies including Pilot Theatre Company, York Theatre Royal, Southwark Playhouse, Sheffield Crucible, Red Earth Theatre, Nottingham Playhouse Roundabout, Unicorn Theatre and the English National Opera Baylis Programme. Her most recent work includes: *East is East* for Pilot Theatre Company (national tour); *The Crane* for Red Earth Theatre (Leicester Haymarket); and *Anansi and the Sky God* (Unicorn Theatre, London). She enjoys designing for a range of spaces, including studios, main stages, parks, community centres, school halls, classrooms and site-specific environments. In 2005 Laura won the *Manchester Evening News* Design Award for *Beautiful Thing* with Pilot Theatre Company (Bolton Octagon).

As well as designing, she frequently works as a creative workshop leader, employed by theatre in education companies, youth theatres, galleries, schools and community groups. Laura has a specific interest in new and devised work and is Associate Director of Red Earth Theatre Company. For more information see www.lauramcewen.co.uk

Prema Mehta

Prema Mehta graduated from the Guildhall School of Music and Drama, London. Her recent theatre lighting designs include: *Year 10* (TJP, Théâtre National de Strasbourg, BAC and Finborough); *Top Girls* and *Two Lips Indifferent Red* (Academy of Live and Recording Arts); *The Trouble with Asian Men* (Arts Depot); *Swingin' in Mid-Dream* (The Albany Theatre); *I Live in Tribeca* (The White Bear Theatre); *Wyrd Sisters* (Upstairs at the Gatehouse); *Cariad* directed by Ken Christiansen and *Free From Sorrow* directed by Robert Bowman (both Tristan Bates Theatre). Dance credits include: *The Robin Howard Commission 2005 - Parallels/ Dissonant/Fine Line* for Rashpal Singh Bansal (The Place); *Dissonant/Parallels* for Dance Umbrella (Lilian Baylis Theatre, Sadler's Wells).
Opera designs for *Opera Scenes*, directed by Martin Lloyd-Evans, include: *Semele, Albert Herring, Così fan tutte, Die Zauberflöte, Manon, Semele, Hänsel und Gretel, Don Pasquale* and *The Rake's Progress* (Guildhall Studio).
Assistant work includes *Death of a Salesman* with Broadway lighting designer (LD) Michael Philippi (The Lyric Theatre); *Così fan tutte, Roméo et Juliette* with LD Giuseppe di Iorio (Peacock Theatre); Associate work includes *Gianni Schicchi* and *Il Tabarro* with LD Simon Corder (Guildhall School of Music and Drama). Forthcoming projects include: *The Trouble with Asian Men* directed by Kristine Landon-Smith (Soho Theatre and UK tour); *Spill* by Sonia Sabri (The Place Prize); and *Year 10* directed by Max Key in Brittany, France. For more information see www.premamehta.com

Fred Meller

Educated at the University of Ulster and Royal Welsh College, Fred Meller received an Arts Council Design Bursary. She has designed for the RSC, Cardboard Citizens, The Almeida, Unicorn Theatre, Eastern Angles, the Watermill Theatre, the Nuffield Theatre, the Gate Theatre and the National Theatre Studio, and Grid Iron.
The synthesis of the live and recorded, performer and image is realised in spaces other than theatre buildings, designing for spaces that include an old hospital, a jam factory, a mortuary, a disused brothel, labyrinthine, Victorian town hall cellars, a supermarket distribution complex and the biggest potting shed in Europe. Fred exhibited at the Prague Quadrennial in 1999 and 2003, winning the *Golden Triga* and was selected to exhibit at the World Stage Design in Toronto 2005. Other awards include the *Jerwood Design Award* and *Year of the Artist Award*. She is a Fellow of the Arts Foundation, and a Senior Lecturer at Central Saint Martins College of Art and Design.

Miranda Melville

Miranda Melville studied fine art at the Byam Shaw School and trained as a teacher, before studying on the Motley Theatre Design Course with Percy Harris. She has designed extensively for theatre, opera, film and dance, while continuing with fine art and more recently sculpture/installation.

This includes co-designing a Gold Medal-winning garden at Chelsea Flower Show, a large earthwork for Westonbirt International Garden Festival and filling the Barbican stage with peas, while designing *How To Live* for Bobby Baker. Her designs for opera and music theatre led to her designing the film biography of Handel, *Honour, Profit and Pleasure*; the opera film *Scipio's Dream* by Judith Weir for the BBC's *Not Mozart* series; and Benjamin Britten's opera *Owen Wingrave*, which he wrote for television. After a period of working solely in film, when she designed a number of dance films including: *Cross Channel* with The Cholmondeleys and The Featherstone-Haughs, and *Outside In* with Candoco, she now has returned to theatre design. More recently, her work has been predominantly for dance and multi-disciplinary companies, notably Yolanda Snaith Theatre Dance and V-tol Dance Company, with whom she collaborated on their large education projects and designed many productions. For Goat and Ricochet Dance Company she has recently designed the *Move*.

Julian Middleton

Julian Middleton joined Arts Team in 1990. He has worked on a wide range of projects, differing in scale and content, across Arts Team's portfolio of buildings. He has also concentrated on the early stages of project development including writing briefs, feasibility and conceptual work. His background in urban master planning helps to locate this work in its broader physical and cultural context. From 2001 Julian also worked as a Scottish Arts Council Lottery assessor, and on the Pier Gallery in Stromness. The Donmar Warehouse for Sam Mendes was his first arts project. He also has a long-standing involvement with the integrated youth theatre company Chicken Shed and was responsible for the design of their permanent home in Enfield, North London. He was responsible for the design of the Auden Theatre at Greshams School in Norfolk, which utilises a natural ventilation system. After working on proposals for a new performing arts centre at Gordonstoun School, Julian designed the new music and drama centre at Chigwell School in Essex. He followed his feasibility study work for Walthamstow Arts Trust with concept diagrams of the proposals for the Walthamstow Arts Centre.
His recent work has included a new performing arts building for University College Chester, extending and transforming Wakefield Theatre Royal, and remodelling Newcastle Playhouse to become a European centre of the performing arts for Northern Stage.

Madeleine Millar

Suddenly, it is 28 years that Madeleine has been working professionally in theatre. In that time she has designed for many companies and directors, mostly for small, medium and large-scale touring productions, with the odd opera and now TV, film and music video. She was very much involved in the theatre in education and the young people's theatre movement, working on several productions for companies such as Leeds TIE, Pit Prop, Theatr Powys and TAG. She has designed for York YPT, Sheffield Crucible Youth Theatre and in 2005 and 2006 with young homeless people in Ashton-under-Lyne in conjunction with Cardboard Citizens Theatre Company. Since the mid 1980s, Madeleine has made and exhibited her own sculpture, based on costume, corsets and crinolines, and portraits and self-portraits of women artists from the past. This work has had an influence on her theatre design, most

apparently in the set for *The Good Soldier* for Public Parts Theatre Company. TV and film credits include: *Last of the Summer Wine* and *Sea of Madness* for One Day Films; *Goodbye Mr Snuggles* for Between the Eyes Films; and most recently the music video for Larrikin Love's *Happy as Annie*, Mezzo Films.

Anne Minors/AMPC

Anne Minors Performance Consultants are devoted to creating the best conditions for making and enjoying performances with all the senses. Since 1996 the practice has been briefing, planning and equipping new performance spaces for the future; working with directors, performers and architects to explore and extend existing spaces and their repertoire; and creating solutions for integrating technology with buildings. AMPC believe in the triumvirate of architect/performance consultant/ acoustician to design facilities with excellent acoustics, sightlines and ambience. The work of the practice includes
● preparing the brief for buildings where people gather;
● assessing existing buildings for their suitability as performance venues;
● advising on the theatrical planning requirements of backstage and front of house;
● advising on the disposition of the audience and the form of the auditorium to achieve good performer/audience relationships;
● integrating and detailing the production equipment within the auditorium to give a cohesive design;
● advising on the facilities management of the performance spaces.
AMPC are performance consultants, not limited to theatre but acknowledging that dance, music, drama and visual and digital art are often combined in the same presentation. AMPC create concepts for performance from the ingredients unique to each project, its client and its siting. There are no formulaic solutions. AMPC combine the knowledge of 21 years experience in the business with the enthusiasm of a recently formed and growing company. Continuity of personnel throughout a project is an aim for a consistency of approach and the carrying through of intent. AMPC are also concerned with how the building and the company prosper post-completion. The creation of a building to enable further artistic endeavour is rewarding in itself, but it is merely the birth of a new era in the company's development. How the company responds to the building and how the building sparks new horizons of creativity is the exciting part.

Nick Moran

Nick Moran has been working in performance lighting for over 25 years. After graduating from Imperial College in 1981, his first professional jobs included stage managing a touring pantomime and lighting designs for several plays on the London Fringe. In 1982 he started working for Theatre Projects Lighting, moving to White Light in 1983 and going freelance in 1985. In 1986 he joined Vari*Lite UK, which eventually lead to the role of programmer for the first use of moving lights on a continuing West End show, *Miss Saigon*. After several successful years working in Germany and Austria, Nick returned to the UK in 2001 to join English National Opera as a Lighting Manager. In this position he helped to create and recreate lighting for some of the best known names in lighting design including: Hugh Vanstone, Mark Henderson, Rick Fisher and Pat Collins, as well as continuing to work on his own lighting designs. Since September

2003, he has held the post of Lecturer in Lighting at the Central School of Speech and Drama. His freelance career continues with lighting design work for music television (MTV Concerts in 2004); drama, including *Bullies House* (Riverside Studios and national tour); *The Comedy of Errors* (Embassy Theatre); and production design for *Love is a Dog from Hell* (Vienna).

Martin Morley

Martin Morley trained at Wimbledon School of Art (1963-1966). He first worked as a design assistant at the Royal Lyceum Theatre, Edinburgh. While there, he designed three productions, including: *Juno and the Paycock* and *The Ha-Ha*.
From 1969-72 he was Head of Design at the Liverpool Playhouse, designing a wide range of plays from Shakespeare to Bond. There followed a lengthy period as designer for Cwmni Theatr Cymru (1973-84). With them he learnt the skills of designing touring productions for a wide range of venues. The repertoire was mainly Welsh and ranged from contemporary writing to translations of European classics. It was a very stimulating period. In 1984 Martin went freelance and also branched out into TV design, which now dominates his output, notably, *Hedd Wyn* (BAFTA Cymru 1993 with Jane Roberts for Best Design) and a string of drama series for S4C. During this period he has designed several productions for Theatr Gwynedd, Bangor, including *Pwy Syn Sal*, a Molière double bill directed by Graham Laker and Firenza Guidi (exhibited in *Time+Space*); *Dyn Hysbys* (Faith Healer) by Brian Friel, directed by Sian Summers (exhibited in *Time+Space* and the 1999 Prague Quadrennial); and *Amadeus* directed by Graham Laker, which was exhibited in the *2D|3D* exhibition in Sheffield. *Hen Rebel* was Martin's first production for the Theatr Genedlaethol Cymru.

Ruari Murchison

Ruari Murchison has designed productions in Washington DC; at the Stratford Festival, Canada; in Stuttgart, Germany; Luzern, Switzerland; Haarlem, Holland; Elsinore, Denmark; and Nilsea and Helsinki, Finland. London work includes: productions at the National Theatre, the Royal Shakespeare Company, the Royal Court, the Young Vic, Hampstead Theatre Club, the Drill Hall and Soho and Greenwich Theatres. He has worked in major regional theatres including: Nottingham Playhouse, Crucible Theatre Sheffield, West Yorkshire Playhouse, Theatr Clwyd, Birmingham Rep, Bristol Old Vic. Recent design work includes: *Mappa Mundi, Frozen, The Waiting Room, The Red Balloon* (National Theatre); *Titus Andronicus* (Royal Shakespeare Company);
The Solid Gold Cadillac (Garrick Theatre); *A Busy Day* (Lyric, Shaftsbury Avenue); *Peggy Sue Got Married* (Shaftesbury Theatre); *Henry IV, Parts 1 and 2* (Washington Shakespeare Company, USA); *West Side Story, The Sound of Music* (Stratford Festival, Canada); *Hamlet* (Elsinore, Denmark); *Hedda Gabler, Electricity, Medea, The Lion, the Witch and the Wardrobe, Alice* (West Yorkshire Playhouse); *Mrs Warren's Profession, The Threepenny Opera, An Enemy of the People* (Theatr Clwyd); *The Life of Galileo, A Doll's House, The David Hare Trilogy: Racing Demon, Absence of War, Murmuring Judges* (TMA Best Design Nomination 2003); *The Tempest, Macbeth, The Merchant of Venice, Hamlet, Frozen, Jumpers, Nativity, A Wedding Story* (Birmingham Rep); *Alfie* (Palace Theatre, Watford). National tours

include; *Twelfth Night, Hamlet, Merchant of Venice, Romeo and Juliet, A Wedding Story, A Doll's House, Dracula* and *Little Sweet Thing*.
Opera work includes: *Der Freischutz* (Opera Cava/ Finnish National Opera); *Peter Grimes, Così fan tutte* (Luzerner Opera, Switzerland); *La Cenerentola, Il Barbiere di Siviglia* (Garsington); *L'Italiana in Algeri* (Buxton); *Les Pèlerins de la Mecque, Zazá* (Wexford); *The Magic Flute, A Midsummer Night's Dream* (Covent Garden Festival). Ballet work includes: *Landschaft und Erinnerung* (Stuttgart Ballet, Germany); *The Protecting Veil* (Birmingham Royal Ballet); *Le Festin de l'Araignée* (Royal Ballet School, Royal Opera House Gala) all choreographed by David Bintley.

Conor Murphy
Conor Murphy was born in Ireland and trained at Wimbledon School of Art, gaining a first class honours degree in Theatre Design and later an MA Scenography in Utrecht, Holland. Designs for opera include: sets and costumes for *The Turn of the Screw* (Nationale Reisopera, Holland); *Pierrot Lunaire* (Almeida Opera); two versions of *Salome* (Opéra National de Montpellier); *Susannah* (Wexford Festival Opera); *The Fair Maid of Perth* (Buxton Festival); *Powder Her Face* by Thomas Adès (Flanders Opera, Belgium); *The Rape of Lucretia* (Flanders Opera Studio); *Greek* by Mark Antony Turnage (Queen Elizabeth Hall and tour of UK and France); *The Country of the Blind* also by Turnage (Aldeburgh Festival and QEH); *The Lighthouse* (Neue Oper Wien, Austria); *The Magic Flute* (Opera Northern Ireland); *The Marriage of Figaro* (Grange Park Opera); *La Bohème* (Augsburg, Germany); Un Ballo in Maschera (Opera Zuid, Holland); and the world premieres of *Facing Goya* by Michael Nyman (tour of Spain and Italy) and *Die Versicherung* by Jan Müller Wieland (Darmstadt, Germany). He has also designed the sets for *Olav Tryggvasson* (Norwegian Opera); *The Flying Dutchman* (Opera Zuid, Holland) and *Il Trovatore* (English National Opera).
Designs for dance include: *The Four Seasons* (Birmingham Royal Ballet); *Attempting Beauty* (Munich); *Giselle, A Midsummer Night's Dream* and *Carmen* (Donlon Dance Company, Saarbrücken)
Designs for theatre include: *The Birthday Party* (Bristol Old Vic); *Major Barbara, The Playboy of the Western World* and *Sex Chips & Rock n Roll* (Royal Exchange, Manchester); *Salome* (Riverside Studios); *Measure for Measure* (English Touring Theatre); *Summer Begins* (Donmar Warehouse); *The Decameron* (Gate Theatre); *Hamlet* and *Pericles* (National Theatre Studio); and *The Rivals* (Abbey Theatre, Dublin).

Neil Murray
Neil Murray is Associate Director and Designer at Northern Stage. Since 1992 his directing/designing credits with the company include: *Great Expectations, Kaput!, Cinzano* and *and Smirnova's Birthday, Pandora's Box* (with Emma Rice), *The Tiger's Bride, The Threepenny Opera, Carmen, They Shoot Horses Don't They?, Therese Raquin, The Swan* and numerous Christmas shows, including: *Beauty and the Beast, The Snow Queen*, and *Grimm Tales*. His latest piece for Northern Stage is *The Little Prince*. He has also designed most of the company's other work, including: *Wings of Desire, Blood Wedding, The Ballroom of Romance, A Clockwork Orange, Animal Farm, 1984, The Black Eyed Roses, Romeo and Juliet, Twelfth Night, Edmund, Not I, The Dumb Waiter* and *Homage to Catalonia* (co-production with West Yorkshire Playhouse, Teatre Romea, Barcelona and MC Bobigny93, Paris). He was Associate Director/Designer at Dundee Rep for ten years and prior to that he was Resident Artist in Theatre at the Arts Lab in Birmingham, where he created mixed-media theatre pieces, which toured internationally.
He continues to work with other companies when time allows.
Recent work includes: *1001 Nights Now* and *Wings of Desire* (Betty Nansen Theatre, Copenhagen); *Princess and the Goblin, Laurel and Hardy, Mrs Warren's Profession* (Royal Lyceum, Edinburgh); *Like Water for Chocolate* (Théâtre sans Frontières) and *Tutti Frutti* (National Theatre, Scotland).

Kimie Nakano
Kimie Nakano studied Costume at ENSATT in Paris and Theatre Set and Costume Design at Wimbledon School of Art. She trained at the Opéra de Paris and at the Saito Kinen Festival in Japan, as an assistant designer and assisted academy award winner Emi Wada in both opera and film, including *8 and a Half Women* by Peter Greenaway. Kimie designed the award-winning *Yabu no naka*, directed by Mansai Nomura, in the Japan Art Festival 1999 and collaborated with choreographer Megumi Nakamura on *Sandflower*, receiving the Gold Award in the Maastricht Festival 2000. Design in the UK includes: *8:15* with choreographer Megumi Eda for Ballet Rambert (Place Theatre); *Kensuke's Kingdom, Big Magic* (Polka Theatre); *Sumidagawa* (The Britten Festival); *Rashomon* (Riverside Studio); *Futon and Daruma* and *Festival for Fish* (New Wimbledon Studio Theatre); *The Picture of Dorian Gray* (BAC); *I Only Want You to Love Me*, with director Yvonne McDevitt (Cambridge and Theatre 503); *Our lady of the Drowned* (Southwark Playhouse); *Karius & Baktus* (Hackney Empire, Bullion Rooms); *Double Tongue* (Old Red Lion); *Lady Aoi* (New End Theatre); *The Conquest of the South Pole* and some short films for Theatre Resource. She directed Snow (workshop) ENO studio with disabled singers. An ambition is to create multicultural and educational projects for both the young and for disabled people, through experimenting in various media, digital animation, film, TV, installation and through workshops in theatre.

Dody Nash
Dody Nash specialises in music-based performance and installation projects. She explores relationships between sound, image, word and movement, and ideas of form and journeying.
In 2000, she started developing *The Early Earth Operas* (ENO) with a composer, librettist, and several hundred children. It was performed en masse at the London Coliseum in 2004. In frame-by-frame animation, Dody evolved the paintings of 300 children into moving scenery. Meanwhile, the exploration of the idea of solid space (initially a *Henry Moore Institute* proposal) has led to a strand of work curating and designing public spaces. She was commissioned by the South Bank Centre to create an installation celebrating Luciano Berio and was creative lead of an international team. *The Berio Lounge* enjoyed thousands of visitors. Designs, notably the *Listening Shell* (co-designed with Julian Brown RDI), have been exhibited in London and Paris, featured globally in print, online, and on Channel 4's *Grand Designs*. She created a sculpture gallery for DuPont to further investigate applications of material technology (*100% Design*).
Dody has developed project briefs for the Royal Designer for Industry Summer School and has devised projects with young people for ROH, ENO, Opera North and Glyndebourne. She was resident designer for *2D13D* exhibition (Plymouth); Visiting Lecturer on the Visual Practice MA (Queen Mary's, University of London). She is a member of the Museum of Learning - curators and educators who meet to brainstorm ideas and methods.

Pip Nash
Pip Nash trained in Art in Social Contexts at Dartington College of Arts, and on the Motley Theatre Design Course. Early design work brought her into contact with new writing, designing productions for the Royal Court Theatre (George Devine Award, Young Writers' Festivals and Royal Court Young People's Theatre). Writers included Paulette Randall, Louise Page and Hanif Kureshi. Several years followed as Resident Designer, firstly with Common Stock theatre company, creating new productions for inner London studio and open air tours, with writers including Bryony Lavery, Tony Coult and Deborah Levy. This was followed by working as Associate Designer at The Dukes Playhouse in Lancaster, working on a number of main house, studio, TIE and open-air productions of devised, classic and contemporary texts. Subsequent freelance design work encompassed main house repertory theatres, including York Theatre Royal and Cheltenham Everyman, and design for dance and theatre in education, including Ludus Dance, Pentabus, Theatr Powys. In 1993 Pip was appointed to run the BA (Hons) Theatre Design course at Rose Bruford College, where she remains as Senior Lecturer. When not teaching, she maintains a freelance career, more recently focusing on devising site-specific, open air and promenade theatre, for companies including London Bubble, Cardboard Citizens, Theatremongers and Garden Opera, in venues as diverse as Billingsgate Fish Market, a Cornish Cave and Oxleas Woods.

Phil Newman
Phil Newman has been in regular demand as a set and costume designer since graduating in Theatre Design from Croydon College in 1999. Since then, he has designed a wide range of productions, from small- and medium-scale tours, through site-specific and devised projects, to main house shows. These have included work *Funnybones* for SNAP Theatre; *You Don't Kiss* and *Monogamy* for Pursued by a Bear; *Treasure Island* for Palkettostage (Italian tour), interactive projects for Ladder to the Moon and Trestle Theatre, and an open-air production of *The Railway Children* for Heartbreak Productions. His design for the internationally acclaimed, award-winning production of John Retallack's *Hannah & Hanna* (*Time Out* Critics Choice) has toured the UK, India and the Philippines since 2001. Over the past six years, Phil has designed seven community tours for Channel/Chalkfoot Theatre (including *The Phoenix & the Carpet, The Sea Morgan's Child* and *The Ragged Trousered Philanthropist*) as well as TIE tours and, most recently, an open-air *Taming of the Shrew*. He has also designed settings for 14 productions at Leicester's Little Theatre and costumes for *The Way of the World* (Pentameters) and *The Dutch Courtesan* (Wimbledon Studio). His ongoing collaboration with director Olusola Oyeleye has produced the world premiere production of *The Playground* (Polka Theatre) which was *Time Out* Critics Choice, in addition to the critically acclaimed *Ma Joyce's Tales from the Parlour* (Oval Theatre).

Pippa Nissen
Pippa Nissen works as an architect and as a theatre designer. She received an MA in Theatre Design from the Slade School of Fine Art, specialising in Greek theatre. She worked for several architecture practices that specialise in the design of theatre buildings before founding the architecture practice Nissen Adams, together with Ben Adams. In 2005 she was selected as one of 40 young architects under 40, as part of the *40 under 40* exhibition at the V&A. She has designed theatre sets both in the United Kingdom and abroad. Recent projects in the UK include: *A Midsummer Night's Dream* (RSAMD); *Transfigured Night* (Opera North); *Breaking The Code* (Northampton Theatre); *The Forest Murmurs* (Opera North); *Kantan/ Damask Drum* by Alexander Goehr (Almeida Opera, Aldeburgh Festival); and *Eugene Onegin* (Clonter Opera/ Buxton Festival) with Netia Jones.
Work with the Actors Touring Company and the director Nick Philippou on productions that toured small venues in the UK, includes: *The Boy Who Left Home* by Michael Wynne and *Faust Is Dead* by Mark Ravenhill. International work with Tim Hopkins includes *The Rake's Progress* (Staatsoper Hannover); *Mare Nostrum* by Mauricio Kagel and *Eugene Onegin* (both at Theater Basel). She has used film increasingly in her work, including an installation *Video Collage* (the Forster Inc. Showroom). She started a theatre partnership that considers the relationship of opera and film, *Live Video Projects*, with opera director Netia Jones. Two projects, *Elevator* and *Transmission Will Resume*, were completed in 2004. Other recent projects include *Elephant and Castle*, with the director Tim Hopkins, for which she received a Research and Development Award from the Arts Council in 2005 and in 2006, *The Paper Nautilus* a new opera by Gavin Bryars, directed by Cathie Boyd (The Tramway). At the Prague Biennale in June 2005 she exhibited a series of films, *The Hospital*, which consider the relationship between theatre and architecture. This was her second exhibition in Prague, following the Prague Quadrennial International Scenographers Exhibition in 1999, where she was part of the British group, and an exhibition at the Theatre Museum in 2000.

Stuart Nunn
In the nine years since graduating from the Nottingham Trent University Theatre Design course, Stuart has worked as set and costume designer in his own right as well as assisting other designers whose work has been an inspiration.
In this time he has been assistant set designer to Tim Hatley on projects including: *Les Miserables* (Gothenburg Opera); *Suddenly Last Summer* (Donmar at The Comedy); *Hamlet, Darker Face of the Earth* and *Sleep With Me* (National Theatre). He has worked with Rob Howell on *Sunset Boulevard* (UK tour); *Our House, the Madness Musical* (The Cambridge Theatre); and *Sophie's Choice* (Covent Garden) amongst others. With Tim O'Brien work includes: *Ulysses Comes Home* for Birmingham Opera Company; *The Ring Cycle* (Lisbon); and with Paul Brown *Die Zauberflöte* (Salzburg Festspiele); and *He Had it Coming / Don Giovanni* for Birmingham Opera Company. He won a Linbury Prize in 1997 for *The Alchemical Wedding* (Salisbury Playhouse) and in recent years has concentrated on his designs for productions including *Close to Home* and *The Crowstarver* for Theatre Alibi; *The Black Monk* (Bloomsbury Theatre);

Pickwick (Basingstoke Haymarket); *Cy Rano* (Hurtwood House); and *Oz* (Unicorn Theatre). Stuart continues to enjoy collaboration with director Graham Vick and frequently acts as assistant designer to Tim O'Brien and Paul Brown on opera projects around Europe and with Birmingham Opera Company. Work continues on *The Ring Cycle* until 2008 and 2009 sees the opening of *Aida* at Bregenzer Festspiele.

Nissen Adams
Nissen Adams was started in 2002 by Pippa Nissen and Ben Adams, who met while studying at Cambridge University. Currently the office is six people based in London Bridge. They have experience of working with a diverse range of clients: commercial developers, restaurateurs, education establishments and private individuals. They have a particular passion for designing theatre spaces, installations and unusual spaces. This has led to the formation of ZNA Consultancy in 2006 with the lighting designer Zerlina Hughes, where they are looking at lighting design for theatre, exhibitions, public art and architecture. In 2005, Nissen Adams were in several exhibitions including the prestigious *40 under 40* exhibition run by the *Architects' Journal* which toured around the UK, from the V&A. Nissen Adams were included in *Föhn*, an exhibition at the Chelsea Space Gallery curated by Rob Wilson. The Chelsea Space is a new architecture gallery run by Chelsea Arts and the exhibition explored the theme of ideal architecture. They were selected for *Vision 05* at the Left Wing Gallery in London, an exhibition of art by architects sponsored by the *Architects' Journal* and Corus. In January 2006 they also exhibited in *Compendium* at the RIBA, Portland Place.

Francis O'Connor
Francis O'Connor was born in Teesside and trained at Wimbledon School of Art. He has designed plays, musicals and operas throughout the UK, Europe, Asia, Canada and the United States. He has worked extensively in Ireland with his regular director, Garry Hynes. Work produced with Garry and her company, Druid, includes: the multi-award winning *The Beauty Queen of Leenane* and *The Lonesome West* (London and Broadway runs); reinterpretations of the work of John B Keane, most recently *The Year of The Hiker*, and *The Synge Cycle*, a marathon staging of the works of John Millington Synge. Francis works regularly with the Young Vic Theatre, where designs include David Lan's production of *A Raisin In The Sun*. He is a regular collaborator with Martin Duncan, most recently on musical productions at Chichester Festival including *Out of this World* and *How to Succeed*.
His opera designs include: *Manon* for Opera North; *Der Vogelhändler* (Komische Oper Berlin); and *Don Pasquale* (Garsington Opera) all with Daniel Slater directing. Francis regularly designs for Grange Park Opera and will design *The Magic Flute* for their tenth anniversary in 2007. His most recent opera design was for *La Traviata* (ENO) again with long-time collaborator Conall Morrison.

Christopher Oram
For the Donmar: *Frost/Nixon, Grand Hotel – The Musical, Henry IV, World Music, Caligula*, which one the *Evening Standard* Award for Best Design 2003, *The Vortex, Privates on Parade, Merrily We Roll Along, Passion Play, Good, The Bullet*.
For Sheffield Crucible: *Suddenly Last Summer* (and Albery) which won the Critics' Circle Award for Best Design, *The Tempest* (and Old Vic), *Richard III, Don Juan, Edward II, The Country Wife, Six Degrees of Separation, As You Like It* (and Lyric Hammersmith).
Other theatre includes: *Evita* (Adelphi); *Guys and Dolls* (Piccadilly); *Macbeth, The Jew of Malta, The Embalmer* (Almeida); *Stuff Happens, Marriage Play/Finding the Sun, Summerfolk* (NT); *Power* (NT, 2004 *Olivier Award* for Best Costume Design); *Oleanna* (Gielgud), *Loyal Women, Fucking Games* (Royal Court); *The Caretaker, All My Sons* (Bristol Old Vic);
Film: *The Magic Flute* (director: Kenneth Branagh).

Ben Pacey
Ben Pacey is a freelance lighting designer, specialising in designing for theatre, dance and devised-performance companies. Ben's recent theatre work includes: *Frozen, After Miss Julie* and *The Birthday Party* (Theatre by the Lake, Keswick); *Shiver* and *Bella and the Beautiful Knight* for Silver Tongue Theatre (touring); *Antigone* for InSite Performance (Walworth Council Chambers); and *This Lime Tree Bower* for the Young Vic (Theatre 503). He is a member of the award-winning devising company Mapping4D, with whom he has collaborated and designed light for *Slender* (2006); *The Pink Bits* (2004) and *Vertigo* (2004). He recently collaborated as a co-devisor and lighting designer on *I Am Waiting For The Opportunity To Save Someone's Life*, for The Other Way Works (Mailbox, Birmingham); and designed light for the Uninvited Guests touring production of *It Is Like It Ought To Be: A Pastoral*. His lighting design for dance includes: Wired Aerial Theatre's *Homemade/Handmade* (Linbury Studio, ROH), *She Lies with Me* (Brindley Theatre and tour) and *Stuffed* (touring). Other work includes: *Augustine* and *Disgo* for the Darkin Ensemble; *Mirage* for Srishti-Nina Rajarani Dance Creations; *Forest* for Maxine Doyle and Felix Barrett; and *Ruins* for Anurekha Ghosh. For more information see www.benpacey.co.uk

Roma Patel
Roma Patel is especially interested in collaborative and multidisciplinary productions. Her work includes set and projection designs for theatre, art direction and set visualisation for film and digital installation art. She has focused on the potential of digital technology within the performance space, and has conducted research into the scalability of virtual reality and immersive interactivity. Graduating in Set Design for Stage and Screen from Wimbledon School of Art, Roma went on to investigate the possible use of digital technology for the purposes of theatre set design for her MA at the UCE. After a period in the Netherlands, where she started to explore real-time software in her own work, Roma returned to the UK in 2004 to complete work on her first artist-curatorship, *The Living Image*, for the London International Festival of Theatre. This real time, 3D, interactive installation, the result of collaboration with two other artists, was exhibited at the Dana Centre, London Science Museum in 2004. Roma has designed sets and projections for several theatre

companies in UK and Europe since 1998. Her most recent designs include the sets for a site-specific production of *The Tempest* and *The Merchant of Venice* for Corcadorca Theatre company, Cork. She has worked with Manchester Library Theatre as visual artist, on stage projections for *Merlin* and *The Real Thing*. The Desperate Optimists worked with her to develop 3D computer visualisations for their short film in Town Hall set in West Bromwich. Roma is also a part-time lecturer at Nottingham Trent University and has worked as a visiting lecturer on the theatre courses at Central St Martins College of Art and Design, Rose Bruford College, and Loughbrough University. She has presented papers on interactivity and theatre in Britain and Germany.

Dana Pinto
Dana Pinto studied Theatre Design at Wimbledon School of Art and has an MA Scenography from Birmingham Institute of Art and Design. With over ten years experience in set and costume design, she has combined her creative role with collaborative work as a production manager, creative skills coordinator, arts manager and youth arts consultant. She currently combines her freelancing with work in schools and colleges around London contributing her skills in set and costume design in workshop settings. Theatre designs include: *What Does it Take?* (Albany); *Soul Sikher* (Watermans and international tour); *AmaZonia* (Bridewell Theatre); *Harmony in Harlem* and *Urban Tales* (George Wood Theatre); *Lost and Found* (Barrow-in-Furness); *Protest* (Old Vic Theatre); NITRObeat (Royal Festival Hall and Contact Theatre Manchester); *One Dance Will Do* (Theatre Royal Stratford East tour); the Ned Rorem operas, *Fables, Bertha* and *Three Sisters Who Are Not Sisters* (Bridewell Theatre); and *Hess – The Prince of Spandau* (Barraca Teatro Lisbon); *Two In One* (Polimedia Theatre, Korea); and *Write This Rhythm: Love* (Bloomsbury Theatre). Production designs and art direction for film include: *Professions of Love* for Unbearable Films Ltd; *Snarl* for Carter White, Shepperton; *Something Gnawing at Me* for Boogle Eyes Productions, which won Best Production Design; and *Almost* for Day for Night Films. For more information see www.danapinto.co.uk

Tom Piper
While studying Biology and then History of Art at Cambridge University, Tom Piper designed over 30 student productions. He then took a two-year postgraduate course at Slade School. This was followed by six months assisting on Peter Brook's production of *The Tempest* in 1990, before starting a freelance career. He has designed for many regional theatres including: *Les Liaisons Dangereuses* directed by Sam West (Bristol Old Vic); *Insignificance* (Sheffield Lyceum); *The Master Builder* (Lyceum Edinburgh); and has a long-standing collaboration with Dominic Hill at Dundee Rep Ensemble, where his design for *Twelfth Night* won the Scottish Critics' Circle Award for Best Design in 2003. He first worked with Michael Boyd at the Tron Theatre designing pantomimes, before the 1993 production of *Macbeth* took him to the RSC. Since then he has designed over 15 productions for the RSC, including *A Midsummer Night's Dream, Hamlet* and the acclaimed *Henry VI History Cycle*. At the National Theatre he designed *The Birthday Party*, directed by Sam Mendes and the touring, big top version of *Oh What a Lovely War*.

For the Donmar he has designed *Three Days of Rain, Frame 312* and *The Lie of the Mind*. His few adventures into opera have included a *Macbeth* for Scottish Opera and *Babette's Feast* in the Linbury Studio, ROH, directed by Tim Supple. Tom was appointed RSC Associate Designer in 2003. Since then he has been involved in the design of the Courtyard Theatre and the on-going collaboration with Bennetts Associates on the redevelopment of the Royal Shakespeare Theatre.

Jacob Polley
Jacob Polley is an award-winning poet living in Carlisle. His first book, *The Brink* (Picador), was a Poetry Book Society's Choice for winter, 2003, and was shortlisted for five major awards, including the TS Eliot, Forward and John Llewellyn Rhys prizes. In 2002 he received the BBC Radio 4/Arts Council of England First Verse Award, judged by Andrew Motion. He is also the recipient of an *Eric Gregory Award* from the Society of Authors. In October 2005, he took up the year-long post of Visiting Fellow of the Arts at Trinity College, Cambridge. Jacob's second collection of poems, *Little Gods*, was published by Picador in 2006. More information can be found at his website: www.jacobpolley.com

Jean-Marc Puissant
Jean-Marc Pussant's career began as a dancer, studying ballet at the School of Paris Opera and the Conservatoire National Supérieur de Paris. He studied Art History and Archaeology at the Sorbonne and then trained at the Motley Theatre Design Course. Now based in London, he designs set and costumes for theatre, opera and dance. He has created original designs for, among others, Royal Ballet, New York City Ballet, American Ballet Theatre, Nederlands Dans Theater 2, Birmingham Royal Ballet, Dutch National Ballet, Rambert Dance Company, Pennsylvania Ballet, Opéra National du Rhin Ballet, San Francisco Ballet, Berlin Ballett – Komische Oper, Hubbard Street Dance Chicago and Royal Academy Opera. He has collaborated with choreographers including: Christopher Wheeldon, on *Tryst, VIII, Quaternary, Klavier, For 4*, and *Swan Lake* (costumes); Javier de Frutos on *Elsa Canasta, Nopalitos, J. Edna and Mother Tolson, El Uno Y Medio*; David Bintley on *The Seasons*; Maina Gielgud on *Giselle*; Marcia Haydée on *Sleeping Beauty* (set); Cathy Marston on *Dividing Silence* and *Viatore*; Adrian Burnett on *Now and Hereafter*; and with directors Stephen Henry on *The Irish Curse*; Toby Frow on *Peer Gynt* and *Of Mice And Men*; William Relton on *L'Incoronazione di Poppea*; Daniele Guerra on *Ciboulette*; and Andrew Neil on *The Tales From The Vienna Woods*. His productions have been performed across Europe, the United States and Australia, on the main stages of the Royal Opera, Covent Garden and Sadler's Wells, the Mariinsky (Kirov) and Bolshoi theatres, New York's State Opera, Lincoln Center and City Center, and the Sydney Opera House. *Tryst*, designed for The Royal Ballet at Covent Garden, was nominated for Best New Dance Production at the 2002 *Olivier Awards*. *Elsa Canasta*, designed for Rambert Dance Company, was nominated at the 2003 *Olivier Awards*. Pennsylvania Ballet's *Swan Lake* was presented at the 2005 Edinburgh International Festival.

Stephen Pyle
In 1979, following a 12-year backstage and workshop apprenticeship, Stephen Pyle established his own studio, This proved to be extremely opportune timing as it was the dawning of a golden age for British theatre design with the emerging talents of a number of designers coupled with supportive and enthusiastic managements in theatre and opera. The workshop's pioneering development and expansion of glass-fibre as a scenic material with its light-weight strength and versatility led to some amazing sets, such as Ralph Koltai's 'lead' *Richard III* (National Theatre); Bill Dudley's Gothic *Richard III* (RSC) and eventually to Maria Bjørnson's Baroque sculptures for *The Phantom of the Opera* (West End, London and worldwide).
Later collaborations with Mark Fisher included two Rolling Stones and one U2 world tour, and a ten-metre *bas relief* portrait of Nelson Mandela for the 46664 Aids benefit concert in 2003. The studio continues to supply scenic sculptures and ornament to the international entertainment industry from its new premises within Elstree Film Studios.

Katherina Radeva
Katherina Radeva studied at the Bulgarian National High School for Fine Arts in Sofia, followed by a degree in Theatre Design at Wimbledon School of Art.
Katherina designs for theatre and dance and since 2003 has been devising her own solo, performance-art pieces, which have been presented at live art festivals including *Expo*, Nottingham and *East End Collaborations*, London. As a designer and performer, Katherina believes in experiencing the entirety of a production. Her drawings and design work is informed by an understanding of what it is to perform and her performances are aided by a knowledge of the concept of design. She believes that a simple representation of an idea lends an importance to the symbolic and the metaphorical as a means with engaging with the now, enabling her to act within the cultural present, whilst remembering the past. Designs include: *Deferral* (WSA Theatre, London); *Daffodils* (The Place, London); *Smother Mother* (a design for film); *Twelfth Night* (site-specific performance Soho, London); *Settling Dirt* (national tour) and *The Underpants* (Old Red Lion Theatre, London).

Michelle Reader
Michelle Reader's work spans the disciplines of design for performance, live art, installation and sculpture. She creates mechanical sculptures, wearable art and objects that interact with performers. She has a degree in Fine Art from De Montfort University and an MA Scenography from Central Saint Martins College of Art and Design. In 2003 Michelle designed *Words Afoot* by Foot in Hand (Derby Dance Centre). She has worked as designer/facilitator for Big Fish Theatre, and works frequently with Bamboozle Theatre Company as the designer on week-long residential projects. In 2004, she assisted Lizzie Clachan with Shunts *Tropicana*, for which she made a leatherette ambulance disguise for a hearse.
In 2005, Michelle designed Greg McLaren's *Riot Pilot* at the Hackney Empire, creating cardboard, scale replicas of buildings and items from the Town Hall Square. The audience participated in recreating a fictional historical riot inside the room, which would spill out into the square itself.
The first manifestation of Michelle's ongoing *Experimental Anatomy* series was a collaboration with performance artist Tessa Wills. This resulted in performances in a shop window as part of *Clockworks* in Brighton, and at the *Fresh* festival (South Hill Park, Bracknell) in 2005. In 2006 she created a mechanical bird in a cage for Garsington Opera's *The Philosophers' Stone*, and an interactive 'Wave' portal for Strandloopers *Silver Swimmers* street performance. For more information see www.michellereader.co.uk

Erik Rehl
Eric Rehl is a production designer, trained at the Moscow Arts Theatre and Central Saint Martins, where he received an MA with Distinction for producing his own stage adaptation of a Gogol short story *The King Is Somewhere Incognito*. Designing for theatre, dance, film and TV he set up his own company *Scenografika* to facilitate his visual arts interests. Erik co-founded dance theatre group Company Q with choreographer Charlotte Hacker and has created the scenography for all their works including *Q*, *KUSAUCHIK* and *Charnik-1*. Other theatre credits include: *Jarman Garden* and *Bloodknot* (Riverside Studios); *Sick Dictators* (Jermyn Street); *Counterpoint* (the Gatehouse); Arnold Wesker's *Letter To A Daughter* (the Assembly Rooms) and lighting design for Di Trevis' production of *The Voluptuous Tango* (Hoxton Hall). He was Associate Designer for the world premiere of the musical *Tomorrowland* (New Opera Theatre, Moscow) and for English Touring Theatre's *Cherry Orchard* with Prunella Scales, and scenographer for Shared Experience's adaptation of *Anna Karenina* with the Quantum Theatre in the USA. Erik production designed his second feature film, Josh Appignanesis' *Song of Songs*, starring Nathalie Press, as well as his short about dementia, *Ex Memoria*, starring Sara Kestelman. He recently art directed Martin McDonagh's 2006 short film *Six Shooter*, starring Brendan Gleeson and an exploding cow, which won the 2006 *Academy Award* for Best Live Action Short Film.

Peter Rice
Peter Rice is currently the Deputy Head of Sound at The Royal Exchange Theatre in Manchester. Most recently he has designed the sound for: *Mary Barton* and *Separate Tables* (Royal Exchange); *Christmas is Miles Away* (the Bush); *Lysistrata* (the Arcola); *Horror For Wimps* for Lip Service; *Crocodile Seeking Refuge* for iceandfire and *On the Shore of the Wide World* (National Theatre), as well as over 20 shows for the Royal Exchange's Main House and Studio Theatres. Forthcoming projects include *Things of Dry Hours* for the Royal Exchange Studio.

Colin Richmond
Colin Richmond is originally from Northern Ireland. He trained at the Royal Welsh College of Music and Drama, gaining first class BA Hons in Theatre Design and The *Lord Williams Award* for Design two years running. He was also a 2003 *Linbury Prize* for Theatre Design finalist and a Resident Designer as part of the Royal Shakespeare Company's Trainee Programme 2004-2005. Recent productions include: *L'Opera Seria* (Batignano Opera Festival, Tuscany); *Human Rites* (Southwark Playhouse); *Speakeasy* (Sherman Theatre Cardiff); *Hansel and Gretel* (Northampton Theatre Royal); *Lowdat* (Birmingham Rep); *Play Not I* (BAC - winning design JMK Young Directors Award); *Twelfth Night* and *Bad Girls - The Musical* (West Yorkshire Playhouse); *Breakfast With Mugabe*, directed by Anthony Sher (Swan Theatre, RSC, Soho Theatre, Duchess Theatre, West-End); *Bolt Hole* (Birmingham Rep); *House of the Gods* (Music Theatre Wales; Restoration (Oxford Stage Company); *Shadow of a Gunman* (Glasgow Citizens Theatre); *One act opera* by Jonathan Dove (London and Italy). Television includes: assistant production designer (set) *Doctor Who* BBC WALES (pre-production and series one).

Malcolm Rippeth
Malcolm Rippeth's designs include: *Cymbeline, Nights at the Circus, The Bacchae, Pandora's Box for Kneehigh; Scuffer, The Lion, the Witch and the Wardrobe, Voodoo Nation, Homage to Catalonia, Medea* (West Yorkshire Playhouse); *Kaput!, Cinzano and Smirnova's Birthday, The Snow Queen, Noir, The Tigers Bride* (Northern Stage); *Mother Courage, Hamlet, Romeo and Juliet* (English Touring Theatre); *Hay Fever, Macbeth* (York Theatre Royal); *Lush Life, Toast, Charlie's Trousers, Keepers of the Flame, Cooking with Elvis* (Live Theatre, Newcastle); *Foyer, The Selfish Giant* (Leicester Haymarket); *Dealer's Choice* (Salisbury Playhouse); *Coelacanth, Black Cocktail* (Edinburgh Festival); *Bintou* (Arcola); *Little Sweet Thing* (Eclipse Theatre), *Monkey* (Dundee Rep) and *Faustus* (Hampstead Theatre). He has also lit: *The Ball, La Vie des Fantasmes Érotiques et Esthétiques, La Nuit Intime* (balletLORENT); *Who put Bella in the Wych Elm, Infinito Nero* (Almeida Aldeburgh Opera); and *The Philosophers' Stone* (Garsington Opera).

John Risebero
John Risebero trained in Theatre Design at Central Saint Martins College of Art and Design. He is co-founder of Antic Disposition, for whom he has co-directed and designed *Romeo and Juliet* (Festival Shakespeare du Quercy and Cochrane Theatre); *Richard III, A Christmas Carol* (St Stephen's, London) and *The Shakespeare Revue* (UK tour and Festival Shakespeare du Quercy). Other designs include: *A Midsummer Night's Dream, Richard III, Macbeth, Hamlet* (French tours), all of which he also co-directed; *Closer* (ADC, Cambridge); *Golden Boy* (Yvonne Arnaud/UK tour); *The Barber of Seville* (Linbury Studio, Royal Opera House); *The Lover* (White Bear); *Evelina, Johnny Simple* (Pentameters); *Waking Up Suddenly* and *Heroes* (Blue Elephant). John has worked on numerous productions as assistant designer, including: *L'Elisir d'Amore* (Glyndebourne); *Edward Scissorhands* (Sadler's Wells and UK tour); *Acorn Antiques: the Musical!* (West End); *Les Liaisons Dangereuses* (Sadler's Wells and Japan); *A Little Night Music* (Leicester Haymarket) and *Whistle Down the Wind* (West End and UK tour). John's design for *Closer* was part of the award-winning British exhibit at the Prague Quadrennial International Exhibition of Stage Design 2003. For more information see www.johnrisebero.com

Francisco Rodriguez-Weil
After obtaining a degree in Architecture at the Universidad Central de Venezuela, Francisco completed a course in Theatre Design at the Bristol Old Vic Theatre School, graduating with distinction in 2000. Having worked as a costume assistant on the series *Teachers* for Channel 4 Television, his stage credits include: *Spring Awakening* (QEH Bristol); *The Beggars Opera* (WNYO); the world premiere of *Daydreaming* by Tim Arthur (Man in the Moon); *When We Are Married* (Bristol Old Vic, at the Theatre Royal); *Miss Julie* (Bristol Old Vic, The Basement); and *The School For Scandal* (Redgrave Theatre, Bristol); *Robin Hood* (National Theatre, Loft); *Anyone Can Whistle* (Bridewell Theatre, London); *A Dangerous Woman* (Jermyn Street Theatre); *Falstaff* (RNT Cottesloe, Platform Performance); *Immaculate Conceit* (Lyric Hammersmith Studio); *Amadigi* (Iford Manor); *Life After George* (Vienna's English Theatre and Frankfurt's English Theatre); *Alice* (touring show, Netherlands). Francisco worked as a set design developer on the musical *The Three Musketeers* (Theatre des Westen, Berlin); *Who Killed Mr Drum* (Riverside Studios); *Othello, Spiel Im Berg* (Young Actors Teatre) and *Fefu and her Friends* (MMU Manchester). He is currently working on *Broadway Shadows* (Grand Theatre, Luxembourg) and *Watercolours* (UK national tour).

Lili Rogué
Lili Rogué was born in France but moved to Britain six years ago. She first trained in Spatial Communication at the Ecole Supérieure des Arts Appliqués et du Textile in Lille, before gaining first class honours in Theatre Design at Nottingham Trent University.
Theatre credits include: *Hobson's Choice* (York Theatre Royal); *Aesop's Fables* (Nottingham Playhouse Roundabout); *Energise & Falling* and *Eyecatcher* (Sheffield Theatres Creative Development Programme).
Assistant designer work includes: *The White Album* (Nottingham Playhouse) and *The Retirement of Tom Stevens* (Lakeside Arts Centre).
She has led Theatre Design workshops for Sheffield Theatres, Lakeside Arts Centre and Sheffield University and also lectures in model making at Nottingham Trent University. Lili is also Associate Designer for Sheffield Theatres Creative Development Programme. For more information see www.lilirogue.com

Peter Ruthven Hall
Peter Ruthven Hall originally trained as an architect. He now works freelance as a stage designer and as a theatre consultant with Theatreplan. He has worked extensively in opera both in the UK and elsewhere in Europe. Productions extend from repertory works to a host of rare operas, many of them premiere performances: *Der Stein der Weisen* (Garsington); *The Turn of the Screw* (Snape Maltings); *Flavio and Ottone* (London Handel Festival), *Jenufa, Le nozze di Figaro, La Bohème, Albert Herring* and *Roberto Devereux* (Royal Northern College of Music); *A Midsummer Night's Dream* (Royal College of Music); *L'Arlesiana* (Holland Park Opera); *Lakmé* (Opera Ireland); Mendelssohn's *Camachos Wedding* and Schubert's *Fierrabras* (Oxford Playhouse); and costume designs for *Tosca* (Malmö Musikteater); *Madama Butterfly* (Royal Danish Opera); *The Turn of the Screw* (Opera Northern Ireland); *Zar und Zimmermann* (Stadttheater Aachen), *Don Giovanni* and *Die Zauberflöte* (Vienna Kammeroper). In musical theatre he has designed original workshop productions of Andrew Lloyd Webber's *Sunset Boulevard* (Sydmonton Festival); *Tutankhamun* (Imagination); and *World Café* (Edinburgh Festival); and in theatre: *Love! Valour! Compassion!* (Library Theatre, Manchester); *Long Day's Journey into Night* (Theatre Royal, Plymouth and Young Vic, London); *The Grapes of Wrath* (Crucible Theatre, Sheffield); *Women of Troy* and *Vassa Zheleznova* (Gate Theatre, London); and *The House of Bernarda Alba* (Oxford Playhouse). For the international design group,

Imagination, his work includes the sets for *Joy to the World* at the Royal Albert Hall (four consecutive years) broadcast on BBC1. He was one of the award winning British designers exhibiting at the 1995 international Prague Quadrennial exhibition of stage design. As Secretary for the Society of British Theatre Designers he jointly organised three major exhibitions of contemporary design. The 2003 exhibition won the top international award - the *Golden Triga* - at the 2003 Prague Quadrennial. He is also joint author of three books on British scenography: *Make SPACE!*, *Time+Space* and *2D|3D*.

Emma Ryott

Emma Ryott trained at Trent Polytechnic. Design credits include: *Rock 'n' Roll* by Tom Stoppard (Royal Court/Duke of Yorks); *Der Sandmann* (Stuttgart Ballet); *Barber of Seville* (Neville Holt, Grange Park Opera); *Damnation of Faust* (Semperoper Dresden); *The Return of Ulysses* (Royal Ballet of Flanders); *Berenice* (Heidelberg); *Oedipus Rex* (Epidaurus Festival, Greece); *One Touch of Venus* (Opera North); *La Peau Blanche* (Stuttgart Ballet); *King and I* (Design Supervisor UK tour); *Pearl Fishers* (Kazan Russia and European tour); *Ragtime* (Piccadilly Theatre); *Lulu Eine Monstretragodie* (Stuttgart Ballet); *La Bohème* (co-designer, Bregenz Festival); *Nine - The Musical* (Malmö Musikteater) *Manon Lescaut* (Gothenburg Opera); *Roald Dahl Revolting Rhymes Concert* (BBC Wales); *Ein Masken Ball* (assistant designer Bregenz Festival); *Manon Lescaut* (associate designer ENO); *Twelfth Night* (RSC); *The Entertainer* (Hampstead).

Penny Saunders

Penny Saunders is an artist, designer and maker of sets and props for theatre, film and exhibitions. Much of her work is mechanical, electronic or otherwise automated. For the past 24 years she has been one of the three Artistic Directors of Forkbeard Fantasy, the theatre and film company, whose innovative and ground-breaking work in new technology and film has established it as the foremost practitioners in their field. Penny likes to work in theatre because it means the pieces she makes are participants in the performance, sometimes as important as the human actors. The technical aspects of the sets and the ways in which they will affect the viewers' imagination are interwoven with the spread of the plot and the meaning of the words. This has enabled her to explore how to combine mechanics with the entertainment and the drama of a show. She has designed and built the sets and props for 23 major Forkbeard shows and numerous smaller pieces for tours of anything up to 60 venues and ten countries. She has built the equipment and effects for nine outdoor shows that have appeared at many festivals in Britain and abroad; this has often involved making special versions for each site. Some have been spontaneous creations designed to catch fire as part of the event. Penny has also built complex sets for six Forkbeard films, including a large room that had to be turned upside down half way through, a moving brontosaurus skeleton and a huge, fantastical, living electron microscope.

Rachel Scanlon

Rachel Scanlon studied Fine Art at Staffordshire University, specialising in 3D, sculpture and installation. She then went on to do a Masters in Scenography at the Birmingham Institute of Art and Design, University of Central England in 2002.

Whilst working towards her MA she was nominated for the *Ryland Award* for innovation and excellence for her original and imaginative concept of creating a child-height, pop-up book, which worked as a tourable theatre set for children.

In 2001 Rachel began designing sets at the Nottingham Arts Theatre, and has worked on a number of productions as set designer, scenic artist and prop maker. She had a solo exhibition at the Herbert Gallery in Coventry in 2005, where she created *Little Big World*, an installation consisting of three giant, fairy-tale, pop-up books with oversized, interactive features. This was based on the Reggio Emilia approach to learning, and encouraged children to use their imagination and play to create their own fantasy world.

Vivienne Schadinsky

Vivienne Schadinsky trained and worked as an interior designer in Switzerland before studying at Motley Theatre Design Course in London. She went on to become Associate Artist of the companies Lightwork and Angelus Arts and works in theatre, film, television and exhibition design. Theatre designs include: *Here's What I Did With My Body One Day* (Strand Tube Station, Pleasance Theatre, London and National Tour); *Invalid* (Barts Hospital, London); *London My Lover* (ICA, London); *Primaries* (Young Vic Studio, London); *Revenger's Tragedy* (Pentameters Theatre, London). Television art direction includes: *Foyle's War* (ITV Drama); *The Murder Room* (BBC Drama); *Silent Witness VII* (BBC Drama); *Beckham/Anthem* (Vodafone commercial); *La Luna* (short film Channel 4). Film and television production designs include: *I love My Job* (Polaroid commercial); *Paint Job* (Smirnoff Ice commercial); *A Place of Execution* (Harper Collins commercial); *Ghost Child* (short film Channel 4); *2 - Sides* (short film); Exhibition designs for Dunhill include: Lighter shaped aquarium with jewellery display for shop in Shanghai; Travel Museum for antiques collection in New York, Tokyo, Beijing, Paris and London; Display for watch fair in the Forbidden City in Beijing. Vivienne is a member of the British Academy of Film and Television Arts and is on the committee of the Society of British Theatre Designers. She exhibited in the *2D|3D* exhibition (2002). Her work was chosen to form part of the British display at the 2003 International Prague Quadrennial exhibition of stage design, which won the *Golden Triga*.

Nettie Scriven

Nettie Scriven is Senior Lecturer in Theatre Design, Nottingham Trent University. Her 25-year career as a designer has encompassed a range of theatre making spaces, including main stages, arts centres, art galleries, studio theatres, schools, and community centres. She represented the UK at the Prague Quadrennial in 1999 with *Best of Friends*. Nettie specialises in developing performance text through collaborative process, and is Joint Artistic Director of Dragon Breath Theatre. She is also a creative development worker for Creative Partnerships, Nottingham, developing and building upon creative teaching and learning in schools. Productions include: *The Secret Garden*, *A Little Princess*, *The Snow Spider*, *Aesop's Fables*, *Plague of Innocence* (1988 Best Young People's Production), *The Waltz*, *The Lost Child*, *Hamlet*, *Dragon Breath*, *Shadow Play*, *In Limbo*, *Journey to the River Sea* and *The Summer Book*.

Ashley Shairp

Planning a Trifle is an infant puppet company formed by: Ashley Shairp graduated in Theatre Design from Nottingham Trent in 1986. He has designed, made props and scene-painted for theatres and companies all over the UK. He was Associate Designer at The Dukes, Lancaster for three years and had healthy collaborative relationships with the Everyman Theatres in both Cheltenham and Liverpool, the Bolton Octagon and Ludus Dance Company. His most recent design was Angels in America (Unity Theatre, Liverpool). He gradually moved into teaching and is now the Course Leader for Theatre & Performance Design at the Liverpool Institute for Performing Arts (LIPA). Sam Heath - trained as a chemist and received a Ph.D. from Leicester University in 1989. He moved into computing and specialised in writing 3D graphical modelling software used for oil and gas exploration. Over the past six years his computing work has diversified to include interactive imagery created using super-computer clusters (which he also built). Sam has had a close personal connection to the theatrical world for nearly twenty years and has always dabbled in video, lighting and electronics. He has spent half a lifetime waiting for the opportunity to try his skills within a creative performance environment. John and Ann Preston - have worked on a wide variety of theatre and TV projects over the last twenty years. John is primarily a set builder and prop maker and is training to be a signer. Ann is a costume maker and wardrobe supervisor currently based at The Dukes, Lancaster. John is learning to be a signer.

Juliet Shillingford

Juliet Shillingford trained at Ravensbourne and Croydon Colleges of Art obtaining a degree in Fine Art and a Diploma in Theatre Design. After being awarded an Arts Council Bursary she spent four years as Resident Designer in Farnham and Manchester. She has worked on a number of productions with Patrick Sandford at the Nuffield Theatre, Southampton most recently: *Cyrano de Bergerac*, *Rattle of a Simple Man*, *Mary Stuart*, *The School for Wives*, *Don Quixote* and *Nelson* a new play by Pam Gems. For New Perspectives, tours of *Last Train to Nibroc*, *Long Way Home* (a new play by Charles Way, at the Pride of Place festival), *Butterfly Lion* and *The Allotment*, a new play by Andy Barrett, which opened in Edinburgh 2006 before touring. Other recent freelance work includes a national tour of *Ballroom*, written and directed by John Retallack, *The False Corpse* by Shaun Prendergast for Zygo (Brighton Festival) and *Novecento* for Mike Moran (Edinburgh Festival and tour). For Rose Bruford College, she designed *Country Wife* (also seen at the National Student Drama Festival in Scarborough), *Lysistrata*, *The Way of the World* and *The Man Who Came to Dinner*. Juliet has recently completed a PGCE and has taught at Richmond and Croydon Colleges of Art and Rose Bruford College.

George Souglides

George Souglides was born in Cyprus and educated in Greece and England. He studied 3D/Interior Design at Kingston University and Theatre Design at Motley. He has worked extensively as a designer for opera and theatre both in Britain and in mainland Europe. His recent designs for the theatre include: *Peace* and *The Acharnians* (Epidauros Festival); *Arcadia* and *Le Bourgeois Gentilhomme* (National

Theatre of Northern Greece); *The Misunderstanding* and *The Talking Cure* (Ilisia Theatre, Athens); *Pterodactyls* (Athinon Theatre, Athens) and *The Private Room* (New End Theatre, London). Designs for dance include: *Mind the Gap* (ICA); *Alistair Fish* (BBC2 Dance for Camera) and as Associate Designer of the award-winning *Fearful Symmetries* (Royal Ballet). His collaborations as Assistant Designer with Antony McDonald include: *Un Ballo in Maschera* (Bregenz Festival) and *L'Enfant et Les Sortilèges* and *Der Zwerg* (Palais Garnier). His recent designs for opera include: Offenbach's *Barbe-Bleue* (co-production of Bregenz Festival, St Polten and Grange Park Opera); *Un Ballo in Maschera* - indoor version (Bregenz Festival); *Maria Stuarda*, *Le nozze di Figaro* and *Il Barbiere di Siviglia* (Grange Park Opera); *Orphée et Euridice*, *Il Prigioniero*, *The Possessed*, *Xerxes* and *L'Elisir d'Amore* for the Greek National Opera; *Aida* and *Così fan tutte* for Scottish Opera; *Arianna in Creta* and *Der Freischütz* (Reisopera, Holland); *Le nozze di Figaro* (Ystad Opera, Sweden). Other opera work includes: *A Midsummer Night's Dream* and *The Rape of Lucretia* (Snape Maltings) and *Semele* (Buxton Festival). He took part in SBTD's *Time+Space* with a design for an installation based on *Aida*.

Daphne Stevens-Pascucci

Daphne Stevens, also known by her married name of Daphne Pascucci, was born in London but studied in Italy and America. She gained her BA in Theatre Arts at Barnard College, with a year abroad at the International University of Ail in Florence winning a RAI-TV scholarship, then returned to take a Diploma in Scenografia at the National Academy of Fine Art studying with Toti Scialoja (Rome) and Gaetano Castelli (Florence). While in Italy she designed costumes for Opera Barga and assisted Giovanni Agostinucci at Teatro in Trastevere. She completed her MFA at Yale University School of Drama under the tutorship of Ming Cho Lee and Jane Greenwood. In America she designed costumes for the original (1984) Broadway production of *Ma Rainey's Black Bottom* with the Juilliard Theatre Department and Santa Fe Opera. She has been assistant designer in Europe and Russia on many costume films in particular, *Rasputin* (1996) starring Alan Rickman and designed several independent feature films in America, including *Easter* (2000) which won acclaim both at New York and California film festivals. In 2002 she designed costumes for a world premiere of the baroque opera *Pompeo Magno* at Varazdin Festival Croatia.

Ben Stones

Ben Stones studied at the Electric Theatre Studios, Barnsley, and subsequently trained in Stage Design at Central Saint Martins College of Art and Design.

He was the winner of the Linbury Biennial Prize commission to design *Paradise Lost* for Northampton Theatres, directed by Rupert Goold. Designs include: *The Musical Of Musicals (The Musical!)* and *Beautiful Thing* for NML Productions (Sound Theatre, Leicester Square); *Paradise Lost* (Theatre Royal, Northampton and on tour with Oxford Stage Company); *Monkey* (Dundee Rep); *The Leningrad Siege* (Tron Theatre and Wilton's Music Hall); *The Shooky* (Birmingham Rep); *Someone Who'll Watch Over Me* (Royal Theatre, Northampton); *Vermilion Dream* (Salisbury Playhouse); *Riders To The Sea* (Southwark Playhouse); *The Marriage of Bette and*

Boo (RADA); *The Arab Israeli Cookbook* (Tricycle Theatre); *The Mighty Boosh* (Phil Mckintyre national tour); *When Five Years Pass* (Arcola Theatre); *Pinocchio* (Theatre Royal, Northampton); *The Vegemite Tales* (The Venue, Leicester Square).

Nancy Surman
Nancy Surman has just returned from designing a tour of Noel Coward's *Private Lives* in the Far East. Other recent work includes: *To Kill a Mockingbird* and *The Waters of the Moon* (Salisbury Playhouse); *The Accrington Pals* (Dukes Theatre, Lancaster); and tours of *Aspects of Love* and *Noel and Gertie* (Gordon Craig Theatre, Stevenage). She designed the world premieres of *Get Ken Barlow* (Watford Palace Theatre); *A Stinging Sea* (Glasgow Citizens Theatre); *The Road to Hell* and *Johnny Watkins Walks on Water* (Birmingham Repertory Theatre). Also, the stage premieres of Hanif Kureishi's *The Buddha of Suburbia* and *My Beautiful Laundrette* (SNAP Theatre Company).
Other productions include designs for a repertoire season of *Much Ado About Nothing*, *Trojan Women* and *Privates on Parade* (Jermyn Street Theatre); *The Duchess of Malfi*, *The Rivals*, *The Secret Rapture*, and *The Winter's Tale* (Salisbury Playhouse); *Private Lives* (Bolton Octagon); and *The Final Appearance of Miss Mamie Stuart* (Torch Theatre, Milford Haven). She has designed new adaptations of *Sense and Sensibility*, *Pride and Prejudice*, *Tom Jones*, *Far from the Madding Crowd* and *Maurice* (SNAP Theatre Company); and tours of *The Hunchback of Notre Dame*, *Beautiful Thing* and *Don Quixote* (Oxfordshire Touring Theatre Company). Nancy designed Maxim Gorky's *Barbarians* (Salisbury Playhouse) for which she was nominated for the *TMA Best Designer Award* 2003.

Takis
Takis was born in 1980 in Sikion, Greece. He studied Scenography at the Romanian National University of Arts (Bucharest), with a scholarship from the Romanian Ministry of Education (1998-2002). In 2002 he continued his studies at the Royal Academy of Dramatic Art on the Theatre Technical Arts Course, graduating with distinction in 2004, with the scholarship "Kiveli-Horn" given by the Greek Friends of Music Society. Takis has worked as Scenic Art Assistant for several productions at the Greek National Opera and the Megaron-Athens Concert Hall; also, as Costume Assistant for the Opera Festival of Rome and as Model Room Assistant at the Royal Opera House (1998 – 2002). He participated in the European Voluntary Service (2002) at the International Youth and Culture Centre Kiebitz in Duisburg, Germany, leading workshops and designing sets and costumes for the centre's theatre company. Since then, he has been leading two workshops per year there. During the academic year 2005-2006, at the Royal Academy of Dramatic Art, Takis provided lectures, design supervision and led the Academy's Theatre Design Summer Course.
Over the past years he has worked as costume and set designer for about 30 productions in Greece, Italy, Germany, France, England and the USA. He is a practice-based PhD student at the London College of Fashion, working on new ways of seeing the contemporary male outfit through an installation, with a scholarship from the *Onassis Foundation*.

David I. Taylor
David Taylor gained a first class honours degree in Drama from the University of London specialising in stage design, and was a scholarship student to the University of Massachusetts at Amherst, USA, where he studied lighting design.
As a freelance lighting designer his work has been seen in over 100 productions in the United Kingdom and around the world, including seasons at Theatre Royal Plymouth, Watermill Theatre Newbury, tours with Wayne Sleep and Naomi Benari Dance Company, shows at the Tricycle Theatre, the Orange Tree Theatre, the San Jose Rep, the American Jewish Theatre, the South Bank Centre and Royal Albert Hall. He has provided set designs for opera in Stowe and Edinburgh, and lighting designs for the Lyric Opera of Kansas City. He was Lighting Designer for the London Theatre Laboratory, an Associate Artist of the new writing company Southern Lights and an associate of Stage One Theatre Company. He was a non-executive director of Temba Theatre Company and also of the Roundhouse Arts Centre Ltd, working to develop a multi-cultural performance space in North London. As an owner and director of Theatre Projects Consultants he has, for over 20 years, created theatres, concert halls and opera houses for some of the leading performing companies around the world, including the Tricycle and Orange Tree Theatres, the Goodman, the Kodak Theatre (home of the Oscars broadcast) and all the main venues for Disney Theatrical.

Ian Teague
Ian Teague has been a designer since leaving Trent Polytechnic in 1982. He has designed a range of productions (over 120) but is best known for Theatre In Education and Young People's Theatre. In the past two years he has formed a strong working relationship with MakeBelieve Arts becoming involved in development work, training and delivering art and design based workshops in schools as well as designing *The Lorax* and *Gulliver's Travels*. He is a member of the Society of British Theatre Designers management committee.
A long-standing member and currently Vice Chair of Equity's Theatre Designers Committee, he has also represented designers at the union's Annual Representative Conference.
He has been a Visiting Lecturer at various colleges including Central Saint Martins College of Art and Design, London Metropolitan University, and the University of Kent. In 2003, his designs for small cast productions of Shakespeare formed part of the British Golden Triga-winning exhibit at the Prague Quadrennial exhibition of scenography.

Yannis Thavoris
Yannis Thavoris was born in Thessaloniki, Greece. In 1995 he graduated with a Diploma in Architecture from the Aristotle University of Thessaloniki. He then studied European Scenography at the Central Saint Martins College of Art and Design, graduating with a Master of Arts in 1997. He was the overall winner of the 1997 *Linbury Prize* for Stage Design. Yannis has worked in opera, theatre and architecture. His designs include: *A Night at the Chinese Opera* (Royal Academy of Music) directed by Jo Davies; *Così fan tutte* (Opéra National du Rhin, Strasbourg); *La Clemenza di Tito* (Danish Royal Opera and ENO, nominated for an Olivier Award for Best New Opera Production); *Madama Butterfly* (Scottish Opera); and *The Rape of Lucretia*

(Aldeburgh Festival and ENO, winner of the *South Bank Show award* and nominated for an *Olivier Award*) all directed by David McVicar; *Candide* (Birmingham Opera Company); and Tchaikovsky's *The Oprichnik* (Teatro Lirico di Cagliari) directed by Graham Vick; *The Rake's Progress* (ENO) directed by Annabel Arden. Also, Irving Berlin's *Annie Get Your Gun* (national tour); Gassman's *Opera Seria* (Netherlands Nationale Reisopera); *Carmen* and *The Daughter of the Regiment* (English Touring Opera); *The Battle of Green Lanes* (Theatre Royal Stratford East); Shakespeare's *Antony and Cleopatra* (English Shakespeare Company) and Wedekind's *Franziska* at the Gate Theatre, London. In preparation: *The Marriage of Figaro* (ENO) and *Les Contes d'Hoffmann* (Netherlands Nationale Reisopera).

Theatreplan LLP
Richard Brett, Roger Fox, Dave Ludlam, Neil Morton, Clive Odom, Peter Ruthven Hall, Charles Wass, John Whitaker: Theatreplan is a specialist partnership, providing consultancy services and design for performing arts and public assembly buildings to clients, architects and engineers. These services include feasibility studies and project development, auditorium design, theatre planning and technical equipment consultancy.
The scope of buildings covered is extensive, ranging from theatres and music venues to conference centres and school halls. These include listed buildings, found spaces and new structures. Theatreplan's achievements demonstrate a flexible and resourceful approach to match the scale and requirements of each project.
Recent and current projects include: Copenhagen Operaen, Hampstead Theatre, Dunstable Grove Theatre, Inverness Eden Court Studios, Singapore Fusionpolis, Singapore Arts School, Belfast Lyric Theatre, Bournemouth New Winter Gardens, Warehouse Theatre Croydon, Frensham Heights School; and refurbishments of the Sydney Opera House, Royal Opera House, Watford Palace Theatre, Belgrade Theatre Coventry, Northampton Royal Theatre, Leeds Grand Theatre, Barking Broadway Theatre, Kingston College Theatre, Barbican Theatre, Sheffield Crucible Theatre and Guildford Yvonne Arnaud Theatre.
www.theatreplan.net

Theatre Projects Consultants
Theatre Projects Consultants has been one of the world's leading theatre design and planning firms since 1957. Our aim is to capture the excitement and energy of live theatre by concentrating on the important details that make theatres successful from both the performers and the audience's point of view. Theatre Projects offers a unique international multi-disciplinary team dedicated to creating successful world-class theatres. Our hands-on experience working in theatres enables us to give practical and comprehensive specialist advice on all elements of theatre planning, design and theatre technologies, ensuring that every project is designed to meet the needs of its users and community. The strength behind Theatre Projects' success lies not only in our understanding of how theatre works, but also in our commitment to our clients and our emphasis on team collaboration to produce the highest quality performance spaces within the timeframe and resources available. Theatre Projects has gained a worldwide reputation for innovation;

innovation in the design of intimate theatre spaces, sensitive renovation and restoration schemes, successful flexible performance spaces, state-of-the-art technology in stage lighting, sound and communications, stage engineering and technical machinery.
Theatre Projects has provided creative design solutions and technical innovation and expertise to more than 1,000 performing arts projects in over 50 countries. Our projects include major performing and visual arts centres, playhouses, opera and ballet houses, lyric theatres, concert halls, regional theatres, educational theatres and flexible performance spaces.

Nerissa Cargill Thompson
Nerissa Cargill Thompson graduated with a BA (Hons) in Theatre Design from Nottingham Trent University in 1995 and works as a freelance designer and maker. She is Associate Designer for Aqueous Humour, a street theatre company which develops community projects and professional strolling shows. She was Head of Design for Manchester Youth Theatre from 1997-2000. In 1998 the team received a nomination for the *Manchester Evening News Fringe Theatre Award* and went on to win the Special Award for the complete season in 1999. She has designed shows for Arden School of Theatre, Proud & Loud, Activ8, DIY Theatre Company, Wise Monkey, Gazebo, Salford University Theatre Company and many fringe productions in Edinburgh, London and Manchester. In the past few years, Nerissa has also started designing/art directing for film and television, including *The Treasure of Albion*, a feature for the British Youth Film Project. Work as a scenic artist and prop-maker includes shows for the Royal Northern College of Music, the Lowry, Bolton Octagon, Library Theatre and Swan Theatre. Nerissa also teaches workshops in visual art, theatre design, masks, puppetry, props and costumes. For more information see www.ncargillthompson.co.uk

Jenny Tiramani
Jenny Tiramani was Director of Theatre Design at Shakespeare's Globe Theatre, London, from 1996 to 2005, collaborating with Mark Rylance (Artistic Director/actor), Tim Carroll (Director) and Claire van Kampen (Director of Theatre Music), and exploring the original playing practices of Shakespeare and his fellow actors. These researches covered the nature of the actors' clothing, properties, the use of the stage, and the decoration and form of the theatre itself. Productions Jenny designed there, exploring these ideas, included: *Henry V*; *Antony and Cleopatra*; *Richard II*; and *Twelfth Night*, for which she received the *Laurence Olivier Award* for Best Costume Design in 2003. Globe shows designed in modern dress included *Cymbeline* and *A Midsummer Night's Dream*, both directed by Mike Alfreds. Jenny's collaboration with Mark Rylance and Claire van Kampen began in 1991 with their production of *The Tempest* at the Rollright Stone Circle, and continues with plans for their own theatre company, Phoebus Cart, including a new production of *Othello* in 2008. Jenny has been associated with the Theatre Royal, Stratford East, since 1977. Productions designed there include: *Thick as Thieves* by Tony Marchant; Nell Dunn's *Steaming* (and Comedy Theatre); *On Your Way, Riley* by Alan Plater; through to the *Olivier*-nominated *The Big Life* (and Apollo Theatre). As a member of Kenneth Branagh's Renaissance Theatre Company, Jenny designed *Much Ado About Nothing*, *As You Like It*, *Hamlet*, *King Lear* and *A Midsummer Nights*

Dream. Other close associations have been with John McGrath, Elizabeth MacLennan and Kate McGrath, designing for 7:84 Theatre Companies England and Scotland, and for Floodtide Theatre Company. Her work with the director/designer Ultz has continued since 1977, with productions at the Theatre Royal, Stratford East, Nottingham Playhouse and Blackpool Opera House. In 2004 Jenny designed the costumes for *L'incoronazione di Poppea* (Théâtre des Champs-Elysées, Paris), directed by David McVicar and she has just designed the costumes for a national tour of *Me and My Girl*, directed by Warren Carlyle.

Johanna Town
Johanna Town's lighting design between 2003 and 2006 include the following productions at the Royal Court (where she is Head of Lighting): *Back of Beyond* (directed by Annie Castledine); *The Winterling* (Ian Rickson); *Live Like Pigs* (Chris Burges); *A Girl in a Car With a Man* (Joe Hill-Gibbons); *Food Chain* (Anna Mackmin); *Rainbow Kiss, The Woman Before, Under The Whaleback* (Richard Wilson); *Way To Heaven, Terrorism* (Ramin Gray).
For Out Of Joint and Max Stafford Clark she designed national and international touring productions of *Overwhelming, O Go My Man, Talking To Terrorists, Macbeth, Duck, The Permanent Way, Rita, Sue and Bob Too/A State Affair.*
In New York: *My Name Is Rachel Corrie* (directed by Alan Rickman) and *Guantanamo Bay* (Nicolas Kent and Sacha Wares). Other theatre credits include: *To Kill A Mocking Bird* (West Yorkshire Playhouse); *In Praise of Love* (Chichester); *Justifying War* (Tricycle Theatre); *A Modern Dance For Beginners, Badnuff* and *Mr Nobody* (Soho Theatre); *Dead Funny* (West Yorkshire Playhouse); *Helen of Troy* (ATC); *East Coast Chicken Supper* (Traverse); *Someone Who'll Watch Over Me* (Royal Theatre Northampton); *How Love Is Spelt* (Bush Theatre); *The Dumb Waiter* (Oxford Playhouse); *Id* (Almeida Theatre); *A Doll's House* (Southwark Playhouse); *Platform* (ICA); *Brassed Off* (Birmingham Rep); *All The Ordinary Angels, Six Degrees of Separation* (Royal Exchange Theatre).

Jamie Vartan
Jamie Vartan trained at Central Saint Martins College of Art and Design, London. He was awarded an Arts Council Bursary to work at Nottingham Playhouse where he has since designed several productions. He was involved for three years as Designer and Artist in Residence with the David Glass Ensemble on *The Lost Child Trilogy*, with residencies involving workshops, research and new productions in Vietnam, Indonesia, China, the Philippines and Colombia. The trilogy was later presented at the Young Vic. *The Hansel Gretel Machine* (part one of the trilogy) was selected for the 1999 Prague Quadrennial Theatre Design Exhibition. He later created an installation at the *October Gallery* based on the work from the overseas residencies. Subsequent collaborations followed with choreographer Darshan Singh Bhuller. He has designed numerous productions at The National Theatre of Ireland (Abbey and Peacock Theatres), including *Mrs Warren's Profession*, nominated for the *Irish Times Awards* Best Production. Designs for opera include: *The Queen of Spades* (La Scala, Milan); *Manon Lescaut* (Teatro Regio, Parma); *A Village Romeo and Juliet* (*L'Opéra magazine* nomination for Best Set and Costume Design 2002); *Aida* and *Carmen* (*Premio Abbiati Awards* 2006, Teatro Lirico di Cagliari, Sardinia) with director Stephen Medcalf; *Der Zwerg* (Teatro Comunale, Florence) with director Annabel Arden; *La Traviata* (Malmö Musikteater, Sweden) with director Thomas de Mallet Burgess; and *May Night* (Garsington 06), directed by Olivia Fuchs.

Janet Vaughan
Janet Vaughan is a visual artist and designer who has designed site-specific and touring performances, and created installation artworks for unusual and digital spaces. Working in collaboration with other artists, or members of the public, on residency-based projects, she uses a variety of media to create her work, much of which is (often temporary) site-specific art for public spaces. Her design for *Talking Birds, Smoke, Mirrors & the Art of Escapology*, formed part of the UK entry to the 1999 Prague Quadrennial and the *Independent* has described her digital art work with the company as 'innovative and unusual...akin to taking part in a David Lynch movie'.
Other recent work includes designing the award-winning *Street Trilogy* for Theatre Absolute; working with young people in Coventry to redesign their school toilets; and an artist's residency running alongside the capital development of Norwich's independent film theatre, Cinema City.
For more information see www.talkingbirds.co.uk

Adrian Vaux
Adrian Vaux studied Design at the Slade School. He has been House Designer at London's Mermaid Theatre (1964 – 1970); House Designer at Leicester Phoenix, and subsequently at the Haymarket (1971-1980). He has designed many productions during this time, some of which transferred to London's West End. These include: *My Fair Lady, Cause Célèbre* and *Tomfoolery*. As House Designer at the Old Vic (1980-1982) credits include: *The Merchant of Venice* and *The Relapse*. He began working in Israel in 1968, designing productions for Habimah, Cameri, Haifa and Jerusalem theatres. Association with Sobol began with original productions of *Weiningers Night, Ghetto, Palestinian Girl, Adam, Jerusalem Syndrome* and *Nice Toni*.
This association led to him working in Germany and United States. Recent credits include: The US tour of *Miss Saigon* and *Oliver!* and most recently, a UK tour of *Miss Saigon*.

Rebecca Vincent
Rebecca Vincent originally trained in Architecture and Interiors at the Royal College of Art before fully embarking on a career in theatre and undertaking a set design course at RADA. She now combines stage design with designing the performance spaces themselves, as a theatre design consultant.
Recent theatre credits include: *Waiting for Romeo* (Hill Street Studio, Edinburgh Fringe and the Gielgud, RADA); *Numbers/Embassyland* (Tabard and Landor Theatres, London); *Requiem for Tomorrow* (Shaw Theatre, London); *Lilita* (Underbelly, Edinburgh Fringe and Piccolo Spoleto Festival, Charleston, USA); *The Elephant Man* (Bridewell Theatre, London); *Accidental Death of an Anarchist* (Teatro Technis, London); *and After Magritte* and *The Real Inspector Hound* (Courtyard Theatre, London). She has more recently ventured into film, as production designer and art director. Film credits include: *Cyrano, The Fix, Trigger* and *Inside Looking Out*.

Martina Von Holn
Martina Von Holn graduated from the Fine Art Diploma Course at the Academy of Fine Arts Hamburg and took the MA Scenography at Central Saint Martins College of Art and Design, London. She is now working as a freelance designer for theatre and performance, both in Germany and the UK. Martina's interest lies in creating innovative and challenging collaborative projects, which are cross-disciplinary merging aspects of installation and performance. Over the past two years, Martina has been developing a site–specific, one-to-one performance practice in which a single member of audience is invited to join the performer and experience a unique performative encounter.
The Tasseographer is a one-to-one encounter created, over the last year, in collaboration with writers Caroline Steinbeis and David Lane and performers, Imogen Smith and Hakan Silahsizoglu. Here the audience find themselves taking part in the ancient ritual of tea leaf reading. Martina is currently developing *Nightshift*, a collaborative performance project with artist Ana Antonio Gill and urban demographers, about people who work at night; and *House Inspection!*, a new one-to-one encounter during which the audience invites the performer into their homes where he provides each audience member with a detailed psychological analysis of themselves on the basis of their personal belongings.

Steph Warden
Steph Warden trained at Bristol Old Vic Theatre School in 2004. Designs for Bristol Old Vic include Peter Barnes' *Red Noses*, costumes for *The Two Noble Kinsmen*, by Shakespeare and Fletcher, and *Anorak of Fire* by Stephen Dinsdale. In 2005 Steph was Trainee Designer at Theatre by the Lake in Keswick. Shows there included the summer season productions for the studio: *Playhouse Creatures* by April de Angelis, *A Number* by Caryl Churchill, *Dead Funny* by Terry Johnson, Patrick Marber's *Closer* and *Stories for Christmas*. Current work includes Patrick Marber's version of *After Miss Julie*. Other design work includes: *Love and Understanding* (Capitol Theatre in association with the Library Theatre, Manchester); *Nobody's Perfect* by Simon Williams; and *Stepping Out* by Richard Harris (Little Theatre, Leicester). Future work includes Arthur Miller's *The Price*, Michael Cooney's *Cash on Delivery* and Mary Jones' *Butterflies are Free*. Design assisting work includes: *Cinderella*, by Martin Johns; *Ultz* at the Royal Court Theatre, London; and Ralph Koltai on a visual arts project at the *Hong Kong Youth Arts Festival* in 1999. It was Steph's interest in sculpture and installation that led her to theatre design.

Libby Watson
Libby Watson trained at Wimbledon School of Art. As Resident Designer at Salisbury Playhouse designs have included: *Beautiful Thing, Secret Garden, The Changeling* and *Tenant of Wildfell Hall*. For Stratford East, she has designed *Cinderella, Night of the Dons, Funny Black Women* and *The Oddest Couple*. In collaboration with director Paulette Randall, she designed *Blest Be The Tie* and *What's in the Cat* (Royal Court); *Blues for Mr Charlie, Gem of the Ocean* (Tricycle); *Urban Afro Saxons* and *High Heeled Parrotfish* (Stratford East); and *Three Sisters* (tour). Libby has designed many touring productions for the Watermill Theatre, all written and directed by Ade Morris. They include: *I dreamt I dwelt in Marble Halls, Witch, Lone Flyer, The Garden at Llangoed, Mr & Mrs Schultz* and *The Comedian*. She designed a site-specific production of *The Wills Girls* (The Tobacco Factory). Her work also includes ongoing collaboration with the Asian theatre company RIFCO, designs include *Airport 2000* (Riverside) and *Deranged Marriage* (UK tour). Libby has designed ten productions for Guildhall with director Wyn Jones and the operas *Beatrice and Benedict, Comedy on the Bridge* and *Mignon*, directed by Stephen Medcalf. Recent projects include the UK tour of *French Lieutenant's Woman, Blonde Bombshells of 1943* by Alan Plater (Bolton Octagon and Hampstead) and a multi-media production of *Macbeth* (Bristol).

Fiona Watt
Fiona Watt trained with Motley at the Almeida. She enjoys exploring the relationship between existing architecture and the designed space, unlocking the hidden dynamics within a building to find the strongest points of exchange between the performer and the audience. Theatre credits include: *A Woman of No Importance* (Pitlochry Festival Theatre); *Further Than The Furthest Thing* (Byre St. Andrews and tour); *The Beauty Queen of Leenane, Boston Marriage* (Bolton Octagon); *Othello* (Nottingham Playhouse); *The Weir* (Lyric Theatre, Belfast); *Dealer's Choice* (Tron); *Outlying Islands* (World Stages Festival, Toronto, Jerwood Theatre Upstairs and UK tour). For the Traverse, she has designed *East Coast Chicken Supper* by Martin J Taylor, *Dark Earth* by David Harrower, and *Outlying Islands* by David Greig (all for the Edinburgh Festival); *The Trestle at Pope Lick Creek* by Naomi Wallace; *Highland Shorts* (seven short plays by Scottish writers); and *Heritage* by Nicola McCartney, a body of work that explored the relationship between people and landscape. Opera credits include: *Good Angel, Bad Angel* (Hebrides Ensemble), *La Traviata* (Haddo House), *Mavra, Riders to the Sea, Gianni Schicchi* and *La Pietra del Paragone* (Royal Scottish Academy of Music and Drama). Her education work includes Aim Higher/Creative Partnerships, part-time lecturing at University of Kent and Guest Lecturer at Edge Hill University where she was also involved in shaping the new design programme. She has exhibited at *Time + Space* (RCA); *2D I3D* (Sheffield Millennium Galleries and UK tour); and the Tron Theatre, Glasgow as part of UK City of Architecture and Design.
As her studio is based in an area of massive regeneration, she is beginning to explore the relationship between artists, urban planners and cultural policy makers, investigating how we might utilise our creative skills to communicate ideas that shape and affect our working environment.

Ian Westbrook
Ian trained at Nottingham Trent University in Creative Arts. His first of many productions for the Lord Delfont Group was with the Lenny Henry, Cannon & Ball Shows. After seasons at Nottingham Playhouse, Leicester and Theatre Royal Plymouth, Ian became Set Designer/Artist with the Theatre Royal Norwich and Cromer Pavilion Theatre, Norfolk.
For the past twenty years, Ian has run his own scenery and prop construction company 3D Creations in Norfolk with his team of skilled artist and craftsmen. His theatre work now totals over three hundred and fifty operas, musicals and plays that include creating special effects for Blythe Spirit at London's Savoy Theatre for the Sir Peter Hall Company, Michael Flatley's Feet of Flames world tour. Designs for *Evita* and

Chicago at the Amphitheatre in Lebanon. Special fire effects for Chichester Festival and Birmingham Stage Company. The Broadway musical *See Saw* by Cy Colman and Dorothy Fields.
Scenery and props for the American illusionist David Blaine, Rock and Pop music arena tours worldwide for Iron Maiden, (five world tours) Robbie Williams Pete Waterman, West Life, Blur, The Spice Girls, Peter Gabriel, Thomas the Tank Engine Arena tour. Disney (TV) Corporation. The Sony Media Corporation and five commissions by HM. Queen Elizabeth 11 at the Sandringham Museum are amongst some of the varied scenic work Ian is involved in.
He also runs his own theatre production company with Desmond Barrit from the RSC and National Theatre London.

Naomi Wilkinson
Naomi Wilkinson trained at the Motley Theatre Design Course after a BA (Hons) in Fine Art at Bristol. Recent credits include: *Just for Show* (Royal National Theatre, with Lloyd Newson, DV8 Physical Theatre); *A Midsummer Night's Dream* (Dundee Rep); *The Misanthrope* (Guildhall School of Music and Drama); *Don't Look Back* (Dreamthinkspeak, a site-specific piece at The General Register House in Edinburgh); *Total Theatre Award 2006*, Edinburgh Festival; *Accidental Death of an Anarchist* (Octagon Theatre); *The Firework Maker's Daughter* (Sheffield Crucible and Lyric Theatre Hammersmith); *Colder Than Here* (Soho Theatre); *I'm a Fool to Want You* (BAC and Tron Theatre). Other credits include: *4.48 Psychosis* directed by Kathryn Hunter (LAMDA); *Wrong Place* (Soho Theatre); *Happy Yet?* (Gate Theatre); *Arcane* with Opera Circus (UK tour); *Don't Look Back* for Dreamthinkspeak (Stanmer House, Brighton Festival/State Cinema Grays/South Hill Park, Bracknell and Somerset House London); *Happy Birthday Mr Deka D* (Traverse Theatre); *Shoot me in the Heart* (Gate Theatre); *Aladdin* (Lyric Theatre Hammersmith); *A Little Fantasy* (Soho Theatre); *I Can't Wake Up* (Lyric Theatre Studio); *Gobbledygook* (Gogmagogs, Traverse Theatre); *My Life in the Bush of Ghosts* and *Heredity* (both Royal Court Theatre Upstairs); *I Weep at my Piano* (BAC); *Two Horsemen* (Gate Theatre, *Time Out Award*); *Mules* (Royal Court Theatre Upstairs).

Simon Wilkinson
Simon Wilkinson designed the lighting for the European premiere of *Mum's The Word* and has recreated this design for all five national tours. He has just designed its sequel *Mum's the Word: Teenagers*, which opened recently at the Kings Theatre, Glasgow. He also lit Gary Wilmot's concert tour *My Kind of Music*, the tribute musical *Always … Patsy Cline*, and this year's English and Irish tours of *Dirty Dusting*. Other theatre work includes *The 39 Steps*, *The Twits*, the European premiere of *Mary's Wedding*, *The Glass Menagerie*, *The Secret Garden*, *Cat on a Hot Tin Roof*, *Honk!*, and *A Christmas Carol* (all for the Byre Theatre, St Andrews); *Snow! The Musical* (Sound Theatre, London); *The Visit* (Dundee Rep); Nottingham Playhouse's revival of the political satire *Feelgood*; the national tours of *A Happy Medium*; the Scottish tours of *Molly Whuppie*, *Passing Places*, *Good Things*, *Dead Funny*, *The Odd Couple* and *Tally's Blood*; *A Sense of Justice* (Perth Theatre); *Aladdin* and *Beauty and the Beast* (RSAMD); *Meat* and *The Play o' the Wather* with Nutshell; *Spoonface Steinberg* with Manick Company; *Ghost Shirt* with Theatre by Design;

Lion in the Streets and *Touch Bass* (Arches Theatre). Simon designed the lighting for the award winning *Last Supper of Dr Faustus*. He lit Act 24's production of *Oklahoma!* at the Edinburgh Playhouse, creating a new world record. His searchlight design for the opening of Perth Concert Hall, *Light Fantastic*, was seen by hundreds of thousands and prompted reports of an alien invasion!

Keith Williams
Keith Williams Architects is multi-award-winning, architectural design practice, with a stream of accolades supporting its fast growing international reputation for the creation of dramatic, innovative architecture. The firm headed by its founder Keith Williams was established in January 2001. During an extremely successful first five years, Williams and his team have been working on an expanding portfolio of high-profile projects across a wide variety of building types in Ireland, Denmark, Germany, Italy and Spain in addition to the UK. A passionate believer in the capability of architecture to benefit the lives of citizens, Williams has devoted much of his career to designing major arts projects including theatres, concert halls and opera houses, museums, galleries and libraries whilst also working on civic buildings and one-off private houses. Based in the firm's central London studio, Keith Williams personally initiates and oversees the design of all of the firm's projects which are developed and implemented with the support of fellow director Richard Brown and key senior architectural staff. Williams' architecture, with its concerns for the interplay of space, light, form and material, coupled with careful consideration for scale history and context, results in buildings that achieve an aesthetic balance between his contemporary, visionary designs and that which exists whether sensitive and historic, or brownfield. Much awarded, he has lectured widely on his work and his projects have been published worldwide.
Principal works:
2005-2008 Wexford Opera House, Ireland
2004-2007 Clones Library & County HQ, Ireland
2001-2006 Private House, London
2001-2005 Unicorn Theatre, London
2001-2004 Athlone Civic Centre, Athlone, Ireland
Selected prizes for completed work:
2006 *BD Public Building Architect of the Year*, Chicago Athenaeum *International Architecture Prize*, *RIAI Overseas Award*, *RIBA Award*, *Irish Concrete Society* Overall Winner
2005 *RIAI Special Award* Best Sustainable Project, *RIBA European Award*, *OPUS Architecture and Construction Award*, *Lighting Design Award*.

Louise Ann Wilson
Louise Ann Wilson studied Theatre Design at Nottingham Trent University and is a freelance theatre designer, painter and visual artist working in performance.
She is the Co-Artistic Director (with Wils Wilson) of wilson+wilson makers of site-specific theatre. Their work includes *Mulgrave* (2005) was a live theatre performance inspired by and performed in Mulgrave Woods. *Mapping the Edge* (2001) transported an audience of 33 on a city-wide journey across Sheffield, on foot, by bus and by tram during which time they witnessed three interweaving stories, inspired by the Greek myth of Medea and the city itself, unfolding around them. The physical living landscape of the city became a stage so challenging the frontier between drama and reality. *News From the Seventh Floor* (2003) took audiences of 25 around Clements, one of the country's oldest department stores, after hours. Journeying the length and breadth of the store, from hellish boiler room to story-book attic and eventually out onto the rooftop car park, they followed a gripping tale of obsessive love, death and redemption. *HOUSE* (1998) transformed two derelict, 19th-century workers' cottages into a unique theatre event where an audience of 15 journeyed from room to room.
It combined visual art/installation, poetry, live performance, live and recorded sound and music and evoked powerful memories and emotions, as well as exploring ideas of evolution, expedition, scientific investigation and religious belief.

Andrew Wood
Andrew Wood studied Theatre Design at Nottingham Trent Polytechnic and worked as a freelance designer before joining Contact Theatre in Manchester, where he filled every position in the design department from Assistant to Associate Director (Design). Designs for Contact include: *Romeo and Juliet*, *Speed the Plow*, *The Trial*, *Ay Carmella* and six *Young Playwrights Festivals*. Since returning to freelance work designs have included: *Neville's Island* and *Blithe Spirit* for Harrogate Theatre; the national tours of *Cold* and *Lockerbie 103* for the Ashton Group; *Oleanna* and *Cooking With Elvis* for Hull Truck; *52 Degrees South* for Big Theatre at the Imperial War Museum North; and *Blast* for the Manchester Poetry Festival. More recently, he co-wrote and designed *The Snowmaker's Grin* for Theatre by the Lake, Keswick, and for the Lowry, led the design team for their new adaptation of *Love on the Dole* and was the designer on the creative team for *Oh, What A Lovely War* He is now working on the development of the *Storytree project*, a format that, within its own distinct geodesic dome space, aims to create a closer link between performance and participation work. He is a Lecturer in Performance Design at The Arden School of Theatre in Manchester and has worked as a Visiting Lecturer at the Liverpool Institute of Performing Arts, Manchester, Manchester Metropolitan and Salford Universities.

Jessica Worrall
Jessica Worrall has been a member of the People Show since 1991 working on many of its productions, most recently designing and performing in no. *117 The Birthday Show* and no. *114 The Obituary Show*. As a designer and director she has worked with them on no. *113 Baby Jane/Film Club*, no. *110 Second*, and no. *107 A Song Without Sound?* She also wrote and directed their short film no. *112 The Art of Escape*. She is also currently working on the *People Show book*, which celebrates their 40 years of performance practice and is due for publication late in 2007. Other design work includes *Wars of the Roses*, a co-production between Northern Broadsides and West Yorkshire Playhouse. Also for Northern Broadsides, national tours of *School for Scandal*, *The Bells*, *Macbeth*, *Oedipus*, *Twelfth Night*, *King John*, *Antony and Cleopatra* and *A Midsummer Night's Dream*. For Bandbazi, the Brighton-based company that uses circus skills she has designed *The Persian Cinderella* and *Breakfast at Audreys*, which won a *fringe first* at the Edinburgh Festival in 2005.
For Oxfordshire Touring Company, she designed *Big Baby*; and for Edinburgh Grand Opera, *Carmen* and *Turandot* (Festival Theatre Edinburgh). Jessica trained at Nottingham Trent University.

Elizabeth Wright
Elizabeth Wright trained at Bristol Old Vic Theatre School and has a degree in Theatre Studies from the University of Leeds. She began her career as a trainee at Theatre by the Lake, in Cumbria where she has continued to design studio plays in repertoire as part of the theatres summer seasons.
Designs include: *The Birthday Party* by Harold Pinter, *Frozen* by Briony Lavery, *Blue/Orange* by Joe Penhall, *Ghosts* by Henrik Ibsen, *Tramping Like Mad* by Julie McKiernan, *Wallflowering* by Peta Murray, *Kiss of the Spiderwoman* by Manuel Puig and *Not a Game for Boys* by Simon Block. Other designs include: *April in Paris* (Haymarket Theatre, Basingstoke); the set for *Cider with Rosie* (Bristol New Vic Studio); *The Dwarfs* (The New Vic Basement); costumes for *Our Country's Good* (Redgrave Theatre, Bristol). On the London fringe, she has designed *Five Kinds of Silence* (Old Red Lion Theatre); *The Christian Brothers* (Etcetera Theatre); and costumes for *Hedda Gabler* (White Bear Theatre). Other designs include *Cocteau's Parade* and *Le Boeuf sur le Toit*, Berkoff's *Agamemnon* and *Hand in Hand* by Sofia Freden, *Behold the Man* for Converse Theatre Company, *Macbeth* and Genet's *The Maids* (Edinburgh Fringe Festival) and *Stags and Hens* by Willy Russell (QEH Theatre, Bristol).

Index of Designers / Collaborators

Keith Allen — 208
Robert Allsopp — 75, 84, 107, 144
Becs Andrews — 94
Richard Andrzejewski — 126
Liz Ascroft — 14, 96
Elroy Ashmore — 40, 172
Mark Bailey — 68
Martyn Bainbridge — 172, 173
Keith Baker — 124, 125
Simon Banham — 8, 142
Donatella Barbieri — 97
Paul Barrett — 85
Dick Bird — 44, 45
Janet Bird — 175
Madeleine Boyd — 48
John Brooking — 176
Lez Brotherston — 74, 75, 143
Julian Brown — 23, 196
Paul Brown — 32, 70, 178
Terry Brown — 172
Paul Burgess — 96
Kate Burnett — 210
David Burrows — 40, 41
Cordelia Chisholm — 142
Bunny Christie — 175
Imogen Cloet — 98, 128
David Cockayne — 46
Rosemarie Cockayne — 145
David Collis — 46
Patrick Connellan — 42, 43
Paule Constable — 75, 80, 87, 109, 119
Kandis Cook — 144
Greer Crawley — 26
Sean Crowley — 48
Gabriella Csanyi-Wills — 144, 145
Anne Curry — 146, 147
Charles Cusick Smith — 62, 103
Phil R. Daniels — 103
Simon Daw — 126, 127
Steve Denton — 180
Es Devlin — 76, 150, 151, 164
Liam Doona — 100
Richard Downing — 148
Atlanta Duffy — 147
Paul Edwards — 78, 79
Mike Elliott — 212
Johan Engels — 84, 108
Lis Evans — 102
Colin Falconer — 41, 143
James Farncombe — 42, 49, 122
Paul Farnsworth — 150
Jonathan Fensom — 78
Rick Fisher — 102
Helen Fownes-Davies — 49, 124
Richard Foxton — 184
Arnim Friess — 101, 162, 173
Bob Frith — 124
Ada Gadomski — 184
Henk van der Geest — 100, 113, 163
Christopher Giles — 130
Paul Gillerion Acoustic Design — 176, 177, 182, 183
Hannah Gravestock — 132
Colin Grenfell — 97, 119
Abigail Hammond — 131
Ken Harrison — 152
Janis Hart — 189
Becky Hawkins — 152, 153
Simon Head — 214

Susannah Henry — 131
Peter Higton — 186
Simon Holdsworth — 50
Pamela Howard — 112, 113
David Howe — 95, 110, 111
Richard Hudson — 80 – 83, 180
Becky Hurst — 188
Martin Johns — 51
Mark Jonathan — 51, 90, 197
Sophie Jump — 32, 154, 155
Simon Kenny — 52
David W Kidd — 91, 99
Bridget Kimak — 52, 53
Kevin Knight — 75
Ralph Koltai — 156
Wai Yin Kwok — 103
Stefanos Lazaridis — 104, 106
Marie-Jeanne Lecca — 84, 106, 108
Adrian Linford — 54, 55, 179
Keith Lodwick — 65
Sophie Lovell Smith — 44
Alexander Lowde — 190
Alex Marker — 153
Tanya McCallin — 109, 119
Gary McCann — 114, 115
Laura McEwen — 132
Prema Mehta — 132
Fred Meller — 14, 156, 186
Miranda Melville — 110
Madeleine Millar — 154
Nick Moran — 86
Martin Morley — 116
Ruari Murchison — 54
Conor Murphy — 58, 59 130
Neil Murray — 60
Kimie Nakano — 158, 159
Pip Nash — 194
Dody Nash — 20, 196
Phil Newman — 86
Pippa Nissen — 116, 117
Stuart Nunn — 160, 161
Francis O'Connor — 134, 135
Christopher Oram — 87
Ben Pacey — 196, 197
Roma Patel — 198, 200
Dana Pinto — 158
Tom Piper — 160
Jacob Polley — 128
Jean-Marc Puissant — 136
Stephen Pyle — 157
Katherina Radeva — 162
Michelle Reader — 127
Erik Rehl — 196
Pete Rice — 75, 97
Colin Richmond — 57
Malcolm Rippeth — 69, 99, 203
John Risebero — 202
Francisco Rodriguez-Weil — 62, 63
Lili Rogué — 88, 89, 101
Peter Ruthven Hall — 202
Emma Ryott — 138, 139, 140
Penny Saunders — 26, 84
Rachel Scanlon — 204
Vivienne Schadinsky — 205
Nettie Scriven — 162, 163
Ashley Shairp — 164
Juliet Shillingford — 91
Adam Silverman — 80, 84, 106, 144
George Souglides — 64, 65
Daphne Stevens-Pascucci — 90
Ben Stones — 90, 91

Nancy Surman — 66
Takis — 137
David I. Taylor — 166
Ian Teague — 164, 165
Yannis Thavoris — 118, 119
Nerissa Cargill Thompson — 159
Jenny Tiramani — 120, 121
Johanna Town — 164
Jamie Vartan — 97, 120
Janet Vaughan — 166
Adrian Vaux — 56, 57
Rebecca Vincent — 168
Martina Von Holn — 168
Steph Warden — 170
Libby Watson — 122
Fiona Watt — 66, 67
Ian Westbrook — 120
Chris de Wilde — 98
Simon Wilkinson — 66
Naomi Wilkinson — 206
Louise Ann Wilson — 92
Andrew Wood — 137
Jessica Worrall — 168
Elizabeth Wright — 128
Sophia Lovell Smith — 44

Index of Theatre architects

AMPC (Anne Minors) — 160, 192
Arts Team (Julian Middleton) — 190
Charcoalblue — 160, 176, 177
Julian Middleton (RHWL) — 188, 189
Keith Williams Architects — 188, 189
Nissen Adams — 194
Theatre Projects Consultants — 204
TheatrePlan — 201
Tim Foster Architects — 182, 183

Index of Photographers

Melanie Alfonso — 197
Marian Alonso — 159
Clive Barda — 104, 105
U. Beuttenmüller — 139
Helen Binet — 189
Ben Blackall — 137
Andy Bradshaw — 121
Eric Brickes (Photo Services) — 121
Dan Buxton — 149
Paolo Calanchini — 120
Louise Callow — 50
Nobby Clark — 50, 94
Anthony Coleman — 190
Edmund Collier — 188
Dee Conway — 196
Bill Cooper — 109
CPNC — 46
Stephen Cummiskey — 180
Fritz Curzon — 97
Kevin Davis — 154
Robert Day — 43, 49, 88, 90, 91, 132, 162, 177
Mike Eddowes — 91
Mattias Ek — 155
Marc Ginot — 59
John Haynes — 164
Steve Hickey — 194
Ken Howard — 70
Dominic Ibbotson — 92

Benjamin Jenner 162
Ursula Kelly (Fluk Photography) 49
Ben King 161
Ellie Kurttz 151
Ivan Kyncl 175
Philip Larter 178
Neil Libbert 86
Peter Litvai 62
Elena Machado 126
Marc Marni 67
Adam Moerk 201
Anthony Morley 145
Chris Moyse 144
Zadoc Nava 168
Maiko Nezu 51
Rowan O'Duffy 44
Eoin O'Riordan 198
Keith Pattison 51, 57, 98, 128, 147, 170
Johan Persson 87, 107, 202
Lara Platman 145
John Reading 52
Douglas Robertson 66
Chris Saunders 89, 154
David Scheinmann 102
Lars Schmidt 201
Tim Sheader 160
Hilary Shedel 131
Brian Slater 144
Derek Speirs 78
Louise Stickland 186
John Tramper 120, 175
B. Weissbrod 139
Jayne West 205
Andrew Whittuck 110
Alan Winn 152
Robert Workman 80 – 83, 111

Index of Productions

25/7 166
A Masked Ball (Un Ballo in Maschera) 86
A Midsummer Night's Dream 117, 176
A Night at the Chinese Opera 118
A Who's Who of Flapland 49
Aesop's Fables 88
After Miss Julie 175
Alice in Wonderland 62
Amadeus 102
An Inspector Calls 172
Anna Karenina 135
Ariadne auf Naxos 51
Barbarians 66
Barbe-Bleue 64
Beautiful Thing 91
Beauty and the Beast 144
Berio Lounge 196
Betrayal 54
Billy Elliot - The Musical 102
bloom 126
BlueBird 145
Bophelo 131
Boxed 154
Breaking the Code 116
Brighton Rock 143
Bugsy Malone 184
By the Bog of Cats (Am Katzenmoor) 44
C-90 131
Cabaret 110
Carmen 120

Cavalleria Rusticana / I Pagliacci 62
Chérubin 79
Chimaera 132
Cliff The Musical 103
Close to Home 160
Closer 170
Consider Rather The River 189
Così fan tutte 119
Daffodils 162
Der Sandmann 138
Der Stein der Weisen oder Die Zauberinsel/The Philosophers' Stone or The Enchanted Island 202
Die Walküre 99
Die Zauberflöte 108
Dog in The Manger 151
Don Giovanni 46
Don't Look Back 206
Dragon Breath 162
Edward Scissorhands 75
Endgame 41
Essence 150
Eva 78
Evita 87
Experimental Anatomy 127
Eyecatcher 89
Faust 134
Festival for Fish 158
Fiddler on the Roof 111
Fine Line 132
Front Window 164
Further than the Furthest Thing 67
Geneva 142
Gianni Schicchi 52
Giselle Reloaded 58
Godspell 152
Gullivers Travels 164
Guys & Dolls 57
Hansel and Gretel 125
Happy yet? 206
Hen Rebel 116
Henry VI   Parts I, II, III 160
Homage to Catalonia 60
How to Live 110
I Am Waiting For The Opportunity To Save Someone's Life 196
Il Tabarro 52
Il Trovatore 98
In The Shadow of Trees 124
Installation 496 137
Invalid 205
Jarman Garden 196
Jesus Christ Superstar 150
La Peau Blanche ... 140
La Traviata 178
Lark Rise to Candleford 153
Le nozze di Figaro 53, 109
Les Liaisons Dangereuses 51, 74
Lilita 168
Little Big World 204
Lucia di Lammermoor 166
Lucio Silla 70
Lulu; Eine Monstretragödie 139
Macbeth 85, 157, 164
Maria de Buenos Aires 46
Maria Stuarda 65
Mary's Wedding 66
Measure for Measure 120
Melody on the Move 68
Messiah 50
Mother Goose 153

Mulgrave, a journey 92
My Home 194
Noir 98
Nopalitos 136
Oh, wot a lovely war? 137
Oliver 56
One Flew Over the Cuckoo's Nest 68
Orestes 2.0 94
Orphée 76
Our Lady of the Drowned 159
Outlying Islands 66
Oz 161
Paradise Lost 90
People Show no.117
The Birthday Show 168
Pericles 165, 186
Pompeo Magno 90
Promised Land 114
Reaching for the Moon 163
Rhymes, Reasons and Bombass Beatz 48
Richard III 202
Rigoletto 97
Risk it? : A Story of Love, Life & STIs 159
Romeo and Juliet 146
Rough Magyck 84
Rusalka 172
Ruthless! 65
Safahd - Telling Tales of a Journey 124
Salome 59
Satin 'n' Steel 49
screwmachine/eyecandy or: How I Learned to Stop Worrying and Love Big Bob 50
Sea House 127
Seaside Special 2006 Variety show 120
Selfish 96
Siobhan Davies Studios 177
Slender 197
Spiel Im Berg 63
Susan and Darren 142
Sweetpeter 124
Tannhauser 75
Ten Belles 130
The Adventures of Tom Sawyer 172
The Borrowers 48
The Burglar's Opera 144
The Canterville Ghost 40
The Comedy of Errors 175
The Country Wife 184
The Crane 132
The Crucible 173
The David Hare Trilogy- Racing Demon, Murmuring Judges, The Absence of War 54
The Dinner 40
The Dubya Trilogy: The Madness of George Dubya, A Weapons' Inspector Calls, and Guantanamo Baywatch 142
The Dwarf (Der Zwerg) 84
The Emperor Jones 180
The Forest 155
The Gambler (De Speler) 45
The Good Person of Setzuan 154
The Government Inspector 115
The Greek Passion 113
The Harmony Suite 180
The House of Bernarda Alba 44
The Lion and the Jewel 147
The Merchant of Venice 199
The Mona Lisas 103
The Philosophers' Stone

or The Enchanted Island/Der Stein der
Weisen oder Die Zauberinsel   202
The Playground   86
The Resistible Rise of Arturo Ui   43
The Ring Cycle   104, 106
The Ring of the Nibelung   80
The Rise and Fall of Little Voice   96
The Romans in Britain   156
The School for Wives   91
The Sunflower Plot   188
The Tasseographer   168
The Tempest   152, 198
The Tunnel of Obsession   41
The Turn of the Screw   130
The Vanishing Bridegroom   55
The Water Banquet   148
The White Album   100
The Winter's Tale   121
This Lime Tree Bower   42
Thread of Gold   145
Three Fragments from
" The Marriage "   112
Three Sisters   122
Timon of Athens   156
Tobias and the Angel   190
Trace   128
True or Falsetto?   52
Twelfth Night   57, 78
Wallflowering   128
Waltz #6   126
What Does it Take?   158

Index of Companies

Adam Cooper Company   74
Angelus Arts   205
Antic Disposition   202
Aqueous Humour   159
Background   78
Belgrade Theatre Company   42
Bill Kenwright Ltd   150
Birmingham Royal Ballet   124
Byre Theatre of St Andrews   66
Cardboard Citizens
Theatre Company   14 – 19, 156, 186
Collective Artistes   147
Collectvie Encounters   180
Company of Angels   124
Contemporary Stage Company   41
Corcadorca Theatre Company 198, 199
Crucible Youth Theatre   154
Daedalus Theatre Company   96
Daily Life Theatre   110
Dartington Summer School   46
Den Ny Opera   99
Donlon Dance Company   58
Dragon Breath Theatre   162, 163
Dreamthinkspeak   206
East Productions   50
Eclipse   122
English National Ballet   68
English National Opera   80, 86
English Speaking Theatre, Frankfurt 110
English Touring Opera   190
Flaming Theatre Company   196
Forkbeard Fantasy   26 – 31
Fran Barbe Dance Theatre   132
Garsington Opera   202
Guildhall School of Music and Drama 94
Gut Immling Opernfestival   62
Harold Finley   48
Heartbreak Productions   85
Higgledy Piggledy Productions   131
Horse + Bamboo Theatre   124
Iford Arts   172
Live Theatre   98
Liz Lea Dance   145
London Sinfonietta   196
Los Angeles Opera   51
Lowry Community and Education   137
Lyric Opera Company
of Kansas City   166
MakeBelieve Arts   164
Mapping4D   197
Mercury Theatre Company   43, 54
Mountview Academy of Theatre   44
National Theatre
Education Department   165
Nationale Reisopera, Holland   130
Neil Laidlaw for NML Productions   91
New Adventures   75
New Vic Theatre   102
Northcott Young Company   152, 153
Northern Stage Ensemble   98
Nottingham Playhouse Roundabout   88
Nuffield Theatre Company   91
Openwide International Ltd   120
Opera della Luna   144
Opera Holland Park   97
Opéra National de Montpellier   59
Opéra National du Rhin   119
Opera North   84
Opera of Thessaloniki   113
Opera Zuid   45

OpusOne   62
Out Of Joint   164
Oxford Stage Company   90
Phoenix Dance Theatre   136
Planning A Trifle   164
Polka Theatre   124
Prime Productions   67
Quarantine   9-13, 142
RADA (Royal Academy of Dramatic Art)
                               115, 137
Rambert Dance Company   126
Really Useful Group   87
Red Earth Theatre   132
Richard Jordan Productions   42
Robin Howard Dance Theatre   162
Royal Academy of Music   118
Royal Lyceum Theatre, Edinburgh   134
Royal Scottish Academy of Music
and Drama   53, 55
Royal Lyceum   135
Royal Opera Company 104 –107, 109
Royal Shakespeare Company 144, 151,
156, 160, 176, 186
Santa Fe Opera   70
Scamp Theatre   50
Second Wave   158
Seven Sisters Group   154, 155
Shakespeare in Education – Schools
Touring, West Midlands   146, 157
Sheffield Theatres   98
Siobhan Davies Dance   177
Skala Theatre Company   40
South Bank Centre   196
Stonecrabs   126, 159
Stuttgarter Ballet   138, 139, 140
Talking Birds   166
Tavaziva Dance   131
Tbilisi Opera   98
The AllieS   168
The Ambassador Theatre Group   182
The London Bubble
Theatre Company   194
The Okai Collier Company   65
The Other Way Works   196
The People Show   168
The Place, London   132
The Royal Welsh College
of Music and Drama   130
The Young Person's
Theatre Company   184
Theater Heilbronn   41, 44
Theatr Genedlaethol Cymru   41
Theatre Alibi   160
Theatre Mélange   103
Theatre workshop Edinburgh   189
Theatul Municipal Ariel   103
U Man Zoo   148
UK productions   111
Vienna Volksoper   108
Walker Dance Park Music   150
Wexford Festival Opera   78
wilson+wilson   92
Yellow Earth Theatre Company   158
Young Vic Theatre Company   190

228

Index of Venues

Adelphi Theatre, Strand, London 87
Albany Theatre, London 158
Albery (now the Coward), London 78
Almeida Theatre, London 143
Anthony Hopkins Theatre,
Clwyd Theatr Cymru 68
Arches, Glasgow 96
Arena di Verona 178
Assembly Rooms, Edinburgh 42, 50
BAC, London 197
Royal Festival Hall. London 196
Barbican Theatre, London 110
Barn Theatre, Dartington 46
Belgrade Theatre, Coventry 42
Birmingham Hippodrome 124
Birmingham Repertory Theatre 54, 122
Birmingham Theatre School 146, 157
Bolton Octagon 49
Bregenz Festival 64
Byre Theatre St Andrews 67
Cecil Sharp House 132
Clore Studio, Royal
Opera House, London 131, 145
Clwyd Theatr Cymru 172, 173
Courtyard Theatre, RSC,
Stratford-upon-Avon 160, 176
Crucible Theatre, Sheffield 154, 156
Crucible Studio Theatre, Sheffield 89
Donmar Warehouse, London 175
Drill Hall, London 52
Dukes Theatre, Lancaster 172
Esbjerg Musikhuset 99, 110
Finborough Theatre, London 153
Garsington Manor, Oxford 202
Gate Theatre, London 180, 206
Gdansk Theatre, Poland 194
Grand Theatre, Leeds 84
Grange Park Opera House 65
Greenwich Playhouse, London 126
Guildhall Theatre, Barbican,
London 52, 94
Gut Immling Opernfestival 62
Haymarket Theatre, Basingstoke 40
Haymarket Theatre, Leicester 132
Herbert Gallery, Coventry 204
Hoxton Hall, London 132
Lakeside Arts Centre, Nottingham 49
Le Corum, Opera Berlioz, Montpellier 59
Lilian Baylis Theatre, Sadllers Wells, 184
Linbury Studio, Royal Opera House,
London 76, 150
London Coliseum 80, 86
Lyric Opera House, Kansas City,
Missouri USA 166
Mc Bobingny'93, Paris 60
Menuhin Hall, Surrey 192
Mercury Theatre, Colchester 43, 54
Municipal Theatre, Larnaka, Cyprus 40
New Athenaeum Theatre, Glasgow 53, 55
New Players Theatre, London 44, 142
New Vic Theatre,
Newcastle-under-Lyme 102
New Wimbledon Studio Theatre 158
Newcastle Playhouse 98, 142
Newport Hall, Japan 74
Northcott Theatre, Exeter 152, 153
Northern Stage, Newcastle 60, 190
Nottingham Playhouse 49, 100, 152
Nottingham Playhouse Studio 88

Nuffield Theatre, Southampton 91
Old Clock Shop, Brighton 127
Old Vic, London 50
Opéra National de Montpellier 58
Opera of Thessaloniki 113
Operaen, Copenhagan 200
Oval House Theatre, London 48
Palace Theatre, Watford 184
Pavilion Theatre, Cromer Pier,
Norfolk 120
People Show Studios, London 168
Perth Theatre 66
Polka Theatre, Wimbledon 86, 124
Prince of Wales Theatre, London 103
Quays Theatre, The Lowry, Salford 137
Queen Elizabeth Hall, Stratford - upon -
Avon 156
RADA, Jerwood Vanbrugh Theatre 115, 137
Riverside Studios, Studio 3 196
Royal and Derngate, Northampton 116
Royal Exchange Theatre, Manchester 96, 124
Royal Festival Hall, London 196
Royal Northern College of Music,
Manchester 46
Royal Opera House, London 104-107, 109
Royal Scottish Academy of Music
and Drama, Glasgow 117
Royal Shakespeare Theatre,
Stratford-upon-Avon 84, 144
RSC, Stratford-Upon- Avon 144
Sadler's Wells,
London 68, 74, 75, 126, 136
Salisbury Playhouse 66
Santa Fe Opera 70
Shakespeare's Globe Theatre,
London 120, 121, 175
Sherman Theatre, Cardiff 48, 130
Siobhan Davies Studios 177
Sir Jack Lyons Theatre, Royal
Academy of Music, London 118
Sound Theatre, Leicester Square 91
Southwark Playhouse, London 159
St Bartholomew's Hospital, London 205
St John's Church Waterloo 190
St Stephen's, Hampstead, London 202
Staatstheater Stuttgart 138, 139, 140
Stadsschouwburg Amsterdam 130
Stafford Castle 176
Stanmer House, Brighton 206
Stratford Circus, London 65
Swan Theatre, Stratford Upon Avon 151
Tactile Bosch, Cardiff 148
Tbilisi Opera and Ballet Theatre,
Georgia 98
Teatro La Scala, Milan 75
Teatro Lirico di Cagliari 79, 120
The Broadway, Barking 183
The Cloister at Iford 172
The Egg Children's and Young Persons'
Theatre, Bath UK 192
The Pit, Barbican, London 147
The Place, London 162
The Sage, Gateshead 204
Theater aan het Vrijthof, Maastricht 45
Theater Heilbronn, Germany 44
Theatre Bet Lessin, Tel Aviv 57
Theatre by the Lake,
Keswick 51, 120, 170

Theatre Romea, Barcelona 60
Theatre Royal, Bury St Edmunds 125
Theatre Royal, Wexford 78
Touchstones, Rochdale 159
Trafalgar Studios at the Whitehall
Theatre, London 182
Traverse Theatre, Edinburgh 66, 131
Unicorn Theatre, The Weston Stage
London 161
Unity Theatre 2, Liverpool 164
Varazdin State Opera House Croatia 90
Victoria Palace Theatre, London 102
Vienna Volksoper 108
Warehouse Theatre, Croydon 41
Warehouse, Batley 164
Waterside, Belfast 156
Waverley Theatre,
Nottingham Trent University 162
West Yorkshire Playhouse 57, 60
Wexford New Opera House 188
Young Actors Theatre, London 63
Young Vic, London 190